Indigenous Films

Series Editors

David Delgado Shorter
Randolph Lewis

Smoke Signals: Native Cinema Rising

JOANNA HEARNE

UNIVERSITY OF NEBRASKA PRESS | LINCOLN AND LONDON

Portions of chapter 3 were previously
published as "'John Wayne's Teeth':
Speech, Sound and Representation in
Smoke Signals and *Imagining Indians*"
in *Western Folklore* 64, nos. 3 and 4
(Summer–Fall 2005): 189–208.
Western States Folklore Society
© 2005. Used with permission.

The appendix was previously published
as "Remembering *Smoke Signals*: Interviews with Chris Eyre and Sherman
Alexie" in *Post-Script* 29, no. 3 (Summer
2010): 118–34. Used with permission.

∞

Index funding provided by the University of Missouri.

Library of Congress
Cataloging-in-Publication Data
Hearne, Joanna.
Smoke signals: native cinema rising /
Joanna Hearne.
p. cm. — (Indigenous films)
Includes bibliographical references
and index.
ISBN 978-0-8032-1927-4
(pbk.: alk. paper)
1. Smoke signals (Motion picture)
2. Indians in motion pictures.
3. Indigenous films — United States.
I. Title.
PN1997..S6115H43 2012
791.43'72 — dc23   2012026247

Set in Minion.
Designed by Nathan Putens.

A portion of the proceeds from this book will be donated to Longhouse Media in support of "Native Lens," a program that teaches digital filmmaking and media skills to Indigenous youth as a form of self-expression, cultural preservation, and social change. Please visit www.longhousemedia.org.

Contents

Illustrations

Acknowledgments

I want to thank Chris Eyre and Sherman Alexie, most of all for making *Smoke Signals*, and also for making time to talk and correspond with me ten years later about the film and its production and reception. I'm also grateful to the indefatigable Christy Cox, Wendy Hathaway, and Tamera Miyasato for keeping communications flowing. Other filmmakers, including Georgina Lightning and Sterlin Harjo, also shared stories about their own films and about *Smoke Signals*, and my thinking has benefited from the performers' insights in print and online venues.

I liked *Smoke Signals* the first time I saw it, in a theater in Tucson, Arizona, in 1998, but I didn't begin to appreciate the film's depth and durability until I began teaching it in a range of contexts — to high school students on the Tohono O'odham Nation reservation, and to college students in southern Arizona and in central Missouri in film studies and Native American studies courses. The film appealed to these wide-ranging young audiences, and I had more to say about it each time I taught it. My thanks go out to all of my students for keeping me connected to their worlds and perspectives, and for helping me to see with fresh eyes.

I'm deeply grateful to series editors Randy Lewis and David Delgado Shorter, and to Matt Bokovoy at the University of Nebraska Press, for inviting me to expand my early work on *Smoke Signals* as part of the Indigenous Films book series. Their astute comments and enthusiastic support for the project — not to mention their patience during the writing process — have meant a great deal to me. I also appreciate the work of copyeditor Sue Breckenridge and the fantastic manuscript editing and production staff. Crucial guidance and suggestions also came from the anonymous reviewers for the press and from conversations emerging from conference panels at the Society for Cinema and Media Studies, the Native American Art Studies Association, and the Native American and Indigenous Studies Association.

Along the way, a number of people shared ideas and important resources for primary and secondary research on *Smoke Signals*, including Aaron Bird Bear, Ned Blackhawk, Jim Cox, Maureen Konkle, Angelica Lawson, and Robert Warrior. Chad Allen, Susan Bernardin, Dean Rader, Michelle Raheja, Ken Roemer, Lisa Tatonetti, and Pam Wilson have been a wonderful and vital circle of support. This book is much the better for the feedback, time, and attention of my writing cohort — Elizabeth Chang, Sam Cohen, and Donna Strickland. Elaine Lawless deserves deep thanks for her unflagging encouragement, as does Anand Prahlad, for saying that *Smoke Signals* is the closest thing there is to a perfect movie. Elise Marubbio and Gerald Duchovnay provided a venue — the volume of *Post-Script* dedicated to Native American and Indigenous film — for the first publication of the interviews that appear in the appendix to this book. And this project took its first baby steps in an essay originally published in *Western Folklore*'s 2005 special double issue on film, which now forms a fragment of chapter 3.

My deepest and happiest debts of gratitude are to my family for their unconditional love and their generosity of all kinds — the daily phone calls, the many photographs, the feasts, the gifts of music, the long walks, the gloriously crowded holidays. My mother, Betsy Hearne, deserves special devotion always, for her sustaining comradeship and intellectual nurture. And my gladdest thanks are to my partner in life, Chris Morrey, for building such a good house in his heart and in the world to shelter us and our beautiful sons, Desmond and Leo, whose stories are just unfolding.

Series Editors' Introduction

David Delgado Shorter, Randolph Lewis

From the earliest moments that we imagined the Indigenous Films series as an antidote to the canonical, Eurocentric approach to cinema studies, we knew we wanted to address *Smoke Signals* as soon as we could. We both believed that *Smoke Signals*'s release in 1998 had been a transformative event in the history of Indigenous media in the United States. Teaming up with the prolific and provocative Coeur d'Alene writer Sherman Alexie, Cheyenne director Chris Eyre, and a team of extraordinary actors had created the first Native film to reach a wide audience in North America. Not only that, but *Smoke Signals* was smart, funny, tragic, insightful, and politically resonant — and perhaps most significant for our purposes, it had pedagogical legs. As soon as it was available on DVD, it became one of the most popular Native films taught on college campuses and in high schools in the United States and Canada, where it was widely used to introduce students to contemporary Native issues in English, anthropology, history, Native American studies, and American studies courses from Maine to California. As if this were not enough pressure on a single text, at times *Smokes Signals* was forced to stand alone in a curriculum designed to exclude certain realities. In other words, college or high school students sometimes learned nothing about Native cultures other than what they saw in *Smoke Signals*.

Despite the unusual nature of this important film and its wide dissemination, scholars had not spoken at length about it. No one was helping students to understand the film in an accessible yet scholarly manner; no one was helping instructors to teach the film with the exception of a few scattered articles; no one was pushing the scholarly conversation forward with a book-length study. Such was the situation that we were hoping to remedy with this film series: we wanted to find the ideal authors to write small, affordable books that would interest scholars, help instructors, and guide students. Moreover, if handled properly, these books would serve as a portal to a deeper understanding of contemporary Indigenous lives. If so much was going to depend on *Smoke Signals*, we wanted to make sure that the film would be richly explicated and carefully situated in relevant contexts. We wanted to treat it with the same care that is afforded a film by Hitchcock or Ford.

Concomitantly with starting the series we were looking for a person to write the book on *Smoke Signals*. We literally could not imagine a series on Indigenous film without prioritizing this film among the many possibilities. We were seeking someone who could "open up" the film without reiterating the tried but true analyses of Native representations in Hollywood. Our hope was to find someone who could read the film as one reads a great work of literature, showing the shifting and lasting impacts across time. Such an author would engage English professors, film experts, and of course the college students fulfilling their required readings. As series editors looking at the complex landscape of scholarly publishing in the United States, we were well aware that not every book represents an ideal and happy marriage between author and subject.

When we came across Joanna Hearne's fascinating article on *Smoke Signals*, "'John Wayne's Teeth': Speech, Sound and Representation in *Smoke Signals* and *Imagining Indians*," in a 2005 issue of *Western Folklore*, we knew that we had found the right person. An English professor with a dual interest in Native literature and cinema, Hearne was already knee-deep in her forthcoming book *Native Recognition: Indigenous Cinema and the Western*. She had already established lines of communication with Sherman Alexie and Chris Eyre. In our first conversations with her, we were impressed by her seemingly frame-by-frame knowledge of *Smoke Signals* and her ability to sustain multiple interpretive readings of the film's significance. We suggested that *Smoke Signals* deserved the kind of book-length treatment we knew she could write. We claimed then, as we do now, that her book would be *the* book on this widely taught film for a long time.

We were very pleased when Joanna agreed to write the book you now hold. We were even more pleased when we saw the early drafts and eventually the final manuscript. We are confident that this book will be useful to the various readerships we described above. Moreover, we believe this to be the companion book that such an important film deserves.

In careful, clear prose, Hearne beautifully explores the complex place that *Smoke Signals* occupies on the contemporary U.S. mediascape. From *Time* magazine to tribal newspapers, *Smoke Signals* was understood as a significant cultural event when it appeared in theaters at the end of the Clinton era. No matter what reviewers thought of the merits of the film when it appeared in 1998 (and most were respectful if not laudatory), they seemed eager to agree that here was something new. Believing the hype that *Smoke Signals* somehow invented Native film in North America, some people imagined that the film was sui generis. Of course, the often-overlooked reality was that *Smoke Signals* was built on a long history of smaller films, going back several decades to the work of Sandra Day Osawa, Phil Lucas, Alanis Obomsawin, Gerald Vizenor, Victor Masayesva, Arlene Bowman, and other Native filmmakers who had made important contributions to the development of Native cinema in the 1970s and 1980s.

Of course, *Smoke Signals* was not sui generis — but it was a genuine breakthrough in terms of perception (and reception). It seemed to announce the arrival of a wry comic realism that could speak equally well to Native and non-Native audiences. Its crossover appeal made *Smoke Signals* an event worth studying, as did the unique combination of elements that went into it: acclaimed writer, a sharp-eyed director, and some extraordinary Native actors. The result of their collaboration was a film that spoke, and continues to speak, to audiences on multiple levels.

In the chapters ahead, Joanna Hearne is attentive to these various levels as well as the diverse relationships that viewers have to the world depicted in the film. Some viewers were astonished and delighted to see a respectful story that resonated with their personal experiences as Native people. Others were astonished and delighted to find themselves drawn into an unfamiliar world that they found compelling and meaningful. For cultural outsiders and insiders, and everyone somewhere in between, the film presented a refreshingly new take on contemporary Native life, one very different from the extremes of romanticism, stereotype, or outright demonization that had distorted mass media in the United States throughout the twentieth century. Coming right at the end of that century of transformation in how Native rights and identities were understood, *Smoke Signals* was a "landmark 'first' in American film history," as Hearne puts it. We are very pleased that Joanna Hearne decided to devote the last few years to working on this book. She helps us understand the film's intentions, receptions, and reflections. And the "landmark" status of the film, we believe, is met with a respectful, attentive, carefully written, and much-needed book.

Introduction — "A Way to Sit at the Same Table"

Indigenizing Popular Culture

Smoke Signals is the most widely recognized and frequently taught film in the field of Native American cinema. The creative duo behind the film's production, director Chris Eyre (Cheyenne/Arapaho) and author/screenwriter Sherman Alexie (Spokane/Coeur d'Alene), marketed it as "the first film to be directed, acted, and produced by Native Americans to have a major distribution deal." Among its many awards were the Audience Award and Filmmakers' Trophy at the Sundance Film Festival. The film has been a critical and financial success and has become a Native cinema classic, appreciated by Native and non-Native audiences and appearing frequently in high school and college course lists. Released in 1998, *Smoke Signals* is both an event — a historical milestone in the development of Native American filmmaking — and an innovative work of cinematic storytelling that calls for sustained critical attention.

For some viewers, this was the first film to tell a story they recognized; for others it was a gateway to understanding perspectives outside of their experience. The film can be seen as a landmark "first" in American film history — although it is important to remember the long history of Native filmmaking that came before *Smoke Signals* — and it can also be seen as a self-positioned first introduction to Native perspectives and Native filmmaking for many of its viewers. These "firsts," like stepping stones, invite us to move from celebrating the film's accomplishment to recognizing its activism. As an intervention, *Smoke Signals* challenges widely accepted misconceptions about Native Americans. Its "firsts" can be seen in different ways as inaugurating a new generation of Native film production; as an important but also problematic industry marketing category; as part of a critical paradigm based on sovereignty; and as a strategic creation of politicized space for Indigenous identity in the public mediascape.

Smoke Signals is a pivotal film for a host of reasons. It signaled a generational shift in Native artistic production toward young writers and artists immersed in the same media they set out to subvert, with its film-school-trained director and media-fluent literary star writer. The film's release in 1998 bookended a decade that began with the 1990 release of the nostalgic, romanticized representations of Plains Indians in *Dances with Wolves*, and the subsequent political struggle over representations of Native American and European contact surrounding the 1992 Columbus Quincentennary. The questions that emerged during that public conversation — Who should be celebrated in such an anniversary, and who should do the celebrating? Why is this history publicly celebrated at all? — are issues that *Smoke Signals* raises with equal intensity in its focus on another calendrical marker, U.S. Independence Day celebrations. *Smoke Signals* also consciously counters representations of Indians in conventional Westerns in iconoclastic, humorous ways. And with all its teasing and playful performativity, the film deflects a certain habit of intrusive public curiosity about Native Americans.

If *Smoke Signals* intervenes in mainstream media's representations of Indians, it also forges a connection between those images, with their mass audiences, and distinctively Indigenous points of view. This intervention is not just a counter-appropriation; to borrow Maori scholar Linda Tuhiwai Smith's term, it is also an "Indigenization" of mass media. Yet *Smoke Signals* is an energetic and ambiguous film in part because it refuses to function as an outsider's guide to Native cultures. It reaches out to both Native and non-Native viewers, yet declines to answer questions or divulge cultural information; viewers are expected to keep up.

Smoke Signals may look like other American films in its use of established formulas — it's a road movie, a buddy movie, a comedy, a family drama — but when we look more closely we see that these familiar conventions take on different meanings, reshaping American cinema from within. Sherman Alexie refers to his pop-culture references as "cultural currency" because popular culture creates common ground: "It's a way for us to sit at the same table. I use pop culture like most poets use Latin." Yet at the same time, audiences are never allowed to forget that Native viewers take in the lingua franca of pop from a radically different position than other audiences: "Superman means something different to me than it does to a white guy from Ames, Iowa or New York City or L.A."[1] This difference is based in history, tribalism, and sovereignty, not appearance. As Alexie stated bluntly to a white reporter in an interview with the *Los Angeles Times* in 1998, "We don't want to be like you. . . . The thing that people don't understand is that we're sitting here at the table with you, we're wearing the clothes you wear, we're speaking English, but we're not like you. We're fundamentally different, and we don't want to change that."[2] Alexie's assertion that Native peoples are "fundamentally different" from other Americans is key to understanding the distinctiveness of Native film and of *Smoke Signals*'s particular intervention in mainstream film. As I argue in this book, *Smoke Signals* creates an oppositional voice within what Stuart Hall calls the "contested arena" of popular culture, while cultivating a broad audience for Native cinematic storytelling.

Yet *Smoke Signals* also shows us that the "common ground" of popular culture is Native ground. The filmmakers invest a media space that has traditionally been hostile to Native people (such as Westerns) with Indigenous contemporary presence and historical imperatives, turning an established sign system to serve distinctly Indigenous political purposes. Taking over and "Indigenizing" the generic forms of American feature film in this way involves taking possession of feature-film production as a tool for telling Native stories, and establishing relationships of speaking and listening, in a venue that has traditionally silenced, ignored, or obsessively misrepresented Native voices and experiences.

Analyzing the way *Smoke Signals* makes meaning involves more than simply mapping the film's revision of past media stereotypes. We must also consider what Ella Shohat and Robert Stam call "questions of address": "Who is speaking through a film? Who is imagined as listening? Who is actually listening? Who is looking? And what social desires are mobilized by the film?"[3] While understanding the way the film is woven into the world requires close attention to screen images and sounds, it also demands attention to information about the film's production and reception from the filmmakers and actors; reviews and articles about the film and filmmakers in the popular press; historical material; and scholarly studies of the film, Native media, and cinematic conventions like flashbacks and voice-over narration. These source materials illuminate different analytical models for interpreting *Smoke Signals* — within the context of the industry, of the film's production, of the film's reception in critical circles and by the general viewing audience, of the film "text" itself, and of authorship and literary adaptation. My goal is to provide not just a close textual reading but also a broad study of one Native film's meaning and effects in the world, with the understanding that contemporary film can function as a politicized way of remembering and forgetting elements of the past, a past that should matter to us as we remake our world in the present. *Smoke Signals* is an example of media wielded as not only entertainment but also a form of activist pedagogy. Eyre and Alexie take advantage of the power of cinema to teach viewers in order to make things happen in the world beyond the screen. My approach to the film in this book pays close attention to the practitioners' own frameworks, particularly their emphasis upon Indigenous political sovereignty. Thus I have tried wherever possible to highlight the voices of the artists themselves by quoting from interviews and other press materials.

Synopsis of *Smoke Signals*

Smoke Signals tells the story of two young Coeur d'Alene men — the tough Victor Joseph (Adam Beach, Saulteaux) and his nerdy, storytelling friend Thomas Builds-the-Fire (Evan Adams, Coast Salish). When Victor's estranged father Arnold Joseph (Gary Farmer, Cayuga) dies far from home, in Phoenix, Arizona, Victor and Thomas travel together by bus from their Idaho reservation to Arizona to retrieve Arnold's belongings and his ashes, and return driving Arnold's pickup truck. In the film's complex chronology, the present (1998) road trip frames flashbacks: to 1976, when Victor and Thomas were babies and a devastating house fire killed Thomas's parents; to 1988, when Victor and Thomas were twelve years old and Arnold abandoned Victor and his mother, Arlene (Tantoo Cardinal, Métis); and to various years between 1988 and 1998, when Arnold Joseph met a mysterious woman, Suzy Song (Irene Bedard, Inuit/Métis) in Phoenix, Arizona. The "smoke signals" of the film's title refer to the house fire at the core of the story, but they are also symbolic — like the radio airwaves of the film's opening sequence — of a broader communication system that travels across boundaries. The image also reframes Western-genre stereotypes of Indians in terms of colonization. Alexie describes the title as "vaguely humorous[;] . . . on the surface, it's a stereotypical title, you think of Indians in blankets on the plains sending smoke signals . . . but in a contemporary sense, smoke signals are about calls of distress, calls for help."[4] Help with maintaining family ties (in the form of storytelling, fry bread, and car rides) also comes from Thomas's and Victor's different relationships with strong female characters, including Thomas's grandmother (Monique Mojica, Kuna/Rappahannock), Victor's mother, Arlene Joseph, Arnold Joseph's friend and neighbor Suzy Song, and their friends and cousins on the reservation, Lucy and Velma (Elaine Miles, Cayuse/Nez Perce; and Michelle St. John, Cree).

The film's emotional engine is the relationships between its key characters. Thomas has a special relationship with Victor's father, Arnold, who both caused the fire that killed his parents and also saved him from the fire and so became a substitute, and somewhat idealized, father figure. Despite Victor's occasional bullying, Victor and Thomas are friends. They are also what their community calls "cousins" (because their families are close, even though they are not related), and in a more symbolic way, "brothers" in their triangulated relationship with Arnold Joseph. This complex and changing relationship is central to the main action, the search for the lost father that motivates their road trip. These characters are also important to the filmmakers, mirroring the creation of the film from their close collaboration, and to Sherman Alexie's style of writing fictionalized self-portraiture especially in the early short stories from which *Smoke Signals*'s story was adapted.

Although the film seems to focus on Victor, we as audience members understand the film's story through Thomas's narration in voice-over, as well as his many stories as an on-screen character. His narration illustrates a critical element of *Smoke Signals*, as well as many other Native films: an emphasis upon the means of storytelling. Victor becomes a character in Thomas's stories, yet Thomas is often an unreliable narrator both for Victor and for the film's audience. This emphasis upon storytelling reveals the way that *Smoke Signals* is not just a passive response to a history of cinematic misrepresentations and geographic inaccuracies but rather a creation of Indigenous reality in a media-saturated world. Thomas is a figure who takes back the power to control Native stories in both public and private ways. And more than a decade after the film was released, his character is still a generative cultural touchstone, judging from the content of the many YouTube parodies and reenactments of *Smoke Signals*.

Media Images of Indians

Smoke Signals responds to both the history of Native tribes in the context of ongoing colonialism, and to the history of Native American images in the media. While an extensive overview of Native American history and representation is beyond the scope of this book, some terms and concepts related to *Smoke Signals*'s embeddedness in these histories need introduction here, and will be explored in greater depth in the chapters that follow. My approach to *Smoke Signals* adopts both film studies and Indigenous analytical paradigms, particularly those frameworks, categories, and imperatives articulated by the filmmakers themselves. In interviews, Alexie and Eyre repeatedly emphasize the importance of political sovereignty. In a dialogue about race with President Bill Clinton on the *McNeil/Lehrer News Hour* in 1998, the year *Smoke Signals* was released, Sherman Alexie again emphasized that "the primary thing that people need to know about Indians is that our identity is much less cultural now and much more political. That we really do exist as political entities and sovereign political nations."[5] We can see this assertion as an invitation to view *Smoke Signals* through a political and historical lens, rather than as an artifact of Spokane tribal culture; its primary aesthetic project is not cultural expression but rather a politicized intervention in the American mediascape. Chris Eyre notes that some audiences make the mistake of seeing *Smoke Signals* as "anthropological because it's about Indians": "One of the biggest misnomers is that *Smoke Signals* is a cultural movie. It's not a cultural movie at all."[6] The film as a product of Native self-representation and artistic vision is distinct, then, not because of culturally defined differences but rather because of political differences that we can begin to explain by thinking about the relationship of political sovereignty to visual culture, including the history of media images of Indians.

Eyre and Alexie address ongoing media discourses of noble, savage, and vanishing Indians in Hollywood Westerns and in other media; their theme of forgiving absent fathers resonates with images of Indian absence, "vanishing," and loss in mainstream media but answers those images with a story about retrieval and return. The economic consequences of outsiders treating Native images as products or commodities, which takes place through industrial production of images, as well as in their reproduction and circulation, is often overlooked in textual analysis. This process of commodification has characterized Hollywood studio treatments of Indian characters from the earliest Westerns to contemporary films.

Smoke Signals speaks back to two films of the 1990s, *Dances with Wolves* (dir. Costner, 1990) and *The Last of the Mohicans* (dir. Mann, 1992), that had a major impact on the industry. These films represent Indians in a classically binary noble and savage formulation: the "good Indians" (the Lakotas in *Dances with Wolves*, the Mohicans in *Last of the Mohicans*) are romanticized and soon to vanish (hence the "last of" the Mohicans), while the "bad Indians" (the Pawnees in *Dances with Wolves*, the Hurons in *Last of the Mohicans*, led by characters played by Cherokee actor Wes Studi in both films) are demonized as "savage." While these films created a Hollywood vogue for Native American subjects and opened up roles for Native actors, the cycle of period films that followed resulted primarily in "loincloth" roles, parts without either emotional nuance or contemporary complexity. Further, control of these films' narratives and structuring scenarios remains with white focal characters, eliding the history of Native agency and resistance. This paradigm of civilization and savagery, or what First Nations scholar Emma LaRocque calls "the civ/sav canopy," has generated "provocations for Native scholars and artists" and at the same time functioned as a powerful "intellectual and recreational play box for the colonizer society."[7] Cinema images of Indians can function as categorizing machines, reducing Indigenous heterogeneity to a set of stock character types and marketing packages, and reducing historical and cultural complexity to an artificial separation of tradition from modernity. Lisa Tatonetti describes the resulting generic "edited-for-TV drama":

> *Front stage*: America is "discovered!"; *Backstage*: Indians, dispossessed of land and voice, are pushed to the outskirts, relegated to the "back walls" of their own countries; *Front stage left*: It's *The Last of the Mohicans*, and Natty Bumppo is sad, sad, sad; *Front stage right*: The Indians dance, "wild and crazy"; (Cue cavalry; swell strings); *Center stage*: The Indians die. As the credits roll, a voice-over in broken English — *the nation's hoop is broken and scattered. There is no center any longer, and the sacred tree is dead* — and the last words that Black Elk never spoke erroneously become the single version of Native "history" into which all Native pasts are subsumed. Pretty soon the whole damn thing is the only film on the all-day History Channel movie marathon.[8]

The clichéd image of the "vanishing Indian" operates on the premise that Native peoples are locked in the past, unable to participate in contemporary time. This vague and generalized assumption carries enormous power in public narratives about Native peoples because it is disseminated across media through news stories, film and television, and books. Stereotypes, even when they seem "positive," actively erode Native sovereignty. Their totalizing constructions focus on a temporally and geographically limited idea of culture, to the exclusion of contemporary and heterogeneous political, economic, and aesthetic elements of Native American life. Influenced by the early anthropological focus on culture as a static category, this approach limits "Indianness" to a narrow range of culturally distinct and aestheticized images.

Contemporary films that romanticize and/or demonize Native characters — Pocahontas (dir. Gabriel and Goldberg, 1995), The New World (dir. Malick, 2005), Apocalypto (dir. Gibson, 2006), Avatar (dir. Cameron, 2009) — exemplify the new expansion of the imperialist adventure film (and its ur-genre, the Western) into other generic forms, such as the science fiction spectacular. The supernatural vampire film New Moon (dir. Weitz, 2009), for example, reimagines the Quileute tribe from the Pacific Northwest as a bestial "pack" of Indian werewolves. The Quileutes are an actual Native tribe — a self-governing political unit within the United States — but neither the novel's author Stephanie Meyers nor the film studio, Summit, offered compensation, or consulted with the tribal council for permission before using the name in the books, movies, and extensive franchise marketing and merchandise.[9] Indian characters in the film repeatedly refer to their "treaty" with the vampire Cullen family, subsuming historical Quileute treaties (the 1855 Treaty of Quinault River and 1856 Treaty of Olympia) within a familiar cinematic and literary racial schema of savage Indians and civilized whites. The public preoccupation with this image also suppresses the radical diversity of Native tribes and languages, including the many distinct tribes of the Pacific Northwest and the interior Salish tribes, such as Alexie's Spokane and

Coeur d'Alene tribes of the upper Columbia River system. Further, the tribe itself and its individual members, some of whom live in poverty, are excluded from the monetary benefits reaped by those who appropriate their name.

Smoke Signals responds to the systemic extraction of profits away from Native artists and communities, and also to the oppressive ubiquity of mainstream representations of Indians as nineteenth-century, feather-wearing Plains tribes so common in the Western. The film works against fetishizing tendencies in commodified representations of Indians, yet also works within that same system of commodification to convert its audiences and redirect its resources, all the while speaking simultaneously to Native and non-Native audiences. Eyre and Alexie produce their vision of contemporary American cultural and political landscapes by depicting common experiences that assume distinct meanings in Native contexts of media misrepresentation, ongoing colonization, and claims to sovereignty. *Smoke Signals* commodifies Indian images differently, using cinema to break down social boundaries and at the same time to shore up tribal differences from other Americans. The film makes the Hollywood scenarios and generic codes accountable to Indigenous politics and histories; it does so by wielding established dramatic forms and sentiments to deliver intertextual critiques of imperialist media representations of Indians.[10]

The stakes of this critique are high because screen images of Indians are so influential in public thinking and debates about Indigenous peoples. N. Bird Runningwater (Cheyenne/Mescalero Apache), programmer for the Native Initiative at the Sundance Institute, writes,

> Inaccuracies and stereotypes undermine Indigenous languages and cultures because the mainstream media promotes assimilation. The inaccuracies also affect the political process that is so vital to upholding tribal sovereignty and the relations between the 557 tribal nations in the U.S. and the federal government. Former Principal Chief of the Cherokee Nation Wilma Mankiller

says "It's hardly any wonder you can go speak with a senator or Congressman and have them know anything about Indians. What little they do know, they get from the media and from movies." . . . The most serious effect media stereotypes have, however, is on Native individuals' thoughts and perceptions of ourselves and the world we live in.[11]

Runningwater's articulation of the real-world effects of media stereotypes — effects on government policy-makers, effects on Native individuals — works to dismantle those stereotypes by exposing their costs. *Smoke Signals* demonstrates this process of dismantling at the level of individual viewers by exploring the ways that its young protagonists become conscious of the dissonance between media images and their own experiences. This process resonates with the experience of Sherman Alexie, who grew up on the Spokane reservation in Wellpinit, Washington, but now lives in urban Seattle; he describes his youthful immersion in a world saturated by popular culture, from sitcoms like *The Brady Bunch* to games like Dungeons and Dragons, and also in the small-town, distinctly Native world of the Spokane reservation.

Political Sovereignty and Visual Sovereignty

The action in *Smoke Signals* is located both on the Coeur d'Alene reservation and off-reservation in rural and urban areas of the American West. Most of the film's characters identify as Coeur d'Alene, and also as part of an intertribal pan-Indian culture (often with English as the common language) that arose during the nineteenth and twentieth centuries as the result of different tribes coming into contact through government boarding-school experiences, relocation to urban neighborhoods, collective political allegiances and activism, and cultural sharing at events such as powwows. James Cox argues convincingly that the reservation is the "privileged landscape and narrative center" of *Smoke Signals*, and further that by emphasizing this land base and community, Alexie "decreases the number of audience members who are cultural insiders."[12] About half of the current Spokane Tribe's 2,441 members live on a 157,376-acre reservation, with the tribal headquarters located in the small town of Wellpinit, Washington. The Coeur d'Alene Tribe, with 2,190 members, has a 345,000-acre reservation. Both tribes now have casinos that provide jobs and income, mitigating the high unemployment and poverty that marked Alexie's childhood. Although their reservations are rural, many tribal members live off the reservation, in cities like Spokane and Seattle, or in other parts of the world.[13] Of course, their sovereignty as politically self-governing entities predates the formal recognition of their nationhood by European and American governments; all of the land in the Americas is Indigenous land, and before colonization was governed completely by tribes with distinct languages, cultures, economies, and systems of law. The Salishan-speaking Spokane and Coeur d'Alene tribes together originally occupied tribal territories of more than 8 million acres across what is now central and eastern Washington, western Montana, and northern Idaho.

My reading of *Smoke Signals* is influenced by Sherman Alexie's assertion that among the most serious problems confronting Native Americans is "the challenge to our sovereignty — artistically, politically, socially, economically. We are and always have been nations within this nation, and any threats to that are dangerous."[14] Alexie's emphatic foregrounding of sovereignty as a primary framework for understanding his script for *Smoke Signals* is temporally specific to the late 1990s, when the film was made; after 9/11 he began to focus more on commonalities between Native and non-Native youth in many of his talks and readings. But attending to different iterations and definitions of sovereignty helps to clarify the ways that *Smoke Signals* articulated a distinct Indigenous perspective.

Native American sovereignty is the recognition of Native tribes as separate and sovereign political entities — and as nations that exist within the larger nation of the United States — as defined in formal treaties made with European nations and with the United States, and as acknowledged in the U.S. Constitution. Scholarly conversations about the history of Native sovereignty stress the tension between tribal nations' political rights to self-government and their relationships with the United States, relationships that have often been characterized by violence and paternalism.[15] Sovereignty is a complex concept with a long history in European thought and international law, and with a specific, contested history and contemporary meaning for Indigenous nations and for Indigenous-U.S. relations. In many cases, Indigenous tribes' nation-to-nation relationship with the United States is acknowledged in legally binding treaties. Political theorist Kevin Bruyneel defines sovereignty, in the context of Native political goals, as a social and political construction that asserts "collective autonomy"; it is "the ability of a group of people to make their own decisions and control their own lives in relation to the space where they reside and/or that they envision as their own."[16] Robert Warrior (Osage), drawing from the historical writing of Native intellectuals such as John Joseph Mathews (Osage) and Vine Deloria Jr. (Sioux), suggests that political and "intellectual sovereignty" advocates a humanizing and "process-centered understanding of sovereignty" in place of "making the rhetoric of sovereignty and tradition a final rather than beginning step."[17] The economic expression of Indigenous sovereignty takes place, for example, in the development of tribal casino gaming, in the tribal management of reservation lands and natural resources, and in the assertion of fishing and other rights to wild harvests guaranteed by treaty. Reclaiming sovereignty in a social context has meant fighting the institutional interventions in Native families, such as the aggressive removal of children from their families through foster care systems and residential schools.[18] The definition and development of aesthetic and intellectual concepts of Indigenous sovereignty are particularly important to the production of *Smoke Signals* as an Indigenous artistic and intellectual work of art.

First Nations scholar Taiaiake Alfred (Mohawk) points out the problematic origins of the idea of sovereignty in a European colonial legal tradition, a discourse that historically does not invite a "fundamental questioning of the assumptions that underlie the state's approach to power, the bad assumptions of colonialism that will continue to structure the relationship,"[19] excluding other frameworks for discourse that come from Indigenous traditions, languages, philosophies and forms of government. Joanne Barker (Lenape) writes that although sovereignty as a concept is "incomplete, inaccurate, and troubled" it has also been "rearticulated to mean altogether different things by Indigenous peoples. In its links to concepts of self-determination and self-government, it insists on the recognition of inherent rights to the respect for political affiliations that are historical and located and for the unique cultural identities that continue to find meaning in those histories and relations."[20] Sovereignty, then, can be seen as a Euro-American construct that has been taken up by Indigenous peoples in tribal, nationalist, and global contexts. While the concept of sovereignty doesn't adequately articulate distinctive, traditional Indigenous social and political structures, it has been an extremely important social justice and legal tool for speaking across the boundaries between peoples to assert Indigenous minority rights. It has served as a discursive marker of the expansion or limitation of tribal autonomy and self-government in the face of ongoing and shifting forms of U.S. colonization.

Indigenous sovereignty is not only, and not simply, an Indigenous issue; it is foundational to the origin of settler nations and central to the ongoing lives of all people now residing in those nations. Canadian journalist and stateswoman Adrienne Clarkson makes this point by emphasizing the reciprocity inherent in nation-to-nation treaties: "In fact, we are all treaty people because it takes two sides to make a treaty, and that's what we agreed to do."[21] Historical studies of treaty-making show us that Natives and newcomers have had changing relationships over time, and have codified those relationships in different ways through trade, kinship (including both blood relations and protocols establishing fictive kinship), oral and written agreements, and military conflicts and alliances. In addition to the extensive critical literature on the international history of U.S., European, and Canadian treaty-making with Indigenous Nations, filmmakers like Alanis Obomsawin (Abenaki) have produced an extraordinary body of documentary film work that historicizes contemporary land and treaty rights disputes in terms of their roots in past violations of treaty agreements.[22]

Sovereignty is not only one of the discourses that "sets Native American studies apart from other critical race discourses," as Michelle Raheja (Seneca) has written;[23] sovereignty is also an important framework for considering the ways that Native arts, such as cinema, take up the colonizers' language, such as cinematic genres and lexicons, for the purposes of shoring up an Indigenous aesthetic autonomy. A number of scholars and artists have expanded upon legal and historical definitions of sovereignty in order to demonstrate the political dimensions of Indigenous identity and nationhood in Native media. Beverly Singer (Tewa/Navajo) defines "cultural sovereignty" as a process involving "trusting the older ways and adapting them to our lives in the present." Amanda Cobb (Chickasaw) has taken up Singer's term in relation to *Smoke Signals* specifically, arguing that the film, as an act of Native self-definition, is also an act of cultural sovereignty.[24] Jolene Rickard (Tuscarora) describes sovereignty in the context of visual art as "the border that shifts Indigenous experience from a victimized stance to a strategic one. . . . Today, sovereignty is taking shape in visual thought as Indigenous artists negotiate cultural space."[25] Scholars translating the concept of sovereignty to cinema include Randolph Lewis, who discusses Native media in terms of "representational sovereignty," and Michelle Raheja, who argues that the concept of sovereignty begins to account for "the space between resistance and compliance" within which Native filmmakers often work. "Visual sovereignty," she writes, "recognizes the paradox of creating media for multiple audiences, critiquing filmic representations of Native Americans at the same time that it participates in some of the conventions that have produced those representations."[26] Visual sovereignty, then, can refer to the way relationships between nations influence (and are influenced by) the shared spaces of visual culture, and to the way Indigenous visual media work to redefine the parameters and significations of mainstream mass media communications.[27]

Although *Smoke Signals* organizes its cinematic discourse explicitly in terms of American Indian relations with the United States — with its frequent references to the U.S. Independence Day holiday and 1976 Bicentennial celebrations, for example — broader frameworks of international cinema circulation and of transnational Indigenism are relevant to the film in a number of ways. Despite their unique histories, there are interrelated and shared patterns of historical colonization among the settler states and Indigenous minority groups across Canada, Aotearoa/New Zealand, Australia, the United States, and the trans-Arctic (such as the Sapmi, or Sami homelands of northern Europe, and northern Asia). Indigenous scholars and artists such as Maori filmmaker Barry Barclay have taken up this transnational perspective to create political and artistic alliances among the Fourth World, or Indigenous minority peoples of settler states. Barclay coined the term "Fourth Cinema" to describe the films by Indigenous minorities working "outside of the national orthodoxies" of colonizing nations.[28] Linked by their assertions of sovereignty and tribal nationhood in relation to specific land claims and treaty documents, Fourth World cinemas also involve considerable regional and international mobility in both production and reception. Film scholar Corinn Columpar describes the "transnational flows" of cinema products that have had an impact on Indigenous peoples, both through dominant film industry products (such as Hollywood's global export of Westerns and British production of colonial epics) and, more recently, the rise of Indigenous filmmaking internationally. This Fourth World cinema has a newly expanded reach through film festivals, digital media, satellite broadcast and other means.[29] *Smoke Signals* provides an example of this, as it circulated worldwide through the festival circuit, in theaters, and, later, through distribution on VHS and DVD. Ultimately, the film should be understood in all of these contexts of media history, political and visual sovereignty, and the historical expansion of Indigenous cinema in North American and beyond.

Scope and Organization of the Book

Listening to these Native voices in cinema involves paying close attention both to the films themselves and to the connections between the films and the producers' and consumers' social and material "media worlds"[30] — including politics and histories as well as production situations, funding, distribution, and audiences. Looking at *Smoke Signals* through these multiple lenses allows us to see the film in conversation not only with mainstream popular culture and the history of Hollywood representations of Indians but also with tribal, regional, and pan-tribal Native issues, including sovereignty, social justice, and environmental history.

In the chapters that follow, I argue that *Smoke Signals*, with its action taking place largely off the reservation on land that was appropriated by the United States, seeks to transform that "public" space back into Native space. Through its reflexivity and wide-ranging historical and popular culture references, *Smoke Signals* "Indigenizes" mainstream cinema, a term Linda Tuhiwai Smith uses to describe a practice that "centres a politics of Indigenous identity and Indigenous cultural action."[31] Projects that privilege Indigenous voices even when borrowing from Western models also provide, as M. Annette Jaimes (Juaneno/Yaqui) writes, "a basis for conceptualization of Indigenism that counters the negative connotations of its meanings."[32] These negative connotations, I argue, circulate through stereotypes circulated in the media. Thinking of *Smoke Signals* as an Indigenizing production brings into focus the ways that this film reappropriates cinematic images of Indians, shifting the meanings and stakes of popular culture images through an insistence that audiences recognize a Native perspective.

I have organized this book into four chapters, which address the historical representation of Indians in the Western and the emergence of "visual sovereignty" in Indigenous media; the production of *Smoke Signals*, from Alexie's literary adaptation of his short story collection *The Lone Ranger and Tonto Fistfight in Heaven* through Chris Eyre's short film *Someone Kept Saying Powwow* and his work with the actors; a chapter on *Smoke Signals*'s intertextual references to popular culture; and an assessment of its reception. In the conclusion, I discuss the way *Smoke Signals* has been positioned within the widely varying definitions of Native cinema from scholars and practicing artists.

Chapter 1 offers a brief history of the Western, an essential background for understanding *Smoke Signals*'s intertextual references to the genre and for unpacking the ways the opening sequences self-consciously position the film as an Indigenous intervention that "speaks back" to the Western's representational history. This chapter foregrounds issues of voice — the voices of media representations as well as relations of speaking and listening in storytelling. The film's opening focus on the radio station DJ demonstrates the power of media to make Native voices heard, just as Thomas Builds-the-Fire's Coeur d'Alene stories become part of a shared public memory through the film's voice-over narration. This overt emphasis on storytelling is the film's most obvious strategy for offering "Indigenizing" perspectives in the public mediascape.

Subsequent chapters follow the trajectory of the film's production, circulation, and reception with discussions of the script, performances, formal images and soundtrack, and reviews. Chapter 2 describes the context of *Smoke Signals*'s production, including Sherman Alexie's screenplay adaptation of *The Lone Ranger and Tonto Fistfight in Heaven*, the development of *Smoke Signals* through the Sundance Film Institute, and the way the filmmakers and actors drew upon personal life stories for their performances. *Smoke Signals* imagines its characters' and its viewers' relationships to cinematic images and stereotypes in terms of both the heterogeneity and the commonalities of Native experiences, especially those of the writer, director, and performers. Their comments about the film tell a cumulative story of seeking social justice through performance and the arts. By engaging as activists in the pervasive field of popular culture, the filmmakers and actors bring the specificity of individual Native histories to bear on a common aesthetic project.

Chapter 3 offers a close analysis of *Smoke Signals*'s images, sounds, editing structure, and location shooting, showing how the film appropriates Hollywood genre conventions and the building blocks of cinematic language itself—such as principles of continuity—to tell a contemporary Indigenous story about events from the past. Both thematically and in its locations, the film embeds politicized references and densely woven allusions to historical events, including the origin of the United States as a nation with the Declaration of Independence and the closing off of Spokane tribal fishing sites with white settlement and dam construction in the Columbia River basin. This extra-cinematic history of nations and lands informs the film's "Indigenizing" perspective on mainstream American culture when characters reflect upon celebrations of Independence Day, discuss revisionist Westerns like *Dances with Wolves*, or tell stories about such mundane activities as basketball games and eating at Denny's.

The final chapter traces *Smoke Signals*'s reception by Native and non-Native audiences, its impact on the careers of the filmmakers and actors, and its influence on the emergence and visibility of new work by Native filmmakers. A key point in discussions about *Smoke Signals* has been its broad appeal; the film is especially significant for its ability to generate shared emotion while keeping the particularities of Indigenous experience at its center. Sherman Alexie has rejected the term "universal" in describing the film, stressing instead its tribalism and the specificity of the characters' experiences.[33] Yet both Alexie and director Chris Eyre have discussed the film as their attempt to reach a mass audience, and its structure conforms to Hollywood road-movie genre conventions and forms.

Not only is *Smoke Signals* one of the most prominent Native American feature films, but it has also functioned historically and politically as a bellwether, a Native cinema "first." The conclusion returns to the issue of *Smoke Signals*'s historical status. What do we mean by "Native cinema"—a category that means different things to different people—and why has it been important to talk about groundbreaking Native features as "firsts"? The book's closing discussion considers these terms beyond scholarly critical constructions to assess their meaning in the practical landscape of industrial and independent film production and distribution, and for Native artists and their networks.

Eyre and Alexie's facility with American pop cultural currency, and their ability to bring so many different viewers to "sit at the same table," has also allowed them to reveal cinema's imperialist history. They ask us to recognize popular culture's colonizing misrepresentations while at the same time inviting us to take pleasure in playing with its field of references, and through that play and humor (as well as drama and affect) to assert power over its exclusions and distortions. In the wake of this media history and in the toxic afterlife of media products, they excel at finding opportunities to resignify an American popular culture imperium to tell a different story. Like changing the captions on old photographs, they offer us a new narration.

chapter one

"Indians Watching Indians"

Speaking to and from Cinema History

Midway through *Smoke Signals*, as the camera tilts upward from a small television screen playing a Western film, Thomas Builds-the-Fire says, "You know, the only thing more pathetic than Indians on TV is Indians watching Indians on TV!" Many critics point to this apparently casual line as a signature of the film's break from the Hollywood tradition of stereotypically stoic representations of Indians.[1] By drawing our attention to "Indians watching Indians on TV," the film asks us to reflect upon issues of media, audience, exhibition, and reception. As is often the case with jokes, this compact utterance makes meaning in several ways, raising a complex set of issues and questions about the history of images of Indians and about film production and reception in Native communities. "Indians on TV" refers of course not only to old Westerns being replayed on television, but also to the characters in the movie, who are watching old Westerns on television in a trailer home in Phoenix, Arizona. It also tips its hat to Native viewers watching *Smoke Signals* itself—a film about Indians with Native actors, which might be playing in a theater or on a television set at home with a Native audience. In this sense *Smoke Signals* speaks directly to its audiences while modeling Indigenous readings of the Western that demystify that aging form of popular culture.[2]

Smoke Signals's intertextual references to mainstream media are part of its Indigenizing political strategy and form the basis for the film's appeal to multiple audiences—and its success as a Native voice that was widely heard. Reflexivity is an important way of taking control of interpretation, the power of meaning-making. Reflecting upon media history also situates Native films—and the Native viewers imagined and addressed in the films—in a modern context, countering tenacious iconographies of Indian primitivity

1. An old Western playing on the TV in Suzy Song's trailer prompts Thomas Builds-the-Fire's comment that "the only thing more pathetic than Indians on TV is Indians watching Indians on TV!"

and the fiction that the Native actors on screen are somehow unaware of the camera, unconscious objects of Western vision rather than artists with distinct agendas.[3] By referring to the on-screen and off-screen Native audience at the same time, the line "Indians watching Indians on TV" bridges the fictional world of the film and the real world of its viewers. This bridge fosters identification between Native viewers and Native focal characters, in direct contrast to the white racial focalization and viewer address in the Western. And like the DJ Randy Peone's (John Trudell, Santee Sioux) greeting both the fictional and actual listeners with *Smoke Signals*'s opening salutation of "Good morning," Thomas's one-liner invites *all* viewers to connect the film's story to the world beyond the screen, thus opening the door for more serious political communications. Ultimately both of these moments ask viewers to understand the film from a Native point of view. "Indians watching Indians on TV" gestures toward the importance of Native actors; the opening credit sequences of *Smoke Signals* take on special significance as the site where the writer, director, producers, and lead actors are named, instead of appearing as "anonymous" Native extras.

Smoke Signals's most important intervention may be its shift in the identity of the narrator. Since the racial identity of cinematic narrators has been assumed (by studios and filmmakers alike) to be a crucial point of focalization for viewers, even Westerns that are sympathetic to their Indian characters — such as *Broken Arrow* (dir. Daves, 1950), *Dances with Wolves, Geronimo: An American Legend* (dir. Hill, 1993), and many others — are narrated by white male protagonists. These Westerns model historiography as the privilege of the settlers; Indian characters are in the story but never the storytellers. *Smoke Signals* foregrounds a pivotal turning point in this media history, establishing a logic of then and now by looking back at the Western with Native eyes.

The phrase "Indians watching Indians on TV" also invites us to think about how media travel and especially about relationships of exhibition and reception — the television rebroadcasting of Westerns, with their mass audience target, and individual homes where Native viewers may view media versions of themselves with (at a minimum) what critic bell hooks has called an "oppositional gaze."[4] *Smoke Signals* adopts this articulated yet oppositional stance with regard to film history, dismantling tropes of Indian "vanishing" with counterstrategies, such as humor and irony, that establish Native contemporary presence. Thomas's comment inserts the movie into a historical trajectory of mediated images of Indians, and in reflecting upon that history and upon the Indians on screen in *Smoke Signals*, the filmmakers engage and speak back to a shared repository of representations. Because *Smoke Signals* so explicitly stages a conversation with dominant Hollywood stereotypes of Indians, and in particular with images of "vanishing Indians," it is worth taking a moment to consider what is at stake in Native filmmakers' continual return to the Western as a referential archive and common heritage of popular signs, and also in their deliberate disruption of that larger history of Native American representations on screen.

"Extras, We're All Extras": Images of Indians in the Western

The images of Indian absence that *Smoke Signals* so often mimics and mocks emerged from the Western, a genre that dominated American film and television screens for much of the twentieth century, and that systematically portrayed and attempted to justify settler domination of Indigenous lands and peoples. Several Western subgenres complicate this pattern, such as the silent-era "Indian drama," and later revisionist Westerns (sometimes called Indian Westerns, or what Amanda J. Cobb calls "Indian sympathy films") — made by non-Native filmmakers — that take Indian-white relations as their central focus.[5] Beverly Singer uses the term "visual genocide" to refer to the way that Westerns obsessively return to the violence of U.S. national origins, yet also mystify, conceal, or attempt to justify that same violence by representing Indians on screen as noble or savage figures that exist only in the past.[6] Westerns disseminate fictions about the history of the United States and its international relations with Native nations, bringing up moral questions for viewers about their relationships and responsibilities regarding the past. They address a basic conflict in the American ideology of democracy: U.S. discourses of freedom and national independence from Europe are rooted in the violent dispossession of Native tribes. The genre has functioned as a form of "bad pedagogy" as well, since many viewers, especially children, uncritically absorb its mythic national charter and misrepresentations of gender, race, and violence in frontier history. As a genre that narrates and envisions internal U.S. colonialism, the Western can also be seen in the context of other imperialist film genres from settler states such as Britain and Australia. Ella Shohat and Robert Stam argue that like the Imperial adventure film — the jungle film, the ethnographic film — "the Western told the story of imperial-style adventures on the American frontier," a domestic imperialism.[7]

Smoke Signals's linked but oppositional relationship to the Western reveals the genre to be a myth-making replay of conquest, and in order to understand how *Smoke Signals* organizes its contrapuntal engagement with the Western's iconic history, we need to know the story of those icons and also of the Western's "vanishing" Indians — the visual techniques of Indian erasure and the resulting marginalization of Native actors in the film industry.[8] In an early (1974) article, "Colonialism through the Media," Gerald Wilkinson (Cherokee/Catawba) wrote that "the fact that these media are so pervasive makes them impossible to escape. . . . We are being defined by outsiders, and the power to define is the power to control."[9] That definition took form primarily through two Western-genre representational devices — stock Indian character types and the trope of the "vanishing Indian" — that cut across historical periods and across popular, political, and scientific discourses.

Historically, the single most pervasive public fiction about Native Americans is that they are vanishing. This "vanishing" is not a single trope or image but rather a series of distinct types of discourse that are collectively informed by a tenacious narrative. These discourses include images that circulate through various forms of popular culture; assumptions that underpin political rhetoric, laws, and policies; and hypotheses or suppositions behind studies and preservation efforts in social sciences such as anthropology.

Indian "vanishing" is part of a broad, structuring ideology that informed various kinds of narratives and images, including demonized images of violent savages and romanticized, sentimental constructions of noble Indian allies, desirable Indian princesses, and magical shamans. As Brian Dippie has demonstrated in his widely cited study *The Vanishing American*, the idea of the "vanishing Indian" — like the interlocking American belief in Manifest Destiny — was rooted in ideas of biological determinism and social Darwinism that imagined Indians as primitive and racially inferior to Europeans, doomed to recede in the face of white expansion across the continent.[10] Images of Indians riding exhausted ponies westward into the setting sun or standing dejectedly at the edge of precipices circulated widely during the nineteenth and twentieth centuries in the form of photographs, postcards, paintings, posters, illustrations in books and periodicals, and, after the invention of motion picture cameras, in the movies.[11] Such representations, which limit images of Indians to the historical past and to tropes of absence, present U.S. imperialism as a fait accompli. Settlers' westward expansion is imagined as an instantiation of temporal "progress" and, further, as inevitable, a force of nature rather an act of human agency. In contrast, many Native writers and filmmakers, including Eyre and Alexie, emphasize Native generational continuation and present U.S. continental expansion as "unfinished business," reminding audiences that treaty responsibilities, court cases, and government and tribal land negotiations are ongoing.

The effect of any individual image is compounded because this "vanishing Indian" representational scenario so completely dominates the Western genre, which is largely lacking in any balancing depictions of contemporary Native people. The consequences of this lacuna are the manufactured absences of modern Indigeneity on screen, and the correlative of that absence, images of Indian decline or death. As documented by such film scholars as Armando José Prats, M. Elise Marubbio, Angela Aleiss, Jacqueline Kilpatrick (Choctaw/Cherokee), and others, Indian absence is envisioned on screen in various forms, including "empty land" or "open" frontiers, signs of threat (such as arrows) that come from off screen, voice-over or screen title narration using the past tense, and stock characters such as the "Indian maiden" who typically dies near the end of the film. These mass media images disseminate assumptions that Indians only exist at a certain historical moment in the mid- and late nineteenth century, or that Indians are chronically incapable of navigating a modernity imagined as the sole purview of urban dwellers — the audience of the movies themselves, who are imagined as homogenous white settlers.[12]

This powerful assumption of Indian vanishing has also structured federal policies, especially legislation and policy aimed at forcing Native people to assimilate into an imagined American cultural mainstream. For example, the 1887 General Allotment Act (or Dawes Act) broke up reservation lands held in common by tribes, assigning plots of land to individuals and opening up the "surplus" land to white homesteading on the assumption that Native people were vanishing, and no future Native generations would need the land.[13] The overarching scenario of vanishing at this time informed legislators' presumptions of Native population decline and degeneracy as well as ideas about assimilation. Native people, it was assumed, would become amalgamated into the non-Native population and simply cease to be Native as a distinct political or cultural group, an assumption that also guided government-run boarding schools where Native children were sent to learn to dress and speak like settler Americans. Native American identity itself has been defined by the government in a way that reinforces the idea of vanishing. Unlike other minority groups in the United States, Native Americans must prove their tribal affiliation to qualify for certain federal services. Currently, Certificates of Degree of Indian Blood ("CDIB cards"), issued to individual tribal members, list their fraction of "Indian blood." The definition of racial identity as a factor of "blood quantum" perpetuates the fiction of race as a biological rather than social distinction and drastically limits the number of people who can claim Native heritage, since the Native population becomes smaller through intermarriage.

A third discourse of vanishing has focused on the study and preservation of Native crafts and languages, not as dynamic, changing traditions but rather as static objects for museum collections and displays and Bureau of Ethnography reports. Anthropologists at the turn of the century, sure that Native populations and cultures were on the verge of extinction, raced to record Native languages and stories, and to collect Native crafts and artifacts, an approach to fieldwork often described as "salvage ethnography." The idea of "salvaging" the remains of Native cultures — including objects and human remains — presumes that they are endangered and in need of rescue and preservation. This assumption that Native objects and languages must be collected and recorded "before they're all gone" hinged on the narrative of imminent Indian vanishing. This impulse was translated to visual culture through the work of photographers like Edward S. Curtis, whose turn-of-the-century portraits posed Native subjects only in traditional garb. His 1914 film *In the Land of the War Canoes* attempted to reconstruct precontact Kwakwaka'wakw life while suppressing evidence of the tribe's contemporary experiences and problems.[14]

Concomitant with the trope of vanishing in the Western is its obsession with the performance of Indianness, an obsession that extends beyond the cinema to cultural practices of "playing Indian" and "going native" on stage, in clubs, in historical events such as the Boston Tea Party, in children's plays and early training through organizations such as the Boy Scouts, and in festivals and parades.[15] Costume is a crucial visual signifier of race and racial allegiance in such performances, especially the Plains feathered warbonnet, face paint, and fringed buckskin (often worn by white gunfighters or trappers — as in *Shane* [dir. Stevens, 1953] and *Jeremiah Johnson* [dir. Pollack, 1972] — who are associated with Indians or with frontier violence).[16] Contemporary TV shows (e.g., the Chumash ghost in *Buffy the Vampire Slayer*, season 4, episode 8, 1999, "Pangs") and films (most recently *Avatar*, 2009) continue this tradition.

Hollywood filmmakers routinely cast Indians as savage or noble, often in the same movie, and part of the work of *Smoke Signals's* comedy is to draw attention to the stock characters and iconic figures that make up the conventional Western's symbolic language.[17] Both noble and savage stereotypes are tropes of conquest and containment; almost invariably, Indian characters lose their lives in Hollywood Westerns. Philip Deloria (Standing Rock Sioux) has pointed out that the word "stereotype" itself traces its etymological lineage to the printing trade and denotes the duplication of identical copies.[18] Thus, the work of mechanical reproduction tends to reinforce the dominance of Hollywood representations while marginalizing Native self-representations. The pervasiveness and uniformity of these images of Indians as anachronisms, lingering problems to be solved, or obstacles to progress (that version of progress being defined as the expansion of the United States as a nation) preclude other images of Indians as, for example, professionals in urban centers; tribal nations engaged in legal battles over land, water rights, and religious freedom; intellectuals using their public voices to intervene in national politics; and communities working to address the social consequences of rural and urban poverty. When Indian characters — especially mixed blood characters — are set in contemporary time frames, they are frequently pathologized as mentally unstable, alcoholic, treacherous, or beset by overwhelming, intractable, and ultimately fatal dilemmas stemming from being "torn between cultures,"[19] as in *Redskin* (dir. Schertzinger, 1929), *Flap* (dir. Reed, 1970), and *Flags of Our Fathers* (dir. Eastwood, 2007).[20]

If the savage Indians in films like *Stagecoach* (dir. Ford, 1939) symbolize physical, racial, and sexual threats to settlers and their homes, travel, property, and prosperity, noble Indians from *The Squaw Man* (dir. DeMille, 1914) to *Dances with Wolves* (1990) sacrifice themselves to enable white settlers to prosper on Indian land. Renato Rosaldo names this form of romanticized representation "imperialist nostalgia," an "elegaic mode of perception" in which "people mourn the passing of what they themselves have transformed." Nostalgic representations of imperialism are a form of symbolic violence employing a "pose of 'innocent yearning' both to capture people's imagination and to conceal its complicity with often brutal domination."[21] Despite efforts at respectful realism in *Dances with Wolves*, the Lakota characters remain outside of the film's power structure. Like the sidekick character of Tonto in *The Lone Ranger* (ABC, 1949–57), the Lakota are in an allied but inferior position to the settler hero, acting as satellites to the white star/protagonist while authenticating his journey of self-discovery. Such characters often willingly bequeath their land and rights to settlers, as the mixed-blood Indian character Pacer Burton (Elvis Presley) does at the end of *Flaming Star* (dir. Siegel, 1960) when he says to his white half brother, "I'm already gone . . . just stubborn about dying. You live for me." Even Indian children are bequeathed to white couples in films like *The Squaw Man*.[22]

Western allegorical storytelling and symbolic consistency are further masked in films with large budgets supporting historical-realist claims and romanticized images. Films such as *Dances with Wolves, Pocahontas*, or *The New World* engage viewers through high production values, including aesthetically rich cinematography, detailed realism in costume and setting, compelling music, and expensive stars, not to mention patronizing sentimentalism. Native characters allied with white protagonists are often beautiful, appealing, and virtuous, as is Pocahontas (Q'Orianka Kilcher, Quechua-Huachipaeri) in *The New World*, but are ultimately powerless against a predestined death. An important point to take from films like *The Last of the Mohicans*, with its painstakingly realistic reproductions of eighteenth-century American colonial material culture, is that stereotypes are not necessarily countered by realism, which can be selectively deployed as an expensive cinematic style supporting commonplace fictions. Politicized stylization, and amplification of Native focalization and voice in cinematic production can function as viable Native aesthetic answers to both stereotypes and a seductive but totalizing "realism."

Hollywood was shaped as an industry by its production of Westerns. The very first feature-length film made in Hollywood was a Western — Cecil B. DeMille's 1914 film *The Squaw Man* — and between 1926 and 1967 more Westerns were made than any other kind of film.[23] Western film production followed broad trends in twentieth-century film history, and is better understood in the context of cyclical production rather than evolutionary progression. For example, Western-genre representations of Indians have not become steadily more sympathetic over time; rather, the "sympathetic Western" has reappeared throughout the century, with production cycles in the early 1910s, late 1920s, early 1950s, late 1960s, and early 1990s.

Before the dominance of Hollywood studios, most early silent-era Western films were actually produced in Europe and imported to the United States. By moving to Hollywood, California, from New Jersey early in the twentieth century, American companies were able to better market their frontier-themed films by claiming greater authenticity in their representations of the West. Yet the proscribed range of Indian roles limited Native off-screen participation in the industry even in its earliest days. In his autobiography *My People the Sioux*, Luther Standing Bear (Lakota) recalls his work in early motion pictures (circa 1912), and upon looking back "cannot help noting how we real Indians were held back, while white 'imitators' were pushed up front."[24] These practices of redfacing, false authenticating, and "loincloth roles" kept Native voices out of the movies even while keeping Indians constantly visible on screen.[25] From this early point in the history of motion picture production, Native American actors were denied influence in productions that cast them in supporting roles as sidekicks, or as "extras," roles in which they functioned as human backdrops to the drama acted out by the white actors in principal roles. When the primary characters were Indian, these roles, too, often went to white actors in redface. Producers could make claims to a film's authenticity based on small roles played by Native actors and un-credited extras, while reaching out to a primarily white audience by casting white stars in lead roles.

Native actors, directors, and viewers have not been passive in the face of this history but rather have been in active conversation with Hollywood representations since the origins of the film industry itself. Despite the racial dynamics of casting that Standing Bear describes, the early silent film industry was far more open to Native participants than the later, more established studio system. Native directors and actors such as James Young Deer (Ho-Chunk) and Princess Red Wing, the stage name of Lillian St. Cyr (Ho-Chunk), were able to exert considerable power over film production for a limited time during the early silent era between 1908 and 1914. In 1911 several delegations of Anishinaabes, Shoshones, Cheyennes, and Arapahos traveled to Washington DC to protest demeaning representations in films like *Curse of the Redman* (dir. Boggs, 1911);

their protests led to industry attempts to increase the "authenticity" of Western films.[26] Between 1910 and 1955, three Chickasaw brothers — writer Finis Fox, director Edwin Carewe (stage name of Jay Fox), and director Wallace Fox — made feature films and serial Westerns (and, in the case of Wallace Fox, television episodes) for both major and independent studios. At the height of the silent era, Carewe was directing lucrative adaptations of literary works such as Tolstoy's *Resurrection* and Jackson's *Ramona*, and had galvanized the careers of stars such as Gary Cooper and Dolores Del Rio. But despite the influential but brief careers of actors and directors like Young Deer, St. Cyr, and Carewe in the silent era, the lack of Native control over screen representations that was articulated by Standing Bear became the norm during the studio era, and this persistence informs our understanding of why creative control and casting Native actors became key goals of Indigenous filmmakers in the second half of the twentieth century.

Aside from prestigious, epic Westerns (such as *The Covered Wagon*, dir. Cruze, 1923), the 1920s, 1930s, and 1940s saw the large-scale industrial production of B-Westerns, including weekly serials starring singing cowboys such as Gene Autry. Higher-budget Westerns from this era, such as *Stagecoach*, also asked viewers to misread history, offering a structural paradigm that inverts the actual history of conquest. Screen Indians "appear to be intruders on their own lands,"[27] making the public space of film screens and the actual space of public lands hostile to Native presence through the symbolic violence of cinematic representations. Like earlier and later films that highlighted racial polarization on the frontier (such as *The Battle at Elderbush Gulch* [dir. Griffith, 1913] and *The Missing* [dir. Howard, 2003]), *Stagecoach* shores up racial and sexual boundaries by categorizing civilization and savagery. Moreover, like *The Birth of a Nation* (dir. Griffith, 1915), another film credited with landmark innovations in film language, *Stagecoach* deploys technical mastery (location shooting, stunt work, casting, and narrative consolidation of generic elements) to imagine and celebrate violence in the form of a race war that charters the dominant imperial social order. In *Stagecoach*, a film organized by what Tom Englehardt calls an "ambush scenario," Indians are exterior to (and represent sexual and social threats to) a vulnerable white domestic stronghold.[28] We never see Indian children or domestic spaces, only images of aggression as Indian men attack the stagecoach carrying, among the other passengers, two white settler women and a newborn baby. Ford's technical virtuosity in representing the climactic attack on the stagecoach through complex editing supports this thematic pattern: shot–reverse shot sequences align viewers' point-of-view with these settlers, thus suturing film audiences to settlers' perspectives through visual and narrative film language and naturalizing political narratives of American triumphalism, expansion and Manifest Destiny. Jon Tuska aptly summarizes the net effect of the final chase sequence of Ford's classic Western: "Killing Indians is shown to be exciting."[29] Spectators are encouraged to identify with white settler heroes and to revisit in the form of play and entertainment the genocidal violence of frontier conquest.

Midcentury shifts in Western-genre production responded to conditions in Hollywood, such as the blacklist of the 1950s, and in turn to the broader national and international struggles over McCarthyism, the civil rights movement, and the Vietnam War. Noble Indian stereotypes have presented powerful tools for American self-criticism in films using sympathetic Indian characters and frontier situations as vehicles for coded progressive or countercultural messages. The Indian Westerns of the early 1950s (e.g., *Devil's Doorway* [dir. Mann, 1950] and *Broken Arrow*) seemed to comment on broad issues of social intolerance and on African American civil rights issues in particular, using the genre as a form of coded social criticism during the era of McCarthyism and the Hollywood blacklist. Later, in the 1960s and early 1970s, as Richard Slotkin has argued, massacre scenes in films like *Soldier Blue* (dir. Nelson, 1970) and *Little Big Man* (dir. Penn, 1970) intentionally alluded to the My Lai massacre in Vietnam.[30] These films tended to stereotype Indian characters as romantic emblems of the counterculture or as "ethnic stand-ins" for other minorities. Limiting critical interpretations of Indian images in terms of their signification of other ethnic groups risks replicating the very discourses of vanishing in the Western itself, treating Indian images and stereotypes as ciphers that can signify almost any social issue, and obscuring nuanced dynamics of power in the film industry, including the work of Native actors and filmmakers.[31]

Although critics have often announced that the Western has reached the point of "genre death," small cycles of Western production continue. *Dances with Wolves* initiated a strong cycle in the 1990s with films like *Thunderheart* (dir. Apted, 1992), and a more recent cluster of Western-themed entertainments include titles such as HBO's series *Deadwood* (2004–6) and films like *The Missing* and *Hidalgo* (dir. Johnston, 2004). The Western's extensive symbolic language and visual iconography have become dispersed into American public culture and available as political allegory and for other rhetorical and marketing purposes, such as photographs on the White House website during George W. Bush's presidency depicting Bush in a cowboy hat, clearing brush from the land on his ranch in Crawford, Texas.

One of *Smoke Signals*'s most effective weapons against the media imperialism of the Western has been humor and irony. The film's comic tone, even in a story about loss, stands out in the history of representations of Native modernity, which are far more often made in a tragic mode (see, for instance, the generally elegiac tone and, in particular, the distressed character of Charles Eastman, played by Adam Beach, in the 2007 HBO film *Bury My Heart at Wounded Knee* [dir. Simoneau]). Thus, in order to understand the way *Smoke Signals*'s humor answers historical film images, we need to recognize how Indian Westerns frequently operate without humor, presenting instead stoic Indian characters and humorless stories of Indian demise (notably, in *Smoke Signals*, Victor tells Thomas to "Get stoic!" in order to act like a "real" Hollywood Indian). *Smoke Signals* comments very deliberately upon the Western's discourse of vanishing and its iconic stereotypes, as when the young Thomas enrages his friend Victor during a schoolyard conversation by applying his expert knowledge of pop-culture Indians to Victor's family situation. Thomas confidently predicts that Victor's father, Arnold Joseph, "ain't comin' back you know. When Indians leave, they don't come back — *Last of the Mohicans, Last of the Winnebago* . . ." At the same time, the elegiac pose in the popular culture image of Indians necessarily complicates our understanding of Victor's more serious feelings about his father's death in *Smoke Signals*, becoming a kind of interference or static in his emotional expression. The film's close commentary upon scenarios of Indian vanishing in popular film (most prominently in *Dances with Wolves*) compels us to juxtapose the posed stance of imperial mourning with Victor's own bereavement and commemoration, and to ask how familial or community mourning takes place in the context of such mediated popular appropriations and stereotypical representations of Indian loss.

Indigenous filmmaking challenges the "vanishing Indian" trope that has structured federal Indian policies. Traversing a media space structured by damaging representations has involved Native filmmakers' reappropriating, mocking, and taking political leverage from Hollywood representations through specific strategies, such as identifying Native actors in Hollywood productions and referring to film production processes in film texts. Eyre and Alexie's repositioning of images in *Smoke Signals* locates Indians both on and off screen, intervening in mainstream cinemas that imagine Indians in contexts of tragedy, death, and disappearance by reworking those older tropes. Native filmmakers who once watched old Westerns on TV are challenging Hollywood's presumptions of an all-white viewing audience that has unified beliefs about the history of U.S. settlement. They retrospectively revise the way those films have been interpreted, offering oppositional readings of Westerns from an Indigenous perspective manifested in acts of seeing, speaking, and listening.

The year 1998 was a breakthrough for Native American features. In addition to *Smoke Signals*, two other feature-length dramatic films screened at Sundance that year: *Tushka*, directed by Ian Skorodin (Choctaw), and *Naturally Native*, directed by Valerie Red-Horse (Cherokee/Sioux). Though each of these films has also been marketed as a first (the first Native action film, the first mainstream feature film to be entirely Native-funded and produced), they, along with *Smoke Signals*, represent a millennial arc in a rich and ongoing history of Indigenous film production stretching back to the origins of cinema and expanding geographically across the globe. The surge in Native-directed feature and documentary films in the 1970s and 1980s emerged in part from the Indigenous rights movements of the 1950s and 1960s, which demonstrated the power of mass communications in social justice struggles. The rise of very different kinds of independent cinema movements influenced Native filmmaking in practical, political, and aesthetic ways, from post–World War II global neorealism, to the activist Third Cinema of Latin America, to film collectives and government-sponsored community filmmaking programs (e.g., Canada's "Challenge for Change" program), to the 1990s Indie film cycle in the United States.

Scholar-filmmaker Beverly Singer offers one of the most complete histories to date of the late twentieth-century emergence of Native American cinema before *Smoke Signals*, describing the work of Victor Masayesva Jr. (Hopi), Sandra Osawa (Makah), Arlene Bowman (Navajo), Randy Redroad (Cherokee), and Loretta Todd (Cree), as well as her own early films, as crucial precursors to *Smoke Signals*'s commercial feature breakthrough.[32] Jacqueline Kilpatrick profiles *Harold of Orange* (dir. Weise, 1984) and *Medicine River* (dir. Margolin, 1993) as important early independent dramas, as well as the work of directors Masayesva, Aaron Carr (Laguna Pueblo/Diné), and George Burdeau (Blackfeet) as exemplary of a vibrant tradition in Native documentary and experimental film production.[33]

Though there was a hiatus in the late studio era between the directing careers of James Young Deer and Edwin Carewe in the 1910s and 1920s and the resurgence of U.S. Native documentary and feature filmmaking after the 1960s, throughout the middle decades of the twentieth century a wide range of Native actors, actresses, consultants, and crews still worked to exert control over their own images and over representations of Indians on screen. In the silent era, this list included artists such as Molly Spotted Elk (Penobscot), Nipo T. Strongheart (Yakama), and many others who were based in Los Angeles or who traveled and performed internationally. In the later studio system and after the advent of television, actors such as Jay Silverheels (Mohawk), who played the stereotyped sidekick role of Tonto on *The Lone Ranger* show, as well as Chief Thunder Cloud (Ottawa), Chief Dan George (Coast Salish), and Will Sampson (Muscogee Creek) used their public visibility to advocate for Native rights off screen.

By the early and mid-1970s, some of the Indigenous actors, who had begun by working as extras in studio films, translated their industry experience into independent projects. Sampson, who played "Chief" Bromden in *One Flew Over the Cuckoo's Nest* (dir. Forman, 1975), hosted the five-part KCTS-TV (Seattle) *Images of Indians* series (1979–81), written, directed, and produced by Phil Lucas (Choctaw) and Robert Hagopian. Larry Littlebird (Laguna/ Santo Domingo Pueblo) and George Burdeau, who had worked as extras on Hollywood studio Westerns, took roles in independent films like Richardson Morse's *House Made of Dawn* (1972) (Littlebird played the lead role of Abel). After studying filmmaking at the Santa Fe Anthropology Film Institute, they directed and produced documentaries for television, including the *Real People* series for KSPS-TV (Spokane) in 1976. Burdeau and Hagopian went on to found the organization that would become the current Native American Public Telecommunications (NAPT) in 1977, and Burdeau has since directed documentaries for PBS, including the *Forest Spirit* series and *Surviving Columbus*, as well as films for the Turner Broadcasting System. Much of the television work emphasizing contemporary Native life was made possible by the 1970s

shift toward more balanced representation in mass communications. The Federal Communications Commission (FCC) ordered
in 1972 and 1974 that local television stations make broadcast time
available to underserved communities, opening the airwaves to
programming such as KFYR-TV's (Bismarck ND) *Indian Country
Today* with the Standing Rock Sioux, and Sandra Osawa's series
episodes for the 1974 NBC-TV *The Native Americans Series* in Los
Angeles, among others.[34]

Some of the leaders and spokespeople of the American Indian
Movement (AIM) during its heyday in the late 1960s and early
1970s took up performing roles in Hollywood films decades later,
including Russell Means (Lakota) (*Last of the Mohicans, Natural
Born Killers* [dir. Stone, 1994], *Pocahontas, Pathfinder* [dir. Nispel,
2007]), Dennis Banks (Ojibwa) (*Thunderheart, War Party* [dir.
Roddam, 1998]), and John Trudell (*Powwow Highway* [dir. Wacks,
1989], *Thunderheart, On Deadly Ground* [dir. Seagal, 1994]). They
also supported independent Indigenous projects, such as Heather
Rae's (Cherokee) 2005 documentary *Trudell* (with John Trudell), and
Dennis Banks's role as Pete Goodfeather in Georgina Lightning's
(Cree) 2008 feature film *Older than America*. In the 1980s, several
Native artists emerged from film schools with short thesis films: Bob
Hicks (Creek/Seminole) directed *Return of the Country* in 1982 as
his thesis film for the American Film Institute, and Arlene Bowman
directed *Navajo Talking Picture* for her University of California, Los
Angeles MFA thesis project in 1986.[35] Many of the feature films made
before (and since) *Smoke Signals* have also involved intercultural
partnerships, including *House Made of Dawn* (dir. Morse, 1972),
Harold of Orange, and the made-for-television movies *Medicine
River* and *Grand Avenue* (dir. Sackheim, 1996), which all resulted
from collaborations between prominent Native writers (N. Scott
Momaday [Kiowa], Gerald Vizenor [Anishinaabe], Thomas King
[Cherokee], and Greg Sarris [Pomo/Miwok], respectively) and
non-Native directors.

Concurrently with these trends in Native American production
has been the emergence of Indigenous filmmaking globally.[36] In

terms of *Smoke Signals*'s own production, the proximity of the Spokane and Coeur d'Alene homelands to Canada calls our attention to First Nations nationhood and cinema history. Most of the lead actors in *Smoke Signals* are Canadian First Nations, including Tantoo Cardinal, Adam Beach, Evan Adams, and Gary Farmer. Many of the actors in Hollywood and U.S. independent features have also been First Nations, including Chief Dan George and Jay Silverheels, as well as contemporary actors Graham Greene (Oneida), Michael Greyeyes (Plains Cree), Georgina Lightning, Eric Schweig (Inuvialuit, Chippewa, and Dene), and Gordon Tootoosis (Cree/Stoney). Canadian First Nations filmmakers such as Alanis Obomsawin, Loretta Todd, Shelley Niro (Quinte Bay Mohawk), Gil Cardinal (Cree), Shirley Cheechoo (Cree), Carole Geddes (Tlingit), and many others have taken advantage of Canada's funding support in documentary and animation — Alanis Obomsawin was a particularly powerful force for Aboriginal film production through the National Film Board of Canada (established in 1967).[37] After challenging the predominantly English-language broadcasting and satellite-licensing infrastructure, northern Inuit communities began making media for themselves through the Inuit Broadcasting Corporation (IBC) in 1981. The IBC served as training for Inuit filmmakers like Zacharias Kunuk and Paul Apak, who later formed Isuma Productions; after making a series of documentaries in the 1980s and 1990s, the company moved on to make feature films, starting with the award-winning Inuktitut-language epic *Atanarjuat/The Fast Runner* (dir. Kunuk, 2001) (followed by *The Journals of Knud Rasmussen* [dir. Kunuk] in 2006 and *Before Tomorrow* [dir. Cousineau and Ivalu], from Arnait Video Productions, in 2007).[38]

Beyond Native North America, film production from Indigenous minority groups in settler nations, such as Maori, Australian Aboriginal, and Sami, has been equally rich. Expanding the circle wider, a huge variety of media, from radio to journalism to digital Internet production, comes from Indigenous populations in Latin America, Africa, Asia, and the international trans-Arctic. The United Nations

Declaration on the Rights of Indigenous Peoples, adopted in 2007, emphasizes access to communications in Indigenous languages as a basic political right. Article 16 states, "1. Indigenous peoples have the right to establish their own media in their own languages and to access all the other non-indigenous media without discrimination, and 2. States shall take effective measures to ensure that the media duly reflect indigenous cultural diversity. States, without prejudice to ensuring full freedom of expression, should encourage privately owned media to adequately reflect indigenous cultural diversity."[39]

Maori filmmaker Barry Barclay terms the feature films from Indigenous minorities in settler states "Fourth Cinema," building on the classification system of First Cinema (First World industrial studios, such as Hollywood and Bollywood), Second Cinema (independent films), and Third Cinema (politically revolutionary cinemas from Africa, Asia, and Latin America). Once comprising just a few titles, Fourth World film production has expanded into diverse and rapidly growing fields. An abbreviated compendium of features might include, from Australia: Tracey Moffatt's experimental film *beDevil* (1993); Rachel Perkins's *Radiance* (1998) and *One Night the Moon* (2001); Ivan Sen's *Beneath Clouds* (2002); Ralph de Heer's *Ten Canoes* (2009). From Aotearoa/New Zealand: Merata Mita's *Mauri* (1988); Barry Barclay's *Ngati* (1987) and *Te Rua* (1991); Lee Tamahori's *Once Were Warriors* (1994); Don Selwyn's *The Maori Merchant of Venice* (2002); Taika Waititi's *Eagle vs. Shark* (2007) and *Boy* (2010). From Rotuma: Vilsoni Hereniko's *The Land Has Eyes* [*Pear ta maˈon maf*] (2004). From the international arctic, across northern Eurasia: Sami filmmaker Nils Gaup's *Pathfinder* (1987); Nenet filmmakers Anastasia Lapsui and Markku Lehmuskallio's *Seven Songs from the Tundra* (1999) and *A Bride of the Seventh Heaven* (2004). From Canada, in addition to the robust film work at Isuma Productions and Arnait Video Productions in Igloolik, Nunavut: Alanis Obomsawin's feature-length documentary *Kanehsatake: 270 Years of Resistance* (1993); Shirley Cheechoo's *Bearwalker* (2000) and *Johnny Tootall* (2007), and many others. From the United States: Victor Masayesva's *Itam Hakim, Hopiit* (1985); Valerie Red-Horse's *Naturally*

Native (1998); Ian Skorodin's *Tushka* (1998); Randy Redroad's *The Doe Boy* (2001); Shonie de la Rosa's (Navajo) *Mile Post 398* (2007); Sterlin Harjo's (Creek/Seminole) *Four Sheets to the Wind* (2007) and *Barking Water* (2009); Blackhorse Lowe's (Navajo) *5th World* (2005); Georgina Lightning's *Older than America* (2008); and Andrew Okpeaha McLean's (Inuit) *On the Ice* (2011). Enormous challenges remain at levels of funding, training, infrastructure, technological resources, licensing, broadcast time, distribution, and language. Despite these ongoing problems, a range of institutions have worked to support the surge in global Indigenous documentary, experimental, and feature filmmaking in the last quarter of the twentieth century in each of these areas. Notably, the emergence of film festivals to curate and host screenings of new work, as well as organizations such as the NAPT in the United States; the Aboriginal Peoples Television Network (APTN), National Film Board (NFB), and IBC of Canada; the Central Australian Aboriginal Media Association (CAAMA) of Australia; and Maori Television of Aotearoa/New Zealand, have contributed to a dynamic, structurally layered Indigenous film world. Given the proliferation of media infrastructures and productions and their increase through the last quarter century and across the millennium, it is no surprise that *Smoke Signals* begins with a clear allusion to Native media communications in the form of DJ Randy Peone and the "K-REZ" radio station.

The "Voice of the Coeur d'Alene Indian Reservation": *Smoke Signals*'s Narrative Intervention

Smoke Signals introduces its story and setting to its audiences with pre- and postcredit sequences that refocus media communications on Indian reservations and establish Native voices and media spaces as the film's center of gravity. The credits are a particularly important moment in this film, because historically Native performers have so often gone unacknowledged in Hollywood movies, their names omitted from screen credits because of their status as "extras," even when their participation was central to the cinematic action. Screen credits acknowledge the work of cinematic storytellers — the scriptwriter, director, editor, actors, and others. Part of *Smoke Signals*'s innovation was to put Native people on both sides of the camera, and the opening credit sequences are freighted with this significant shift in visibility and identification.

The film announces itself as a form of Indigenous media in the opening shots that link the reservation landscape with the voice and then the image of the K-REZ radio headquarters — a weathered trailer home — and its MC, DJ Randy Peone, played by John Trudell, a prominent AIM activist whose biography and political work intersects powerfully with his screen appearance in *Smoke Signals*. This casting and the history of Trudell's radio work politicizes his role as a radio DJ in *Smoke Signals* through the intertextual associations with past media coverage of AIM. Trudell's mellow, humorous performance as a radio host suggests the film's self-conscious presentation as a new Indigenous voice in popular culture. Significantly, this self-presentation is projected through the medium of sound, and especially radio. Radio Westerns once played a crucial role in disseminating stereotypes of Indians as "Tonto" sidekicks in shows like the long-running *Lone Ranger* series, while local radio stations on reservations were important early instances of Native appropriations of broadcast media.[40]

Casting John Trudell as Randy Peone lends considerable depth to this seemingly small opening moment in the film. Trudell currently sustains a multifaceted career as an activist, poet, recording artist, and performer (both on stage and on screen), and he has been an important and highly visible public figure for decades.[41] He was a prominent leader during the early days of AIM, serving as the organization's national chairman from 1973 to 1979, and before that he was the official spokesperson for the Indians of All Tribes occupation of Alcatraz Island from 1969–71. He issued broadcasts for Pacifica community radio from Alcatraz during the occupation on his *Indian Land Radio* show: "Aircheck Alcatraz," and "Indians on Alcatraz: First Anniversary." In the 1970s, Trudell's work as an activist spokesperson conveyed AIM's new ability to amplify

2. John Trudell as DJ Randy Peone, in the K-REZ Radio studio trailer.

3. Thomas Builds-the-Fire's portable radio.

Native public speech with mass media, making the organization's political goals reverberate on the national and global stage. In their files from this period, the FBI describes Trudell as a target because he is "extremely eloquent and therefore extremely dangerous" to U.S. government interests.[42] In 1979, shortly after Trudell burned an American flag on the steps of the FBI building in Washington DC during a protest, a suspicious arson fire destroyed his house on the Shoshone Paiute reservation in Duck Valley, Nevada, killing his young family. Many have assumed that the arson was a retaliatory act of violence intended to silence Trudell's speech and end his political activities. Trudell's casting brings these devastating events in the history of Native activism, public speech, and protest to bear on the more internally symbolic world of *Smoke Signals*.

Randy Peone shares the airwaves with Lester FallsApart (Leonard George, Coast Salish), who keeps an eye on the highway traffic, the weather, and the community, from the roof of his van. FallsApart's name is a deliberate allusion to Nigerian author Chinua Achebe's 1957 novel *Things Fall Apart*, about traditional Ibo village life in Nigeria and its social disruption in the wake of Christian missionary conversion and British colonization. Achebe's title itself comes from the line "Things fall apart; the centre cannot hold" in the W. B. Yeats poem "The Second Coming." The name FallsApart carries additional weight because Alexie has returned to it so consistently in his poetry and fiction and as a performative identity, sometimes dramatizing the character on stage. He chose the name as his online identity for his Facebook page and extensive website (http://www.fallsapart.com). "I first wrote that guy, Lester FallsApart, in 1987, after I read that fucking book," Alexie said in an interview. "Basically that's a Sisyphus novel, and there's no identity in the world more Sisyphean than Native Americans."[43]

"FallsApart" is a self-conscious reflection on the way an African novel about the destruction of Ibo tribal systems of law under European colonization speaks to the experiences of a Spokane poet; it is about the importance of intellectual and artistic community among Indigenous peoples. The name connects the Nigerian Ibo

4. Lester FallsApart's van, "broken down at the crossroads since 1972."

tribe and the Native American Spokane and Coeur d'Alene tribes as Indigenous peoples, and points to global parallels in histories and systems of colonization. This connection also reframes viewers' understanding of the United States not as a bastion of freedom and democracy but rather as a colonizing entity, as were the British in Nigeria. Achebe's novel, considered a founding work of African literature in English, is widely taught in college courses, from English and history to anthropology. Alexie's reference to it is also a comment, then, about the relationship between researchers and those they study, and about the circulation of information about Native people among scholars in the very institutional settings that often exclude Indigenous peoples. The name FallsApart is also a comment on non-Native tendencies to romanticize the aesthetics of Native American names (a tendency illustrated in the film *Dances with Wolves*, which panders to white fantasies of being assigned an Indian name in its title character, and with names like "Wind-in-His-Hair" that summon up rock-star images). The name "FallsApart" is a reality check for those mystically inclined viewers who idealize Native relationships with the natural world. Instead,

Alexie's moniker tells a story about dispossession, although, ironically, the character also signifies taking possession of the means of communication, from radio airwaves to Internet superhighways. It is especially appropriate for Lester FallsApart to be reporting his observations on the radio, a medium that emphasizes his voice. In his novel, Achebe gives his Ibo characters an elevated English to indicate the richness and eloquence of the Ibo language, just as Alexie invests his Indian characters with immense gifts of language and an expansive capacity for storytelling. The expressive fluency of the Indigenous characters in Achebe's novel and Alexie's literary and cinematic work is the opposite of the stereotypically stilted English, or sometimes the inarticulate silence, of Indian characters in many Westerns and other films produced by dominant cinemas about colonized peoples. Lastly, because Alexie's homage to Achebe takes the form of an intertextual joke, it becomes a paradigmatic instance of his propensity for finding humor even in the dystopia of colonization — in fact, for making humor a tool of survival.

Laughter is a powerful and sustaining force of resilience in the face of adversity, and it is a profoundly social act. Laguna Pueblo author Leslie Marmon Silko has observed that Laguna teasing reminds people of their place within the Laguna community, so that "you're never lost."[44] Teasing and joking can function as an inclusive, leveling social glue that binds individuals together as a community, strengthening social bonds. Native humor, then, can be a subversive strategy that fosters social cohesion and is simultaneously a way of confronting complex issues. It is difficult to write about Native humor and irony in a scholarly context, not only because it is next to impossible to define, but also because one of the many useful ways of thinking about Native humor is as an effective evasion of the more objectifying qualities of academic discourse. Cherokee author Thomas King, who wrote and performed for the *Dead Dog Café Comedy Hour* radio show from 1997 to 2000 on the Canadian Broadcasting Corporation's (CBC) Radio One, writes: "I'm not sure that a valid definition of Native humour exists. If I were threatened with bodily harm, I would probably find myself saying that Native humour is humour that makes Native people laugh, and hope that you didn't ask me to define a Native."[45] In the essay "Indian Humor" from his landmark manifesto *Custer Died for Your Sins*, Vine Deloria Jr. writes, "The fact of white invasion from which all tribes have suffered has created a common bond in relation to Columbus jokes that gives a solid feeling of unity and purpose to the tribes." Another example of Native ironic humor wielded against serious historical events is amply demonstrated in Alexie's frequent references to U.S. Independence and to General Custer in *Smoke Signals*. Deloria writes, "The most popular and enduring subject of Indian humor is, of course, General Custer. There are probably more jokes about Custer and the Indians than there were participants in the battle."[46] *Smoke Signals*'s opening sequences establish the film's ironic, humorous tonal range with Lester FallsApart's deadpan commentary on the meager highway traffic, Randy Peone's peaceable orchestration of the local airwaves, and Thomas Builds-the-Fire's lyrical, earnest yet wry narration of the devastating backstory that informs the film's present-day action, marked by his likening of the house fire to General Custer.

FallsApart is stationed atop a van that has been "broken down at the crossroads" since 1972. In spite of—or rather because of—this suggestion that things are perpetually broken down or "falling apart" on the reservation, there is a need for an activist at the mic who can hold the community together by providing practical information (who's having a house party, when the school bell has just rung) and by reminding residents that "our reservation is beautiful today" and that "it's a good day to be Indigenous." In acting as the "voice of the Coeur d'Alene Indian reservation" Trudell embodies the filmmakers' conception of *Smoke Signals* as a cinematic Indigenous voice intervening in the contested arena of American popular culture (a role taken up in the film by Thomas Builds-the-Fire). The forest of antennae on the rooftop of FallsApart's broken-down van represents not a lack of technology but rather an inventive mastery of airwaves, and we see Peone's makeshift recording and broadcasting studio in front of his trailer home as if it were through the windshield of a bus, with Peone in the driver's seat. Trudell's character of Peone is comparable to Samuel L. Jackson's character DJ Señor Love Daddy, a radio announcer who calls both characters and audience to "wake up, wake up, wake up!" in the opening shots of Spike Lee's *Do the Right Thing* (1989).[47] The comparison between these films, often made in reviewers' assessments of *Smoke Signals* after its 1998 theatrical release, is helpful in understanding how both Spike Lee and Chris Eyre took advantage of the rising independent film scene to energetically seize and direct public attention toward issues of race and social justice, and to reposition minority film perspectives as an essential rather than marginal element of the American film landscape.

Introducing *Smoke Signals* as a road movie, these opening images establish the highways and the airwaves as intersecting, mediated spaces, "crossroads" where people from different communities encounter one another. Both are what Mary Louise Pratt would call a "contact zone," which she defines as a "space of colonial encounters, the space in which peoples geographically and historically separated come into contact with each other and establish ongoing relations, usually involving conditions of coercion, radical inequality, and intractable conflict."[48] A concept frequently invoked in relation to the frontier and the Western, the contact zone is by definition characterized by copresence and interaction rather than separation. Indigenous media spaces are envisioned in *Smoke Signals* within this relational (rather than separatist) model. In a film focused entirely on Native concerns, and with no white lead actors, the history of colonial interactions is manifest in its effects upon characters and in images of poverty, alcoholism, media images, Independence Day fireworks, and stories about basketball games against Jesuit priests. *Smoke Signals*'s intertextual references, mixed audiences and stylized political drama actualize this relational model in concrete ways and further define its screen space as one of colonial encounter characterized by politicized transactions.

After the opening sequences featuring images of the reservation and shots of Randy Peone and Lester FallsApart, the second image sequence in the film is the raging house fire that kills John and Maggie Builds-the-Fire and sets the events of the film in motion. Their son, Thomas Builds-the-Fire, narrates the story in voice-over as images of the burning house fill the screen: "On the fourth of July 1976, my mother and father celebrated white people's independence by holding the largest house party in Coeur d'Alene tribal history. I mean every Indian in the world was there. And then at three in the mornin', after everyone had passed out or fallen asleep on couches, on chairs, on beds, on the floor, a fire rose up like General George Armstrong Custer, and swallowed up my mother and father. I don't remember that fire. I only have the stories. And in every one of those stories, I could fly."

The burning house that creates the "smoke signals" in the title sequence is symbolically freighted, a site where cataclysmic national and historical events are made visible in the emotional field of interpersonal relationships at the microlevel of the family and the reservation community. Yet even here, Alexie's trademark hyperbole and irony surface in lines comparing the house fire to General George Armstrong Custer, a reference that sets up the film's ongoing political references. As I discuss further in chapter 3, the destructive celebration of white independence suggests not only internal colonization and generational loss, but also the twin thematic threads of nation-to-nation relations between the United States and tribes, and the quality of "independence" as a negative personal trait or value because it encourages the dissolution of family ties (when Arnold Joseph achieves "independence" by leaving his wife and son). The party as a symbolic gathering ("Every Indian in the world was there") is echoed later when Suzy Song describes the Gathering of Nations Powwow that she attended with Arnold, and may suggest the Ghost Dance movement prophecy of the return of past Native generations.[49]

This opening voice-over also functions as an address to all Native viewers, making the storytelling situation in *Smoke Signals* a "party" or gathering place specifically for them. Thomas's ability to "fly" in his stories of origin parallels his ability to narrate, implying that storytelling itself is a superpower analogous to flight—something that can help Native children survive ongoing colonization. And this moment is made literal—Thomas actually does fly when he is thrown out the window of the burning house and is caught by Arnold, making flying (like the "lightness" that comes with laughter and humor in storytelling) into another image of resilience. These scenes also establish the narration in first-person voice-over—the storytelling voice of Thomas, who, like the filmmakers, will not allow us to forget the way the past continues to shape the present.

Thomas's voice begins and ends the film, and marks some of its most significant moments. Film scholar Sarah Kozloff describes the way first-person direct address in voice-over can create intimacy between the narrator and the viewers, serving "as a means of winning the viewer's understanding and identification."[50] Pointing to the close relationship between cinematic voice-over and radio, Kozloff also suggests that the use of voice-over calls up oral storytelling situations by emphasizing speech as a transaction between narrators and listeners: "Cinematic storytelling is one of the youngest, most technologically dependent, and most expensive modes of narration; oral storytelling, the most ancient, fundamental, and widely accessible. In films with voice-over narration the older form has been superimposed on top of the newer."[51] With his stories about generational connections that counter Victor's stories about familial rupture, Thomas's narrative presence is itself generative of Native familial continuity even when his stories are clearly based on idealized visions. By producing stories, and through the literal work of the voice-over in the film, Thomas (as a character and as a cinema narrator) offers a specific and concrete model in the same way Native media "answer" and "speak back" to mass media images of Indian vanishing.

If Hollywood productions deny Indigenous futures and turn that denial into a commodity intended to convey visual pleasure, Thomas's joke about "Indians watching Indians on TV" imagines an Indian audience that by its very existence and participation in the quintessentially modern act of watching television defies the image of vanishing Indians on the television screen. In bringing viewers' attention to the recirculation and afterlife of Westerns on broadcast television, there is a further implication of both the continuing damage of absorbing these images and the possibility of mitigating or balancing such damage by talking back to the image and by producing new images of Indigeneity. *Smoke Signals* consistently returns to the issue of media effects of popular representations upon Native and non-Native viewers by reminding us that watching a Western constitutes a representational return to genocidal wars and expropriation of land. Eyre and Alexie ask audiences to recognize Native viewers as meaning-makers rather than on-screen empty signifiers, and to resist media products that invite audiences to take pleasure in images of imperial domination. They reassess prior systems of Western image-making through references to earlier films, as well as through editing techniques, mise-en-scène, cinematography, and especially sound — including storytelling and song in voice-overs and sound bridges. The use of sound in recoding images represents an especially powerful way in which Indigenous media makers assert their voices in the present while reclaiming images taken in the past and fused with Euro-American scenarios.[52] Popular culture is common ground, and it is also contested ground; Eyre and Alexie's investment in media intertextuality speaks back to the history of cinematic images of Indians and the exclusion of Native voices from Hollywood power structures, using the power of cinema instead to amplify and disseminate an Indigenous story in the public arena.

chapter two

"The Storyteller Is Part of the Story"
Making Smoke Signals

In *Smoke Signals*, Thomas Builds-the-Fire's joke that "the only thing more pathetic than Indians on TV is Indians watching Indians on TV" seems to function as the film's defining moment, a cinematic statement of thesis that is worth returning to in contemplating the relationship between the film's production and its audiences. The joke characterizes both televised Indians and the Native audience that consumes Hollywood's images of them as "pathetic." But Thomas's blithe tone finds a counterpoint in moments of more understated pathos in the film, such as when the young Victor Joseph (played by Cody Lightning, Cree), Thomas Builds-the-Fire's friend, occasional tormentor, and symbolic "brother," witnesses his mother and father fighting in the living room in front of a small television set playing an old black-and-white Western. "Indians watching Indians on TV" becomes part of Victor's household environment as he is presented with both televised and familial forms of psychological trauma at once, and his father Arnold's abandonment of the family following this fight is linked metonymically and metaphorically to the screen tropes of military suppression and vanished Indians. The broadcast images assault and transform intimate spaces in the film, and the young Victor, as the "spectator" of both screen and domestic performances of conflict, absorbs and learns from the scripts and scenes he witnesses. The generic media images come to stand for the effects of colonization in the home and in Victor's own psyche, while his parents' domestic disputes take on the magnitude of genocide, war, and dispossession. Parallel with the characters — Arnold and Arlene fighting in front of the television screen, Victor watching — the Native actors are also performing what are to some extent scripted roles against the backdrop of the screen, communicating to, among other audiences, young Native viewers — a layered configuration that, in a media landscape saturated with stereotypes, raises complex issues of performance, spectatorship, and reception.

The image of a young Native viewer making meaning from pop-culture symbols broadcast into the home is a central fixture in Sherman Alexie's autobiographical anecdotes and in his poetry, fiction, and filmmaking. Alexie adapted the screenplay for *Smoke Signals* from his short stories in *The Lone Ranger and Tonto Fistfight in Heaven* (1993), a title that refers to the staging of Indigenous resistance and revitalization in the arena of mass entertainment. Images of media relations in Alexie's fiction and screenplay speak to issues of accessibility, adaptation, and the performance and re-production of Indigeneity in the public sphere — elements that are brought together in the way young Native spectators are imagined as both the objects of representation and as interpreters of media. This figure is important, too, because the very existence of Native audiences works against narratives of Indian vanishing (since the "vanishing" trope presumes that there are no Native people in the contemporary world, only in past, or in the virtual playground of the screen) and disturbs fixed assumptions of audience homogeneity embedded in mass-media content. This idea of Native spectator-ship as an image of both colonization and resistance — as well as the idea of performative address to such spectators through Native acting — helped to carry the production of *Smoke Signals* from script to screen.

Performances involve heightened, specially framed relationships between performer and audience, thus forming and playing with the boundaries of staging and inviting audiences to understand the performed communication in a particular way. Performance, then, can be seen as a form of display, a way of saying, "Look at *this*, not *that*." Like the lens of a camera, performative framing focuses our attention and opens up the content of the performance within the frame for special scrutiny. Theories of performing arts have often focused on the relationship of performance to fixed texts: to what extent does an actor change the meaning of a text through his or her interpretation of it? To what extent does a text establish and hold a stable core of meaning across various performances? Employing a different approach, folklorists and anthropologists have theorized performances as socially and culturally communicative events: how are performances used to accomplish social actions? Theorizing the performance of Indigeneity in *Smoke Signals*, then, represents a key bridge between the script text and the filmic characters, and between the film and its viewers (or spectators). The term "spectator," indicating an abstract or ideal viewer position, is also distinct from the actual viewers who make up the audience. This distinction will be especially important in chapter 4's discussion of *Smoke Signals*'s reception, when the filmmakers' intentions and projections before the release of the film, based on imagined spectators, are measured against audience reactions, box office sales, and reviews in the press.

There are also magical qualities to performance as a form of play. Performances essentially conjure up make-believe characters and embody them as "real" in the world, if only for a brief space of time, even as performers must rely on their own bodies and experiences to carry out the actions. Through role-play, performances can invite audiences to mentally step outside of their own experiences, to imagine the experiences of others, and to see their world and themselves from these other perspectives, or alternately to share similar experiences in solidarity.[1] This quality facilitates the political work of performance and of performative genres such as jokes. Jokes are often about the very process of looking at something in a different (funny) way; to get the joke, the listener must acknowledge or even adopt a certain perspective on the world. *Smoke Signals*'s many funny moments and storytelling performances hinge on this special, performative relationship between speakers and listeners, filmmakers and viewers. The film's stylized storytelling also calls attention to social actions in relation to specific audiences. What does it mean to tell a Native story to a Native audience, or to a non-Native audience, or to both simultaneously? How does the film's address to these audiences intersect with the actors' processes of improvising performances out of life experience?

Performing Indigeneity complicates these general ideas about performance, because issues of race, identity, and history, of visual marking and political difference, enter so powerfully into the field of interpretive possibilities. That is to say, relations of colonization and Indigeneity enter into already complex performative relationships with audiences. In Hollywood, "playing Indian" is a profitable enterprise if it is done within certain restrictive parameters — such as the scenarios of primitive "vanishing" Indians and stereotypes of noble savages discussed in the previous chapter. Hollywood studios have, in that sense, attempted to steal the right to perform and socially "speak" the definition of Indigeneity to the public. Indigenous political activism has involved performances that contest the Hollywood versions of Indianness that, in their domination of film and television screens, have already saturated the public imagination. Specifically, Indigenous activist performances — and Native filmmaking as an instantiation of such performance — draw attention to Indigeneity as contemporary rather than past, present rather than vanished, human rather than stereotype. An important element of the staging of Indigeneity on film is the marking of Indigenous distinctiveness from (and sometimes commonalities with) both mainstream Americans and minority groups in the United States. Native self-determination and sovereignty is extended to the realm of mass media representation through the performative work of defining identity for a heterogeneous audience.

Smoke Signals's relationship to popular culture emerges from the social relations of media both in and beyond the film's actual content. Following the trajectory of the production — Sherman Alexie's autobiographical short stories and screenplay, Chris Eyre and Sherman Alexie's development of the project through the Sundance Institute, and the actors' performances — reveals complicated processes of literary adaptation, collaborative authorship, and activist performance. Although we often tend to think of film adaptation in an orderly way as a linear progression from fiction to screenplay to production to exhibition and reception, tracking issues of Indigenous spectatorship and performance shows us instead a more circular, porous, and flexible production model across these stages. Attributing authorship in the necessarily collaborative world of filmmaking is a fraught practice, and the authorship of *Smoke Signals* was particularly contested at one point immediately after its release. As I do elsewhere in this book, in tracing the film's authorship here I have tried to privilege the voices of those important to the production — especially Eyre, Alexie, and the actors — whose contributions form a complex matrix of individual Native experiences and performances filtered through media cultures and institutional structures of film production.

"You're Always Auditioning": Sherman Alexie's Autobiographical Fiction

In many ways, the engine of Sherman Alexie's writing is autobiography, and he makes a political point of writing about "what I am, not what I want to be."[2] Even his characters' names come from his family — names like Polatkin, Aristotle, Joseph, Arnold. He was born in 1966 and grew up in Wellpinit, Washington, on the Spokane reservation. He is enrolled Spokane on his mother's side, which also includes Spokane, Salish, Kootenay, and Colville; his father is Coeur d'Alene. All are Salish-speaking tribes: "My parents are both fluent in Salish but they didn't teach us [children]. . . . When I was very young, my mom told us 'English will be your best weapon.' My own language wasn't going to save me. English would. And it has."[3] He grew up sharing his father's compulsive reading of pulp novels, playing Dungeons and Dragons in the basement of the family home, and watching movies — all contributing to the profound influence of media in his life. "My literary influences are Stephen King, John Steinbeck, and my mother, my grandfather and the Brady Bunch."[4] While Alexie describes Coyote as "in my database," he also says that when he goes home, he and his family "watch TV together and play board games. That's the family culture."[5]

"It's a complicated mix," Alexie says in a 1999 interview. "That's what colonialism does to an Indigenous person. To succeed in the white world, I had to be better at their culture than they are. I grabbed it, held on to it, and absorbed it with all of my heart, because I knew that was the way I would survive."[6] As an example, Alexie frequently narrates an early, determining experience at a drive-in screening of *The Texas Chainsaw Massacre* (dir. Hooper, 1974) when he was about seven years old:

> I was terrified, of course, but I loved it, being scared. I remember thinking, "White people are crazy." That always fascinated me, the things white people did to each other. You never hear about Indians taking chainsaws after each other, eating each other. I remember being fascinated by that, sort of anthropologically, even as a seven-year-old. That was my first conscious thought about a movie. I didn't sit there as a seven-year-old and think, "Wow, the power of cinema!" but I was amazed that something could make me feel that strongly. I was growing up in a pretty rocky environment — I mean, a rez, and my parents were both drinkers. There was a lot of partying. For a seven-year-old to be in the midst of that, it was a pretty crazy life. To protect yourself from that, you become numb. You try not to feel anything, so you really cut yourself off from your emotions. But *Texas Chainsaw Massacre* did not allow me to remain numb. . . . It pushed me outside of my world, it pushed me away from being numb. Books did the same thing, but movies are much more visceral. Movies became my drug, in a way.[7]

Alexie tells the same story in the opening pages of his introduction to the published screenplay for *Smoke Signals*, although some of the details differ. In that introduction he also describes his family spending too much money on an early VHS machine, and then moves on to recount the first day on the set of *Smoke Signals*, on location in DeSmet, Idaho, on the Coeur d'Alene reservation, "just a few feet away from the exact spot where my father was born."[8]

These narratives don't say much about the adaptation of fiction to screenplay and text to image in *Smoke Signals*; instead, they tell a story about the transition from being a viewer to a producer of images on Native ground. Alexie's stories about watching movies complicate the linear narrative impulse of adaptation studies in which a book becomes a screenplay and then a film, because his anecdotes situate pop-culture *reception* as the primary experience — prior to and formative of the short stories, rather than flowing from them. His stories about film reception locate this reproduction of popular culture in the relationship of movies to Indigenous homes and families. Alexie is of course not recycling or remaking *The Texas Chainsaw Massacre* through his scripting of *Smoke Signals*, and the makers of *The Texas Chainsaw Massacre* probably never intended the film to be either an ethnographic document of whiteness or a tool of assimilation. Rather, Alexie's film tells stories about Native relationships with film screens — spectatorship, and the reproduction and repurposing of that spectatorship through performance — to reveal the way media reception functions to assimilate ("It pushed me outside of my world") and to both source and ameliorate the familial damage wrought by mediated colonialism. His stories about immersing in popular media are survival stories, resembling his story about generational movement from Salish to English as the household language. To borrow Joy Harjo and Gloria Bird's phrasing, by "reinventing the enemy's language" through a generative model of spectatorship, Alexie inserted himself into the mediascape as a celebrity, using the social power that comes with public attention and public voice: "I've created this public figure . . . I'm an Indian pop-culture figure. I like that social power. . . . I want to be accessible. I want to be populist."[9]

The Lone Ranger and Tonto Fistfight in Heaven

The Lone Ranger and Tonto Fistfight in Heaven came about largely because of the demands of the literary marketplace for fiction over poetry. After reviewer James Kincaid called Alexie "one of the major lyric voices of our time" in a front-page *New York Times*

Book Review article on Alexie's first book of poetry, *The Business of Fancydancing*, Alexie fielded calls from publishing agents asking if he wrote fiction, "because that's what they could sell."[10] He was then only twenty-five, working as an administrative assistant at a Spokane, Washington, high school exchange program. He had some short stories filed away (from a college fiction-writing course), but he wrote many of the stories in *Lone Ranger and Tonto* in the months following Kincaid's review and went on to sign a two-book contract that led to his first novel, *Reservation Blues*. "I got pushed into it by economics," Alexie says.[11]

Alexie took the title for *The Lone Ranger and Tonto Fistfight in Heaven* from a dream that located the Western-genre white settler hero and his devoted Indian sidekick in a spiritual boxing match: "In this dream, I was sitting in a huge arena. I could see people boxing, miles away it seemed. This gentleman with a hawk face, dressed completely in red — boots, shoes, cap, top hat — sat down beside me. I said, 'What's going on down there?' He said, 'Oh, that's the Lone Ranger and Tonto. They're boxing. The winner gets to go to heaven and the loser has to go to hell.' I said, 'Oh, my gosh.' Then I realized this was the devil. . . . I really started getting into it, 'Go, Tonto, hit him, hit him!'"[12]

Alexie's story about the origin of *The Lone Ranger and Tonto Fistfight in Heaven* — its chartering image — casts himself not as a performer but rather as a spectator trying to make sense of stock characters on stage. In *Smoke Signals*, the characters of Victor and Thomas are informed by an implied backstory of such spectatorship; they have clearly watched and puzzled over many a John Wayne movie (not to mention *Dances with Wolves*). Alexie's translation of this dream to a short story (the title story in the collection) about contemporary interracial romance suggests the proximity of antagonism and attraction in relationships of colonization. This central image, as it functions in the story, also envisions the way that intimate relationships are filtered through the visual language of mass-produced popular figures. "I think this is the theme between all Indian-white relationships," he says, "not only as individuals, but as races, as colonials to colonized."[13] The idea of a staged contest (and of a contested stage) is theorized in strikingly similar terms to Alexie's image by Stuart Hall in an essay from 1981, in which he characterizes popular culture as a shifting "arena of consent and resistance," literally a "contested ground."[14] For Alexie, the "contested ground" of the media is not just the virtual space of broadcast signals but also the domestic space of media reception in Native homes. Thus, an Indigenous refusal to play along with colonial fantasies of the "domesticated" Indian sidekick is revealed by the title to be the books' own strategic performance. Further, this refusal locates the potential for active resistance and critical vision, as well as the potential for passivity and damage, in Native spectatorship. As in other stories, Alexie casts interpersonal interactions (not to mention Catholic religious iconography) in terms of spectators and visual spectacle, as he does when Arnold Joseph tells the story of Victor's basketball game against the Jesuits (as I discuss in chapter 3).

Scholars in Native studies have pointed to the recurring focus in Alexie's poetry and fiction on television as an invasive force. James Cox writes that Alexie not only revises the stereotypes, but also "illustrates how these narratives and representations have a destructive influence on the lives of many of his characters" and how "images and stories of archetypal Tontos colonize the reservation and the imaginations of its residents."[15] In the short stories, Alexie consistently refers to television as racially inflected "white noise" invading and damaging Victor Joseph's home; it mystifies, distracts, twists, and drowns out the voices and emotional interactions of the Indian characters. In the title story, which presents television as one index of a virtual relationship to the Western, the narrator avoids coping with a failed interracial relationship by returning to the reservation and watching television: "For weeks I flipped through the channels, searched for answers in the game shows and soap operas."[16] In the story "Family Portrait" the television is "always too loud." It dominates the narrator's memories of childhood: "I don't know where all the years went. I remember only the television in detail. All the other moments worth remembering became stories that changed with each telling, until nothing was aboriginal or recognizable."[17] The personal telling of history here takes on a broader significance with the reference to Native stories. Stories that are unique with each performance suggest oral stories, which tribes relied on to incubate cultural values and histories, but these come to be seen as unreliable and ephemeral in the face of the mechanical reproduction that standardizes audiovisual storytelling.

In Alexie's fiction, television is an index of damaged relations and an erosion of familial resources, yet it also represents an ever-present, stable constant in a changeable domestic scene. Television both invades and stands for other invasions; it interferes with the memory and voice of the characters, destabilizing the ability of Native storytelling to either offer testimony or simply hold a family together. "Every conversation was distorted, fragmented," he writes — words and phrases are misheard and misapprehended in the cacophony: "'Dinner' sounded like 'leave me alone.'"[18] This confusion of domestic and media speech results in a multiplication of histories and an incoherent and surreal disconnection between family members. The narrator's family is erased as "we hid our faces behind masks that suggested other histories." Televised images and narratives represent an incursion of acculturating "masks" and "histories," and faces-as-screens become metaphors for social interactions in which Indigeneity is screened out of the character's public face. The temporal and spatial patterns of the characters' domestic lives and emotional intimacies are structured by the distances and interruptions of television programming, generating an environment in which "we stared across the room at each other, waited for the conversation and the conversion," and "every emotion was measured by the half hour."[19] Television works like celestial bodies here to mark time for the characters, as when two characters "kissed until the television signed off and broke into white noise. It was the end of another broadcast day."[20]

Because Alexie saturates his fiction and poetry with mass-media allusions — especially cinema and television — and because of his visibility and celebrity (including a second career in stand-up comedy), he has become a magnet for issues surrounding commodification and stereotyping of Native peoples in the public sphere. He remains at the center of debates about Native artists' relationships with their Native and non-Native audiences and about how Native artists should represent Indians in print and on screen. Spokane poet Gloria Bird, writing in 1995, was one of the first to compare Alexie to Spike Lee in his interpretation of his "insider's perspective to the mainstream audience." Pointing to the ways that Alexie's novel *Reservation Blues* resembles a screenplay and "relies on readership exposure to film," Bird assessed Alexie's "exaggeration of despair" on the reservation as both exploitive of Native readers and misleading to a mainstream audience that might mistake those representations for reality: "Stereotyping native peoples does not supply a native readership with soluble ways of undermining stereotypes, but becomes a part of the problem, and returns an image of a generic 'Indian' back to the original producers of that image."[21] Elizabeth Cook-Lynn (Crow Creek Sioux) also rejects Alexie's pop inclinations, calling his representations a "deficit model of Indian reservation life";[22] similarly, Louis Owens (Choctaw/Cherokee) calls Alexie's first three books of prose "commodified Indian fiction."[23] It is primarily Alexie's relationships with his audiences that are at issue in these criticisms, which measure his fiction according to its potential to impact perceptions of reality among different segments of the population.

Bird, Cook-Lynn, and Owens particularly target Alexie's images of alcoholism and vanishing; their claims have been addressed at length by critics such as James Cox, Dean Rader, Jennifer Gillan, and others, and Alexie himself has responded in a number of venues. In the new introduction to the 2005 edition of *The Lone Ranger and Tonto Fistfight in Heaven*, he writes that "in writing about drunk Indians, I am dealing with stereotypical material. But I can only respond with the truth. In my family, counting parents, siblings, and dozens of aunts, uncles, and cousins, there are less than a dozen who are currently sober, and only a few who have never drank. When I write about the destructive effects of alcohol on Indians, I am not writing out of a literary stance or a colonized mind's need to reinforce stereotypes. I am writing autobiography."[24] He goes on to discuss the events in his family life that are retold in stories such as "Every Little Hurricane," "Amusements," "The Fun House," "Witnesses, Secret and Not," and the story adapted for *Smoke Signals*, "This Is What It Means to Say Phoenix, Arizona," which he calls "thinly disguised memoir" and an example of "reservation realism."[25] Other scholars have defended Alexie's work based on the conventions of satire and irony as well as on close readings that reveal the complex dynamics of revisionism in Alexie's representations.[26] Alexie resists the pressure to perform Indigeneity as a spokesperson, arguing that his experience is not representational of all reservation experiences. In fact, he writes that he was always a misfit in his own community: "I was a divisive presence on the reservation when I was 7."[27]

Alexie's autobiographical stories — being a reservation basketball star, losing beloved family members in a house fire — and his interest in Native youth as both subjects and audiences are shared themes across texts and films from *The Lone Ranger and Tonto Fistfight in Heaven* to *Smoke Signals* to his most recent book, *The Absolutely True Diary of a Part-Time Indian*, which won the National Book Award for Young Adult Fiction in 2007 (according to Alexie, a film adaptation of that book is in "strong and serious negotiations . . . right now with a very, very, very famous guy").[28] Each of these narrative iterations of his reservation childhood move the artistic center of gravity further from the distilled rage of his earlier writing and toward a humanist vision that Alexie says became important to him after 9/11: "Since September 11, I've let go of making decisions based on tribalism."[29]

Although the critical debates about Alexie's work are primarily focused on his fiction and poetry, they are relevant to *Smoke Signals* as well, a film that poses similar questions about the politics of Native artists' and intellectuals' relationships to mainstream and

Native audiences. Alexie answers some critics by focusing not only on his own early autobiography but also on potential Native youth audiences. In his first novel, *Reservation Blues* (written while *Smoke Signals* was in development), Alexie forecasts his own movement from describing media damage and Native spectatorship in his fiction to intervening more directly in media representations by making films that allegorize modes of mass communication production and reception. Victor Joseph, Thomas Builds-the-Fire, and Junior Polatkin (all characters who carry over from *The Lone Ranger and Tonto Fistfight in Heaven*) form an Indigenous blues band, Coyote Springs, and enter into negotiations with a recording label called Cavalry Records — clearly a figure for the popular culture industry as a colonial enterprise extending the violence of historical military incursions into Native territory.[30] These characters, not yet arrived at actual screen presence in *Smoke Signals*, already perform on the page what Dean Rader calls Alexie's "vision of spliced celluloid and self."[31] Fragmented by media images into "split selves," Victor and Thomas self-consciously occupy media scripts: "You sound like we're in some god-damn coming-of-age movie. Who the fuck do you think you are? Billy Jack? Who's writing your dialogue?"[32] Alexie's characters' split selves often emerge during these moments of comedic distantiation, when irony creates a critical self-awareness, separating readers from the very stereotypes that Alexie has been accused of promulgating, while at the same time naming and describing them. Telling the story of mass-media modes of production and how they affect what is visible in the mediascape, as Alexie does in his poetry, in *The Lone Ranger and Tonto Fistfight in Heaven*, and in *Reservation Blues*, highlights issues of audience reception not only as an economic and ethical issue for Native artists and audiences but also as an artistic point of origin. By articulating so profoundly his characters' immersion in mediated environments, Alexie shows us how popular culture becomes not secondary or separable but rather formative to identity and even to the very way that we see.

"I Can Hear the Audience": Performance and Adaptation

In several interviews, Alexie has described his filmmaking as an attempt to reach Native youth, who are often tuned into mainstream media rather than poetry and novels: "Probably five percent of Indians in this country have read my books. Maybe that much. Probably more like two percent, or one. You take a thing like *Powwow Highway* and 99% of Indians have seen it."[33] Indeed, we can see *Smoke Signals's* use of popular culture references not just as an attempt to be broadly accessible, but also as one of the elements that makes the film Indigenous.

In both his writing and his film, Alexie focuses on Native youth and their experiences with media, often offering an empathetic vision of an emerging critical spectatorship. This preoccupation in his writing has helped Alexie to find a Native youth audience. His focus in his writing and films not only on "the younger version of me,"[34] but also on the relationship between that younger self and his current position as a successful Native intellectual and performer functions as a model for Native artists' relationships with their Native readers and viewers. His interviews and essays are full of stories about his own earlier relations with movies. In "I Hated Tonto (Still Do)" he recalls his early (and formative) love for films like *The Searchers* (dir. Ford, 1956), *Billy Jack* (dir. Laughlin, 1971), *Powwow Highway*, and *Little Big Man*. Profoundly and sometimes painfully aware of the economics of artistic production and distribution in American markets, Alexie equated his early media exposure with the dumping of government commodity food on reservation communities: "Being colonized, you have to adapt, and it's not like we get colonized with the best the culture has to offer. Nobody comes in and starts slapping us with Shakespeare. . . . You take what's given to you, which is generally the lowest of the low, the worst food, the worst culture, and try to blend it into yourself."[35]

Alexie's characters are often confined by cinematic definitions of loss and vanishing, trapped in a mediated national imaginary that has already scripted their despair and demise. In *Smoke Signals*, Victor's inner conflicts are related to spectatorship: he wants to find a way to mourn his father, but the very definition of "Indian" mourning has already been canned and distributed by Hollywood as a sentimental, melodramatic scenario of Indian vanishing. Charles Bronson, John Wayne, and Kevin Costner act as decoys in his search for a model of adult masculinity and Native paternity. This cinematic portrait of the way a Native viewer's emotional range becomes interpellated within scripted scenarios and colonial schema, however, is often rendered consciously comedic in Alexie's work. The distancing effect of Alexie's ironic style and satirical social commentary insists that audiences and characters, in recognizing the script, regard such media forms as the constructions that they are rather than the naturalized, defining orders that they sometimes seem to be.

And in holding up media representations for scrutiny and ridicule, in dramatizing the destructiveness of their mismeasures, Alexie shows how his characters chafe at the boundaries of the script. His characters sustain damage but are neither stupid nor totally silenced; rather, they model a range of spectatorial strategies, including precisely the kind of sharply satirical debates about mainstream media stereotypes that lead to critical distance, demonstrating not just the dangers of apathy in viewing but also the power of heuristic insight through engagement. In this sense, Alexie's writing shares certain qualities with forms of mass media resistance that turn corporate media back onto itself (such as culture jamming) as well as with less high-tech politicization of communication (such as street theater).[36] Alexie's Indigenization of media stereotypes successfully addresses both Native and non-Native audiences in part because these audiences converge in their avid consumption of popular culture: "That's one of the reasons I really got ambitious about movies, because I know they'll see the movie. Ninety-nine percent of Native Americans in the world have seen *Smoke Signals*. Native culture is pop culture, so to reach them, you have to work in that idiom."[37]

Despite this allegiance to the reach of popular culture, Alexie consciously positioned *The Lone Ranger and Tonto Fistfight in Heaven* within the history of Native American literature, with the collection's opening dedication to Native literary giants Joy Harjo (Muskoke), Leslie Silko (Laguna), and Simon Ortiz (Acoma). The final screenplay for *Smoke Signals* retains a sense of the literary in a way that few screenplays do, and Thomas's closing monologue, adapted from the poem "Forgiving Our Fathers," by Dick Lourie, a non-Native poet (and Alexie's poetry editor at Hanging Loose Press), contributes to the film's address to both Native and non-Native experiences and suggests the film's commitment to voice-over as a literary element as well as a form of action. "There's this national fear of poetry, especially in movies — everything has to be very clear cut and very forward," Alexie says, "I wanted to break that apart. Because I'm naturally a poet."[38]

The film, in turn, bridges Native literature and popular film (as authors like Thomas King and Greg Sarris have done) by translating a wide range of characters into a few primary focal characters; by using a cinematic flashback structure to compress multiple stories into a coherent screen narrative; by using an established Hollywood genre (the road movie) as a framework; and by emphasizing comedy. Translating the short stories to a road movie was "a time-honored structure, and also very cheap to do[;] . . . you can let the landscape tell a lot of story."[39] Alexie also shifted the tone of the film toward a gentler portrait of contemporary Native reservation life; a line spoken by the protagonist from "This Is What It Means to Say Phoenix, Arizona," "It was the beginning of a new day on Earth, but the same old shit on the reservation,"[40] for example, is transformed as one of DJ Randy Peone's lines in *Smoke Signals*, "Coeur d'Alene people, our reservation is beautiful this morning. It's a good day to be Indigenous" (which is in turn a revision of the line "It's a good day to die" from *Little Big Man*). Alexie also wrote many of the songs for the film, including "Father and Farther" and "A Million Miles Away," describing songwriting as composing "accessible poetry."[41]

Two of the key elements from Alexie's literary readings that carry through in his entertainment industry career are performativity and comedy. Comfortable on stage, he was the only four-time winner of the World Heavyweight Poetry Bout Championship, and he then moved into stand-up comedy, film directing, scriptwriting, and script doctoring. Alexie's stand-up comedy work infuses his writing with a subversive humor that activates an alternative imaginary for viewers, in part by offering a playful (and thus less threatening, more inviting) view of the world from another perspective. In order to "get" and enjoy the jokes, viewers must imaginatively occupy an "other," even oppositional position, even if only partially. This politicized use of humor captures the attention of both Native and non-Native audiences through what Gerald Vizenor calls "tricky scenes" of active Native presence and "survivance."[42] Vizenor uses Bakhtin's theories of dialogism to help define Native "trickster discourse" as a literary strategy; the "intertextual dimension" of texts is historically situated utterance, such that "all discourse is in dialogue with prior discourses on the same subject. . . . There is no utterance without relation to other utterances."[43] Coyote, the trickster character from Spokane and other tribes' traditional stories who creates the world through mistake and disorderly conduct, is never mentioned in *Smoke Signals*. But the connection between humor and world-making creativity, and the emphasis on teaching through funny stories, is discernable in *Smoke Signals*'s use of jokes and in its purposeful use of irony in the project of changing public perceptions.

Alexie's years on the road performing stand-up comedy, poetry slams, and literary readings for audiences has become his version of Native oral tradition in that his fiction, as he says, "really is sort of audience-tested. At this point, after nine years of being on the road, when I'm writing I can hear the audience. In fact, I can hear different kinds of audiences. I *know* what Indians are going to laugh at, I know what non-Indians are going to laugh at, and I know what they're going to laugh at together. Or even when they are laughing at the same joke, I know the different reasons why they're laughing."[44] Humor, in Vizenor's model, is audience-dependent and intertextual, forcing different audiences into (different) relations. In *Smoke Signals*, non-Native audiences are exposed to reservation in-jokes and Alexie makes fun of "oral traditions" while at the same time translating his own performative, storytelling impulse to a mainstream comedy form. In reaching out to audiences through funny stories, the "accessible poetry" of songwriting and the "lingua franca" of popular culture, Alexie emphasizes humor as "the most effective political tool out there, because people will listen to anything if they're laughing."[45] Pointing out that books aren't technically part of Native oral traditions — "I type it" he points out[46] — Alexie nevertheless incorporated a more direct performative venue for storytelling: "And the way to be a part of that is through performance, and improvising, and changing the story based on the audience, and the mood of the audience[;] . . . the whole thing is just as much about me, as the storyteller, as it is about the story. People would call that postmodern, but the fact is that that's been the case forever. The storyteller is part of the story."[47]

Chris Eyre's "Home Dramas"

Chris Eyre is one of the first generation of Native directors to receive formal film school training, a filmmaker's "very traditional route to a career."[48] He discovered a love for images and landscape photography in high school and then pursued an associate's degree in television in Portland, a BA in media arts from the University of Arizona and an MFA from New York University's prestigious Tisch School of the Arts for Graduate Film (the institution where African American filmmakers Spike Lee and Ernest Dickerson received their training before going on to make groundbreaking films like *Do the Right Thing*). When he read Sherman Alexie's collection of short stories, *The Lone Ranger and Tonto Fistfight in Heaven*, in 1994, Eyre had just won several awards for his short film *Tenacity*, about a fateful roadside encounter between two young Native boys and a group of drunk white high schoolers on prom night — the film won NYU's Best Short Film award and a Mobile Award, and was screened at Sundance in 1995.

He asked a mutual friend for Alexie's telephone number and, as he tells it, "called Sherman out of the blue and asked if he'd be interested in trying to adapt one of the stories into a feature-length film." Eyre favored adapting "This Is What It Means to Say Phoenix, Arizona," in part because it would translate well to the dramatic arc of the road movie that tracked characters through a narrative and spatial circuit "from point A to point B and back to point A."[49] He was also struck by one of the story's central images:

> When . . . Victor gives half of his father's cremated remains to Thomas, it really struck me that . . . he actually gifts his father to his best friend, which filmically was something I'd never seen. And that was the thing that struck me in the twelve pages of short story — the Indianness of it and the giving part of it. I mean, this is a guy who has nothing to give except a thank you, and in this Indian way he wants to give him a gift and the only thing that's available are the essence of what he's been looking for, which is his father.[50]

Alexie had already turned down other offers to buy the film rights, because he wanted an Indian director for the movie, so he was receptive to Eyre's proposal.[51] Eyre calls their relationship "generationally easy" — both were in their midtwenties when they began working together. Eyre drafted an initial script, but Alexie quickly took over the writing. Eyre recalls that "I think I incited Sherman to turn to screenwriting by trying to write the first draft of the screenplay. I think that it infuriated him so much that he said, 'That's not how you do it, let me show you how to do it,' and he literally commandeered the screenplay and whipped out forty-four pages in like two weeks. He called himself a binge writer, and he definitely was a binge writer in creating that screenplay."[52]

They continued to develop the screenplay over fourteen months, including a stint in the Sundance Writer's Lab.[53] They were also invited to attend the Sundance directing workshop, where Eyre shot

5. Victor gives half of his father's ashes to Thomas.

a four-scene adaptation from Alexie's screenplay as a test start, titled *Someone Kept Saying Powwow*, with mentoring from established Hollywood insiders like Robert Redford, screenwriter Steve Zaillian (*Schindler's List, American Gangster*), and cinematographer Allen Daviau (*E.T., The Color Purple*).[54] During the making of that film, Eyre found actor Evan Adams through a casting director and began working with him to develop the nerdy, bespectacled character of Thomas Builds-the-Fire.[55]

In part because of the Sundance Institute, the film's writing and visual development took place simultaneously. Both Eyre and Alexie credit the four-week Sundance workshop for allowing them to nurture the project, including guidance, support, and encouragement to experiment with strategies that might fail. Alexie notes that his experience in the Sundance lab helped him to adapt the story to commercial screenplay conventions: "At Sundance it was much more straightforward, Syd-Field, 120-page, three-act-er. They talked a lot about basic structure. For me, that was film school in a week, and I needed that."[56] According to Eyre, "In four weeks at Sundance, I probably got as much as I did at four years at NYU," in part because the training was intensely practical ("It was all shooting") and in part because it facilitated relationships with industry professionals.[57] *Someone Kept Saying Powwow* won the NHK Award at Sundance in 1996, which Eyre notes was "definitely a catalyst for some financiers to like the project"[58] and to see it as "a viable commodity"[59] — including Shadowcatcher Entertainment in Seattle, which produced the movie.

During the mid-1990s, when Eyre and Alexie were seeking a financier to invest two million dollars to produce *Smoke Signals*, independent film was booming, with the Sundance Institute as its epicenter: "We were lucky enough to be part of that whole crescendo of independent film that . . . was a national catchphrase and piece of social consciousness," Eyre said.[60] But despite Eyre's short-film awards, Alexie's visibility as a writer, and the backing of the Sundance Institute, deals with two other investors fell through as Alexie and Eyre sought financing for the film before they found Shadowcatcher. According to Eyre, part of the difficulty was that he and Alexie held out for ownership and artistic control: "We had deal breakers in that year and a half . . . because Sherman and I wanted to own part of the movie. We wanted to be producers on the movie. We knew we had something that was special. John Sayles said it best when he said, 'Financing a movie is like hitch-hiking: just because the car stops doesn't mean you get in.' . . . As desperate as you are to make your movie, just because the car stops doesn't mean that you should get in."[61] Another factor was the on-location production: "Sherman had said that he wanted to shoot it on his reservation, which he was reluctant to do unless the producers were somebody that he wanted to stand next to on his reservation. And that was another issue — who are the people you're inviting to your home?" Those people were Larry Estes and Scott Rosenfelt, who produced the movie through Shadowcatcher, and David Skinner, executive producer for the movie, who, along with his family, financed the entire project. Alexie acknowledges Skinner's support in his introduction to the published screenplay: "There was one man, a white man, who believed so much in this film by and about Indians, that he completely financed it. Amazing."[62]

Eyre shot the film in twenty-three days on location in Idaho and Washington, in April of 1997. After working on the script and financing for four years, he describes the initial days of the shoot:

> I'll never forget after all these years of wanting to get up this great big hill, and doing a month of preproduction on location — I'd never stayed in a hotel for a month before in my life. . . . I'll never forget waking up one morning and looking out my curtains and seeing semi-trucks in the parking lot, and thinking to myself, "Huh, that's strange, wonder whose those are?" And then it dawns upon you that these are our trucks for our show and it's all equipment and it's all camera packages, it's all props, it's all grip equipment. You sit there thinking it's honey wagons, it's trailers, all this stuff, and you say, "What have I got myself into?" You dream that it comes one day and then you're like, "Wow, now I have to perform." . . . It's just a matter of having the bravery to own it.[63]

During the shooting, Eyre worked with Director of Photography Brian Capener to keep the film simple, in part because of the small budget and in part to keep the focus on the storytelling: "I didn't want a glossy or a flashy type of film[;] . . . it was a less is more kind of thing. When non-Indians shoot Indians, they always make it very romantic[;] . . . it's so over the top. That's not the movie I wanted to make at all."[64] He drew on his early love for landscape photography in translating the Coeur d'Alene reservation landscape to film: "I love the West and I love looking out the windows and I love taking drives and I love framing the shots that way. . . . All reservations are different. . . . For me, there's a whole context that you have to place a story in filmically. My biggest high is to look at the landscape and try and incorporate that into the volume of the sensibility and feel of the movie."[65]

He also drew on his own feelings of empathy with the characters. Before making *Smoke Signals*, Eyre, who was adopted as an infant and grew up with a non-Native family in Klamath Falls, Oregon, spent several years searching for his birth parents and exploring his tribal heritage. He talks about directing *Smoke Signals* as part of that process: "I had love out there but I didn't know where it was and I think in my movies what's happening is these characters are yearning for each other. . . . I knew I might never meet my mother, and as fate had it she was in good health, but it was possible I'd never have the ability to reconcile with my birth culture. . . . In my movies I'm trying to convince my audiences to . . . go home."[66] Eyre says that he wasn't thinking of the film's future audience but rather making a movie he himself wanted to see: "I wanted to see Thomas Builds-the-Fire and this whole near miss, which is Victor trying to find his estranged father. . . . I'd missed my own parents in that sense for twenty-five years, and . . . I could empathize and relate to Victor so deeply. . . . It was literally about being an artist and investigating through the actors and the emotions this thing that I was really close to. . . . I met my biological mother about two years before I made this movie, and I understood that genetic pain and memory."[67] This emphasis carried over to the actor's performances behind the scenes as well — Eyre notes that "in this movie, we're all searching for home to different degrees."[68] The shoot itself was pan-Indian: "When we were making the movie we were many different tribes, but that's like a powwow. You go to a powwow and it's many different tribes, but it's one people . . . it's a sense that we were making something that was ours. And inventing ourselves. . . . The actors in *Smoke Signals* told me it was a very trusting thing."[69]

"No Italians with Long Hair":
Acting Indian in *Smoke Signals*

The performative qualities of Sherman Alexie's script and Chris Eyre's directorial style created opportunities for the Native cast, who improvised lines and drew on personal experiences in preparing for their roles — a collaboration in production that marks the film's departure from the old studio system's two-tiered practices of casting white stars in "redface," to be supported by anonymous Native "extras." For example, in Alexie's notes accompanying the published script for *Smoke Signals*, he writes that although he wishes he'd written the line "Indians watching Indians on TV," "Evan Adams improvised it a few months previously while shooting a short film based on the second act of this screenplay."[70] Alexie repeatedly emphasizes the importance of casting in his various commentaries about shooting *Smoke Signals*, pointedly asserting in interviews that there were "no Italians with long hair."[71] In the annotations to the screenplay, he repeats three times his "LESSON LEARNED: Note to all other filmmakers: Cast Indians as Indians, because they'll give better performances."[72] This stress upon the identity of the actors asks us to think about the politics and ideologies of performing Indianness as it has been entwined in a long history of Hollywood production systems. Consciously hiring Native actors for Native roles represents an intervention in an industry that has traditionally excluded Native actors from screen credits. Historically, Hollywood directors turned to highly paid, non-Native stars such as Sal Mineo, Rock Hudson, and Anthony Quinn to play Indian roles in redface, while Native people worked as sometimes uncredited, usually underpaid extras who lent a physical but anonymous form of authenticity to the production and its narrative and stars. Theatrical performances of Indianness have been marked as authentic in different ways — in fact, it is a long standing trope of Hollywood film marketing to claim to represent Indians accurately for the first time, locating the idea of new realism in the filmmakers' consultation with experts, Native participation, location shooting, authentic or expensive costumes and props, and other aspects of production.

When talking about *Smoke Signals* in interviews, Alexie has called attention to the value of performative moments in the film that remind him of people he knows. For example, he was moved by Tantoo Cardinal's performance as Victor's mother, Arlene: "When Arlene Joseph stands up to Arnold, she is being the kind of powerful Indian woman I've known all my life."[73] Similarly, he claims that actors Michelle St. John and Elaine Miles (as Velma and Lucy) "give what may be the most rezziest performance in cinematic history. There is no non-Indian actor in the world who could have given these performances. These performances are not the result of years of training and study on how to 'act' like an Indian. They are the result of years of living as an Indian, of years of 'being' an Indian."[74] Alexie's emphasis on being Indian as a primary resource for the actors' performances is corroborated by some of the actors' stories about their work on *Smoke Signals* and other films.

Many of the actors related to Alexie's autobiographical stories because of their own experiences surviving the losses in their families that came directly or indirectly from systems of colonization, problems that the production itself addressed. They described drawing their performances from the position of their own personal knowledge of these political circumstances and consequences, and out of an understanding that performance is always a reworking of transmission. Actor Adam Beach drew from his own experience to portray Victor Joseph's distress over the absence of his father; Beach lost both of his parents when he was eight years old. "Living with that loss and not understanding it, you kind of feel you're not in the right place. I'm kind of looking for the right place in this movie." While filming the final scene at the bridge, Beach says, "I remember I was crying on Chris's shoulder and saying, 'It still hurts.' And he'd say, 'Well, you have to go do it again.'"[75] Tantoo Cardinal describes how she became an actor out of rage at losing her family, eventually using performance as a way to speak out:

> That's how I got into this business in the first place — it was rage. Absolute, livid rage. . . . I've felt the injustices and I've seen the injustices. I wasn't allowed to have my mother. I didn't have my father. My grandparents were there in my life and my grandfather was gone by the time I was ten, and my brother had an early death. . . . There's so little left of our family, and it's such a struggle to live as a full human being in this society when your family's been demolished and your community's

been demolished and it's all been demolished. And that's my passion, is that I will live, and I will live to tell. And that was, at a certain point in my life, that was the only reason to live, is that I wanted to tell on them. . . . Because I've seen things, and I know things. . . . And that's why I'm in the arts.[76]

For Cardinal and for many of the other actors, performances can emerge out of activism and function as a form of testimony or witnessing. Moving from the impulse to perform as a form of political action — a way to "tell on them" — to Hollywood "loincloth" roles as professional work could be frustrating. *Smoke Signals*, as a cinematic revision of those Hollywood performances, allowed some of the actors to use their own emotions and experiences to testify, as Cardinal describes here, rather than to facilitate fantasies that cover over systematic injustices. Such crossover casting includes not only Tantoo Cardinal's prior role as Black Shawl in *Dances with Wolves* but also Adam Beach's lead role in *Squanto* and Irene Bedard's role voicing Pocahontas for Disney's 1996 animated production of that title. Gary Farmer's role as "Nobody" in *Dead Man* (dir. Jarmusch, 1996) and *Ghost Dog: The Way of the Samurai* (dir. Jarmusch, 1999) presents, as I discuss in chapter 3, a different kind of crossover casting, one taken up deliberately in *Smoke Signals* as part of its intervention in cinematic discourses of Indian vanishing. Farmer became involved with acting initially through work with Native youth, and although he gives a powerful performance as Arnold Joseph in *Smoke Signals*, he has since distanced himself from that role because of its negative representation of Native fathers. He is the figure who most strongly connects *Smoke Signals* with *Pow-wow Highway* in his role as Philbert, *Powwow Highway*'s version of Thomas Builds-the-Fire. Like *Powwow Highway*, *Smoke Signals* created a range of opportunities for actors to perform versions of Indigenous masculinity on screen; and while Farmer is ambivalent about the role of Arnold Joseph, Evan Adams describes feeling an ancestral connection to his role as Thomas Builds-the-Fire.

Translating Thomas Builds-the-Fire

The actors in *Smoke Signals* maintain a richly productive tension between naturalistic acting and a more stylized performativity, a balance that draws attention to the way Indianness has been staged in the media and the effect of that staging on viewers. The actors' stories about drawing on their own experiences for their performances in *Smoke Signals* call to mind Stanislavskian or Method acting training, in which actors rely on their own affective memories to generate naturalistic performances (a connection made by Eyre as well, as I discuss in this section). Yet despite the realism of the performances, rooted in the actors' experiences, at pivotal moments *Smoke Signals* denies viewers the kind of naturalism that would facilitate easy, uncritical access to fantasies of Indianness so common to films such as *The Last of the Mohicans* — fantasies that depend on the studied sincerity of naturalistic acting for their air of earnest authenticity. For example, Thomas's storytelling scenes involve a somewhat showy style of delivery, while in the narrated flashback sequences Tantoo Cardinal and Gary Farmer overplay gestures and mouth their lines with an exaggerated theatricality, a style that indicates performance-within-performance since their scenes are taking place in Thomas's mind as he speaks.

Throughout the film, Victor and Thomas continue to debate the correct theatrical presentation of genealogy, locating their Indigeneity in the terms of both heredity and staging. Evan Adams's rich and complex performance as Thomas Builds-the-Fire presents a number of insights into the larger issues of performing Indianness that are taken up in *Smoke Signals*. Because Thomas also acts as the film's narrator in voice-over early on in the film and in the closing sequence, he takes on qualities of both author and director and stands in for these figures as a guide for the audience. His voice structures the film and its "magical" moments, controlling our understanding of the memories that are at the core of the characters' journey (although it is uncertain whether Thomas himself is aware of Arnold Joseph's most closely kept, most destructive secret — that he started the fire that killed Thomas's parents). In a sense, Thomas speaks with Alexie's poetic and storytelling voice, making audible the performative qualities of Alexie's writing and the lyricism that Alexie brought to the production. Adams has worked very closely with Alexie, recalling that "[Alexie] calls me his 'Injun-ue'; while he's been thinking about his film projects, he imagines me as his on-screen persona."[77] Here the joking reference reverses the gender of a stock character type — the ingénue, or virtuous young woman of film melodramas — while maintaining the term's implied tension between the naïveté of the character and the deliberate artifice of the actor playing the role and even the writer's own projection of self into the action. Alexie's stamp on the production is perhaps most evident in Thomas's character and in his lines, which mark the most literary aspects of the film; as Sarah Kozloff notes, voice-over narration is often imagined by viewers as the "mouthpiece of the image-maker."[78]

Thomas's stylized artifice in the storytelling scenes becomes the sign of his legitimacy and authority as a narrator for the film as a whole. His voice-over narration takes on the serious work of transmission — in the form of both storytelling and broadcasting. In that sense, Adams's performance (and Thomas's character) represent a generational model of film production as a "mediation of rupture," the term Faye Ginsburg uses to describe the way Indigenous media begins to address the social fractures of colonization. The social relations of telling and listening here mimic the relations of film production and film audience, reflexively reminding us that we are attending a communicative event. The "Indian trying to make a social statement" in Thomas's on-screen story to Velma and Lucy in an early scene from *Smoke Signals* also describes the film and its filmmakers.

This scene, in which Coeur d'Alene characters Velma and Lucy offer Victor and Thomas a ride to the bus stop in exchange for a story, and in which Thomas tells the story of Arnold Joseph's participation in a 1960s-era antiwar protest, is one site of the film's metacommentary on Native storytelling. The relations of speaking and listening are dramatized by Velma, whose framing comments gently mock Thomas's "fine example of the oral tradition" and so remind us of the ways that Native storytelling has been co-opted by outsiders. But Velma also demonstrates rapt (and somewhat stylistically exaggerated) attention during the storytelling itself, and Lucy is likewise so taken with the story that she turns to Victor for confirmation: "Did your dad really do that?" Victor's response, "Thomas, you're so full of shit," pulls viewers back toward an immersion in Adam Beach's more naturalistic manner and away from the heightened performativity of the storytelling, while at the same time distancing viewers from all performance and from romanticizing "oral traditions."[79] Alexie's script in this and other scenes also emphasizes Native women's spectatorship and commentary, as well as women's performances; like Velma and Lucy, Suzy Song says "Wow, that was a good story!" after Victor narrates a scene, pictured in flashback, of Arlene Joseph "on stage" delivering her miraculous fry bread to an appreciative crowd. This inclusion of a female Native audience in the film's imagination of Native spectatorship and performance is especially significant in light of the limited roles for Native actresses in Hollywood productions.[80]

Evan Adams's storytelling scenes in *Smoke Signals* are his most stylized and self-referential, and yet also the moments most anchored in his own identity. His thoughtful description of his relationship to the character of Thomas Builds-the-Fire demonstrates the opportunities presented by the context of the production:

> I really committed to Thomas, more so than I ever had to be. I tried to be really pure with him, because the feeling of Thomas — because he was the feeling of my grandmothers, and of my people. And so I said, "I know this feeling." I'm not putting on tricks. It's not casual behavior. I have to really immerse myself in a memory in wanting to do it. So I wasn't posing[;] . . . it was a very deep feeling. . . . I really did it for the Indians who came after me, so that they would know what it felt like to be an old-time Indian. Because I know that even my nephews and

nieces, they didn't know my grandmother. They didn't know how beautiful she was in her Indianness. . . . Anyway, I tried to capture that feeling and I would pray that I could capture it. It was holy because I was copying people who were dead. I was paying homage to them. It was my tribute to their lives, to how they had become. How they had stayed so loving in the face of horrible tragedies — most of them had terrible lives — so many people they lost so young, poverty . . . you know the whole shtick. To me they were heroes, and I was playing a hero. I was playing an icon. . . . For me, telling those stories, it's this wonderful thing in my mind. I'm just saying the words and closing my eyes. Often I'm closing my eyes, I'm speaking, telling this story, and I'm getting this warm feeling of I'm my grandmother; I'm my grandmother passing on knowledge, telling, being funny, being light at the same time.[81]

Adams's description of his turning inward to generate an expressive truth based on emotional recall seems to conform to a Method acting model of naturalistic performance because, as he describes it, his immersion in the role was rooted in his own identity and his empathetic and fulfilling relationship with his grandmother, whom he took as a model of traditional Indianness. Chris Eyre says that Adams "retranslated the literature" in his role as Thomas: "I told all the actors . . . you're creating contemporary Indian characters. And as contemporary Indians, talk about a sense of memory. Method acting. There's really no wrong they can do as long as they stay in the story and in character."[82] Adams claims that he wasn't "posing" in his storytelling scenes, yet his performances seem very posed, even stylized, as he tips up his face and closes his eyes (even peeking occasionally, in an exaggerated way, to check on his audience), holding his hands folded together except for emphatic gestures that punctuate key moments in the story. He speaks with a cadence reminiscent of poetry recitation, shifting out of this intonation and inflection when voicing characters in his story, and ending his stories with a brief axiom that resembles something between a

6. Thomas telling a story to Velma and Lucy.

7. Thomas assesses his audience while telling a story.

homily and a punch line.[83] Adams's carefully cultivated appearance in an old-fashioned suit and immaculate braids (and a prosthetic front tooth that contributed to the actor's expression of physical awkwardness) — and his mannerisms, such as his sudden wide smile and slightly exaggerated facial expressions, which contrast with his still face and closed eyes while telling stories — contribute to the stagy and sometimes even deliberately hammy effect of Thomas's stories, framing the performances and setting them apart from daily life. And extending Alexie's play with "ingénue" as a theatrical term associated with female characters, Adams's performance is also ambiguously gendered — perhaps even transgendered — in its primary modeling on a female ancestor. In the humor and the stylization of his storytelling performance there is also a hint of Brechtian distanciation, which disrupts the Method notions of coherence and unity (the "unbroken line" of characterization) based in the actor's recourse to the self.

Traditional, European-derived acting theory maintains a somewhat overdetermined division between stylized and naturalistic acting. Stylized acting is marked by an actor's overt performativity; at its extreme, an actor might look directly into the camera, acknowledging his or her own address to the audience. James Naremore writes that an antirealist or Brechtian actor is "more like a comic than a tragedian, concerned less with emotional truth than with critical awareness; instead of expressing an essential self, she or he examines the relation between roles on the stage and roles in society, deliberately calling attention to the artificiality of performance, foregrounding the staginess of spectacle, and addressing the audience in didactic fashion."[84]

Lines from the script that frame Thomas's first storytelling performance serve to remind the characters (and the viewers) that Indians have been treated as objects of scrutiny by outsiders, especially anthropologists, who have defined them in limiting ways (Indians barter, Indians have oral traditions) that deny Indigenous modernity. Velma comments (delivered with a stylized exaggeration), "We're Indians, remember? We *barter*," and, after the story,

"Well, I think it's a fine example of the oral tradition!" Such lines coming from Lucy and Velma — the "Indian audience" of Thomas's performance — underscore a performed *disunity* or fragmentation of Native selves, because a double vision is necessary to recognize Native social relations and performances occurring within and alongside outsiders' defining and ubiquitous representations. Adams's performance, then, like Alexie's script, requires a critical, politicized stance from the film's spectators. Instead of reflecting a unified self back to viewers, media constructions of Indianness are destabilized, and their underlying ideologies are revealed by the fragmentation of social relations and social roles.[85] In one sense, then, *Smoke Signals* resembles political theater at this moment in its distancing of spectators from an immersion in the seemingly realist drama that has so often offered up fantasies of Indianness.

But Adams's description of his approach to his role suggests an interpretive framework beyond the Brechtian and Stanislavskian continuum that often dominates discussions of acting. He sees his performance as an homage to his elders, documenting an older generation through performative embodiment addressed specifically to a younger Indian audience ("the Indians who came after me"). Rather than inviting outsider audiences into a fantasy, Adams attempts to bring together his contemporary Native audience with his Native ancestors through his own performative retrieval of genealogy. The stylized aspects of the performance and its reflexive framing by Lucy and Velma cast that return to ancestors in a politicized, activist context (an appropriate mode, since the story is about Arnold Joseph's violent antiwar protests in the 1960s). To do this, Adams accesses a specifically Native dramatic idiom — his grandmother's storytelling style — that involves "passing on knowledge, telling, being funny, being light at the same time." The "beautiful Indianness" that he ascribes to "old-time Indians" comes, he suggests, from their ability to be "loving" in the midst of the life-and-death struggles and calamities of colonization that can stress and weaken the bonds between family members. This struggle to maintain love for one another in the context of colonization is the primary emotional challenge for the Joseph family in *Smoke Signals*. This focus also counters the emphasis upon Indians-as-victims in many politically weighted productions, both documentary and dramatic. Adams further describes this aspect of his approach to the role in spiritual terms, and in a way that reflects the intergenerational aspect of *Smoke Signals*'s appeal as children take up parental legacies: "It was holy because I was copying people who were dead."

In this interpretation, Thomas's storytelling comes closest to what Hopi videographer Victor Masayesva calls "Indigenous experimentalism," Native artistic innovation that reaches back toward ancestors. Masayesva writes that "the tribal person's trans-cultural performances . . . are at their most profound when inherited skills and ancestral knowledge dominate the stage." Unlike Eyre and Alexie's Indigenization of American popular culture, however, Masayesva distinguishes between "Indigenous culture" and "popular culture," defining "the Indigenous aesthetic" as "the language of intercession, through which we are heard by and commune with the Ancients."[86] According to Masayesva, an Indigenous aesthetic, as he has said elsewhere, "begins in the sacred." Evan Adams's description of his performance suggests that Masayesva's model of Indigenous experimentalism is an important part of *Smoke Signals*'s artistic success. For all of the film's immersion in the language of popular culture, Adams infuses the key role of Thomas with a distinctly Indigenous aesthetic even when his stories incorporate references to such icons of mainstream Americana as the National Guard, Charles Bronson movies, and Denny's restaurants.

Beyond questions of popular culture and the question of who is a real Indian — a discourse that is exploded in the "Dances with Salmon" scene (discussed below) — Thomas's stories also engage in narrative transmission as a form of political consciousness. Adams has described his conviction that "acting is holy work" as a form of activist teaching, framing the idea of changing the world through artistic performance in explicitly spiritual terms. He also sees acting as intellectual work; throughout his acting career, he continued his studies in medical school, completing his residency at St. Paul's hospital in downtown Vancouver. In an interview, he linked his work as a physician with his acting: "I like to think that my work is as an intellectual," involving social commentary about contemporary Native communities.[87] In the context of his second film with Sherman Alexie, *The Business of Fancydancing* (2002), he notes:

> I'm not here to sell dreams, I'm not here to flirt and to titillate. I'm here to teach important lessons and to bring forward important ideas that could potentially change your life. . . . So I think that at its purest an actor puts forward dramas or puts forward stories — histories — for others to see and experience and to learn from. . . . To learn about the race riots and slavery. To learn about feminism and abortion, to learn about gay and lesbian identity and struggle, to learn about children's rights. Those are important issues. An actor has a hand in that. And that's when it becomes holy.[88]

For Adams the *political* work of acting entails not only mediating between ancestors and audiences through the retrieval of familial relations but also dramatizing history in service of a transformative pedagogy. Competing with mainstream movies-as-teachers, Thomas's stylized storytelling is an instance of metanarrative, as folklorist Barbara Babcock would describe reflexivity in storytelling performance: narrative communication that situates itself within a set of social dynamics in order to call attention to the story's meaning in relation to a particular audience. In this case, Thomas's performed metanarrative dramatizes the way the history and politics of media images of Indians is absorbed by an Indigenous audience.[89] As critic Amanda Cobb suggests, *Smoke Signals* is made up of "stories within a story" as well as a "story about stories."[90]

One of the funniest and most beloved scenes in *Smoke Signals* — the "Dances with Salmon" sequence on the bus to Phoenix — also offers the film's most intense commentary on media images of Indians and on the pressure felt by some Native youth to conform to those images in their everyday lives. In the scene, Victor, expressing his impatience with what he sees as Thomas's incoherent rambling, equates "talking about nothing" with "trying to sound like some damn medicine man." He accuses Thomas of having seen *Dances with Wolves* too many times ("100? 200?"), and finally challenges him: "Don't you even know how to be a real Indian?" "I guess not," Thomas answers. Responding with, "Well, shit, no wonder. Jeez, I guess I'll have to teach you then, enit?" Victor then proceeds to give Thomas an explicit acting lesson on "being Indian," which is (ironically) drawn from the very same media source he's accused Thomas of copying — the Kevin Costner film *Dances with Wolves* (1990). Unlike the "old-time" Indianness that Thomas (and actor Evan Adams) hopes to provide for Indian audiences — modeled on his grandmother's ability to maintain her light humor and commitment to "telling" and "loving," to relationships within a community, in the midst of poverty and loss — Victor's imagined warriors and medicine men are serious, silent, isolated, and emptied of affect:

> VICTOR: First of all, quit grinning like an idiot. Indians ain't supposed to smile like that. Get stoic!
> *Thomas tries to look serious. He fails.*
> VICTOR: No, like this.
> *Victor gets a very cool look on his face, serious, determined, warrior-like.*
> VICTOR: You got to look mean or people won't respect you. White people will walk over you if you don't look mean. You got to look like a warrior. You got to look like you just got back from killing a buffalo.
> THOMAS: But our tribe never hunted buffalo. We were fishermen.
> VICTOR: What? You want to look like you just came back from catching a fish? This ain't *Dances with Salmon*, you know? Thomas, you got to look like a warrior.
> *Thomas gets stoic. He's better this time.*[91]

8. Thomas, wearing an apron and kitchen towel, makes fry bread for his grandmother.

9. Thomas tries to follow Victor's instructions: "You have to look like a warrior."

In the screenplay (but not the scene as filmed) Victor goes on to say that in order to "have some mystery . . . you don't talk. You just nod your head or something." Significantly, performing the dangerous masculinity of movie Indians requires silencing Native voices, surely a commentary on the silence and stilted speech of Indian characters in Hollywood movies (indeed, Victor is forever telling Thomas to "shut up!"). Such characters are delineated by their costumes instead, and Victor goes on to instruct Thomas on the topic of assembling the visible signs of Indianness that are recognizable in the wider world, specifically his hair and clothes.

Underlying Victor and Thomas's conversation about pop-culture versions of Indian masculinity are the synchronous images of Indian stoicism and absence of expression. The serious warrior stereotype depends for its dramatic success upon the audience's belief in the premise that stoicism isn't a performance but rather a sign of authenticity (that is, a nonperformance). Yet Victor and Thomas's discussion of the warrior figure reveals just how profoundly theatrical this image is, particularly as they catalog the assembly of props, gestures, facial expressions, costuming and especially hairstyle necessary to carry it off. In trying to perform the "authentic" Indian warrior they see in *Dances with Wolves*, they demonstrate the artifice of movie Indianness and the ways it is learned ("I'll have to teach you then, enit?"), the way Indianness, in the movies, is made available to anyone rather than remaining politically and genealogically specific.

The way Victor and Thomas's media-saturated ideas about Indians influence their self-presentation is particularly apparent in their conversation about hair. Since the two men are modeling their current versions of idealized Indianness on characters from *Dances with Wolves*, Victor's line of reasoning in convincing Thomas to unbraid his long hair ("You gotta free it!") suggests that he is emulating the warrior character Wind-in-His-Hair (Rodney Grant, Omaha) from that film. Victor's comment to Thomas that "an Indian man ain't nothing without his hair" prepares viewers for the gravity of the scene later in the film in which Victor cuts his hair to mourn his father's death, while at the same time summoning the construction of visibly racial Indianness through hairstyle in movies. Barbara Babcock argues that costuming functions as a crucial racial marker of Indian identity in popular images: "In the absence of a significant difference in skin color, what is on the body, particularly the head, becomes 'the key signifier of cultural and racial difference' in the stereotypes of the Native American."[92]

In a short film about Native identity, titled *Half of Anything* (2004) and directed by Jonathan S. Tomhave (Hidatsa/Hocak/Prairie Band Potawatomie), Sherman Alexie describes "being a real Indian" by talking about shifting reactions to his hairstyles:

> Indian identity has almost exclusively become something physical. . . . Well, it's interesting how my hair, and the length of my hair, has become such an issue. . . . I wore a mullet for a long time. And I knew it was out of style in terms of pop culture, and out of style in my class, what I did for a living. It got cute and fashionable to hammer on mullets . . . which is really elitist. So I enjoyed wearing the mullet after that as well just to fight against elitism. But I wore it because it's a reservation hairstyle. And I didn't want to lose my connection to the rez. So, my hairstyle as a mullet was sort of the last-gasp effort to retain my reservation identity . . . at least physically. . . . I don't live there, I won't ever live there, I don't speak my language, I don't dance, but I'm from there, I grew up there and my family's still there. So, I mean, my hairstyle was nostalgia. I was guilty of nostalgia, and thinking I had to look a certain way to send a message to people about Indianness. And then when I just started wearing it all one length, which was more Indian-fashionable, people loved it. And I got so many comments about the hair, constantly. And then, when I cut it, 'cause my dad died — which was the ironic thing, that my fans didn't know why I cut my hair, when 99% of them have seen *Smoke Signals*, where Victor cuts his hair because his dad dies — and it became such a subject during the book tour last year. Every reading somebody would ask

the question and then everybody would laugh, cause it was funny to talk about the Indian's hair. That was the measure of identity, was hair. And now that I've cut my hair I've become even more ambiguous — my identity. Which is weird because . . . among the Spokane Indians I'm dark, and I also grew up in Eastern Washington, which is sunny 300 days a year so I was darker skinned than I am now. And I'm a writer who lives in Seattle, so I'm pale as hell right now . . . and with short hair, I blend, now, into Seattle. I could be Asian, I could be Mexican, I could be Middle Eastern, I could be Italian, you know, I could be generic northern European, I could be, you know, some dark German descendant, I could be just a white mutt. I could be half of anything. And earlier on in my career, that would have bothered me, and it did bother me when people didn't know what I was, or people commented, you know, "you don't look Indian." And now I don't care. I am not interested in sending obvious and shallow signals to people about who I am. I'd no sooner wear turquoise, dream catcher earrings . . . that just feels to me like costumes.

Alexie's extended discussion of the way his own public image hinges on hair style indicates how the critical discourse around Adam Beach's wig in *Smoke Signals* reveals a racialized public preoccupation with the most visible (or what Alexie calls the "obvious and shallow") signs of Indianness.

Given the scope of this discourse about hair as a manifestation of Victor's confused identity in *Smoke Signals*, the wig of black shoulder-length hair worn by actor Adam Beach (after Victor cuts his hair in an emotional scene in his father's trailer) has provoked an interesting commentary among viewers. Unlike Evan Adams's prosthetic tooth, which he wore to get in character and to give Thomas's smile a slightly crooked look, Beach's wig has drawn criticism from viewers who feel that the artificiality of the false hair is distracting. In fact, Chris Eyre never asked Beach to cut his hair. According to Eyre, the "unspoken rule with Native American actors is that you really can't ask them to cut their hair," in part for cultural reasons and awareness of the history of coerced haircuts Native children were subjected to in boarding schools and other institutional settings. There are also industry-based reasons for Native actors to keep their hair long, "because this is something that they live by" in term of ongoing auditions for roles in period films and television programs. As Eyre tells the story, the limited time and budget for the film were also determining factors:

> The way that it worked was that we were about nineteen days into twenty-three days of shooting and I'd approved the wig, and when it showed up on set, it was much worse than what I remembered it to be. We had two wigs, because they're so expensive, one to cut and one to wear, just because of budget. And on the nineteenth day when he showed up, Adam looked at me and said, "How do I look, dude?" I looked at him and I said, "You look great." I said, "Give me just a minute." I turned around, I walked behind a trailer, and I thought to myself, I think I've just ruined my movie. Because at the time I knew there was nothing else to shoot except his scenes with the wig, and I knew that we weren't going to take a day at a cost of $75,000 and not shoot, and I knew that in order to get a wig, a new wig, it would take two days. There was no way we were going to do anything but shoot. So in fact, we did keep shooting. And when Harvey Weinstein bought the movie, he said, "The wig's fine." Because we did entertain doing a reshoot, and Harvey Weinstein, who owned the movie then, said, "The wig's fine, the wig stays, we're not going to reshoot it."[93]

The artifice of Adam Beach's wig, though unintentional, extends the film's dialogue about the theatricality of "authentic" Indianness, exposed in the "Dances with Salmon" sequence, to consider the positioning of Native actors in a film industry that often limits their work to period rather than contemporary roles.[94] The performance of stoic Indianness in Hollywood films demands both visible signs of traditionality and silence — a visibility without speech — and Evan Adams's performance of the chatty, sociable Thomas Builds-the-Fire is a breakout role in this regard. Thomas's loquaciousness has been noted critically as an example of Indigenous oral story-telling,[95] but his characters' range of human emotions and social modes, conveyed through his abundant verbal capacities — to be funny, poetic, dreamy, annoying, wrong, right, loyal, sly, hyperbolic, dorky, empathetic — are also, importantly, one of Alexie's deliberately scripted interventions in movie-Indian silence.

The temporary silencing of Thomas in the "Dances with Salmon" sequence amounts to a momentary erasure of stories and of the memories that those stories carry; Thomas's Indigeneity (in the sense of his familial identity) resides in his stories. As he says of his family origins in his opening narration, "I don't remember that fire, I only have the stories," suggesting both loss and retention of his heritage through memory and the recounting of memory. The line also deepens the fire's broader signification of European settlement as a cataclysmic historical event that continues to be remembered through repeated narratives. To suppress Native stories about themselves — and the memories from the past reactivated in the present through stories — is also to erase the politics carried and taught through those memories and the activist self-determination inherent in self-definition. Conforming to media images of silent and stoic Indians, then, amounts to an erasure of Thomas's Indian identity and of history itself — especially the rights (to land, to resources) that come with treaties and other events from the past. Victor's media-made self-image makes visibility (rather than history) the term of recognition — Indianness is racialized by the movies.[96] Thomas's narrative voice, in contrast, represents the ongoing work of the past — media history, political history, family history — in the present, as these histories are intertwined in his own generation's needs and projects. As a stand-in for the movie's director (as he scripts and narrates sequences, including voicing the characters), Evan Adams's presentation of Thomas answers the cinematic Indian-as-commodity with other models of performance and spectatorship, other relations of speaking and listening in the film itself and in its production.

For the writer, director, and actors, *Smoke Signals*'s production involved translating personal experience to the screen in a complex address to multiple audiences. This translation took place in a number of ways and by a variety of means — including literary adaptation, supportive infrastructures like the Sundance Institute, outside financial backing, and casting and performance. I have argued here that one of the most important elements of *Smoke Signals*'s production is the coordination of various kinds of performance, from the performances of and within Alexie's writing to the performances of actors in production and the performance of Native ironic humor by characters like Lester FallsApart and Thomas Builds-the-Fire. *Smoke Signals* is a film about the staging of Indigenous revitalization in a visual and performative mode, drawing in non-Native viewers while simultaneously addressing Native viewers as insiders (the trick that Alexie has often called "Indian trap-doors").

Evan Adams's improvised line about "Indians watching Indians on TV" is perhaps the paradigmatic example of an alternative production trajectory that highlights the communication between performer and audience across the borders of the screen (while complicating linear, text-to-performance-to-screen models of adaptation). This is a crucial point for understanding Native performances of Indigeneity as a form of activism — and of visual sovereignty — that opposes the dehumanizing traditions of Hollywood spectacle. In particular, linking Native film production to life experiences that include media reception (as in Alexie's stories about the drive-in movies of his childhood) challenge popular assumptions that Native peoples are somehow either outside of the contemporary circuit of production and consumption, or trapped in the display case of pop-culture content. Understanding *Smoke Signals* as emergent from the filmmakers' immersion in — and facility with — pop culture as consumers and producers situates them in the contemporary moment rather than outside of it. In a broader sense, seeing links between Native reception and Native film production explodes the temporal divisions between the separate, homogenous worlds of modernity and primitivism promulgated by the mainstream film industry's focus on nineteenth-century Indian images. Instead, Native film production and reception emphasizes the way we live together in a world that is also marked by political boundaries. These distinctions matter, not least because of their link to political rights and responsibilities. The distinctiveness of Indigeneity is made clear by *Smoke Signals*'s Indigenous performances in the public sphere, performances that speak about the relations of power in the contemporary world we all share.

chapter three

"Dances with Salmon"

Reading Smoke Signals

Recalling the experience of scripting and filming *Smoke Signals*, Sherman Alexie has said, "It's pretty amazing to be in charge of our own images. . . . I think we were immediately aware that we were doing something revolutionary, that it was a revolutionary moment." Yet he also describes the film as "tamer" and "gentler" than his books, in part because "it was purposely written to be a PG, PG-13 movie": "It's the only [Native] film that ever went even remotely mainstream."[1] Alexie and Eyre's investment in visual sovereignty, in being "in charge of our own images," complicates the film's emphatic use of established codes of cinema and film genres, with their sure appeal to mainstream audiences. How does the film reconcile these seemingly contradictory "revolutionary" and "mainstream" impulses, its function as both an intervention based on distinct political identity and a gathering place based on commonality? One strategy is the way *Smoke Signals* marshals temporal and spatial cinematic language to infuse mainstream American stories and discourses about independence, freedom, and Western settlement with Indigenous significations. The film's continual return to the image and metaphor of the bridge or intersection suggests both historical conflict and intercultural gathering. It is an image that brings together material elements of Spokane and Coeur d'Alene geography and history — the film's references to actual events and places — with the virtual landscapes and histories of pop-culture representations.

In one of *Smoke Signals*'s many self-reflexive moments, its protagonist Victor Joseph seems to deny that he's a character in a Spokane Indian movie when he says "This ain't *Dances with Salmon*, you know." His cinematic self-assessment distances *Smoke Signals* from both the aestheticized romanticism of revisionist Westerns like

Dances with Wolves, and also from the traditionalism represented by the fish that were once a primary source of food for the inland Salishan tribes. In its disavowal of "Dances with Salmon," the line also seems to proffer a reflexive characterization of the film's actual project as it relates to the harmful and sustaining qualities of commodification as well as more traditional forms of sustenance. The food metaphor is amplified as Victor and Thomas argue about how to position themselves as Indians within the purview of mainstream (non-Indian) popular culture — or, as they say, how to be a "real Indian." In the "Dances with Salmon" sequence on the bus, as Victor emerges from a harrowing memory (shown in flashback) of the day his father Arnold left the family, Thomas recalls a more heroic vision of Arnold eating fifteen pieces of fry bread to win a fry bread–eating contest ("It was cool!"). Victor accuses Thomas of "talking about nothing" like "some damn medicine-man" from the movies: "I mean, how many times have you seen *Dances with Wolves* — 100? 200? Ah jeez, you *have* seen it that many times, haven't you?" This exchange associates Arnold's capacious consumption of food with Thomas's equally exaggerated consumption of movies. These different commodities — fry bread and film — can be unhealthy in quantity yet also pleasurable and energizing. Indeed, in the same scene Thomas transforms himself from nerd to superhero with a "Fry Bread Power" T-shirt designed to look like Superman's costume (he later confidently but erroneously claims that Arnold looks like Charles Bronson from *Death Wish V: The Face of Death* [dir. Goldstein, 1994]). In a critique of the generic (white) American superhero, Thomas becomes an Indian pop-culture hero empowered by a food made with commodity flour, a powdery-white staple food emblematic here not of precolonial tribal traditions but rather of reservation life and Native ingenuity and physical survival in the face of colonization.

Smoke Signals's "Indigenizing" work takes place not only in the performances and production but also in the film's textual workings; by "being in control of our own images," Eyre and Alexie make something new, sustaining and specifically Native out of the commodified forms of pop culture. The film's politicized references, symbolic places, and techniques of film language — sound, editing, and mise-en-scène — incorporate densely woven allusions to both historical events and popular representations (including Westerns, road movies, and films by Jim Jarmusch and John Ford). Alexie and Eyre's images of crossroads and intersections, use of sound (especially music and voice-over narration), and sound bridges allude to Western genre films and frontier history. Disjunctive editing brings together multiple time frames, continually redefining the relationship of the past to the present even within the context of the road movie genre's linear movements across the Western landscape. The flashback sequences, in which Victor remembers events from his childhood, suggest the impact of systemic, imperialist infrastructures on individual Native families and children, and on the tribe as a whole.

The figure of Arnold Joseph activates a broad range of such references: he holds the promise of rejuvenation, "like a salmon," yet also reminds Thomas of Hollywood's constructions of masculine retribution, "like Charles Bronson in *Death Wish V.*" His character connects the film's discourses of nationhood, especially the references to "Independence Day" and the spectacle of fireworks, to its images of fatherhood and masculinity. The relationships between Victor, Thomas, and Victor's father provide an emotional axis in the film that links the general theme of loss accessible to many audiences with distinctly Native issues of colonization and repatriation, and specifically with questions of guardianship and masculinity suggested by the metaphor of the United States as a "Great White Father."

The film's sovereigntist position is also advanced through the politics of location shooting on the Spokane River. Conversations in *Smoke Signals* about salmon and rivers allude to U.S. expropriations of Indian land and the loss of salmon runs following the construction of the Grand Coulee Dam, which devastated the traditional economies that had sustained tribes along the Columbia River and Spokane tributary. The film's images of rivers, empty of fish, come together with its discourses of hunger and fast food in the character of Arnold Joseph, a figure representing both scarcity and plenitude. Media representations, historical U.S.-Native relations, and private memories are intertwined in the film to suggest their combined influence on the characters' present lives.

Arnold Joseph's Independence

The entire structure of Smoke Signals is based on Victor and Thomas's retrieval of Victor's father's ashes, and in the process Victor's discovery and then forgiveness of his father's tormenting secret — Arnold's careless use of fireworks that started a house fire and ultimately killed Thomas Builds-the-Fire's mother and father. The film's constant movement between national and local frames of reference — between affairs of state and affairs of family — is established in the film's opening narrative of that disastrous Independence Day celebration. The house fire introduces the film's focus on fatherhood and nationhood in the same image, while impressing upon the film's different audiences the ways that these threads are connected. Seeded by fireworks, the July 4th house fire materializes U.S. nationhood as an invasive power that consumes and destroys Native families. The celebration of Independence Day deliberately recalls symbols of U.S. origins — the Declaration of Independence, the historical image of the nation's "founding fathers," and the troping of the U.S. president as the "Great White Father."[2] Ralph Armbruster-Sandoval presses this parallel between biological fathers and founding fathers in the film, suggesting that Arnold Joseph is a metaphor for the United States and that "Arnold, Victor's biological father, acts like our 'founding fathers' did" in causing the destructive Independence Day fire.[3] Armbruster-Sandoval goes on to consider the logical extension of this argument, whether the film's closing poem about forgiving our fathers advocates Indigenous forgiveness of the United States, and what that forgiveness might mean, suggesting that the film's final question — "If we forgive our fathers, what is left?" — should provoke a realization that what is left after forgiveness is reparation. While reparation is a compelling way of viewing both U.S. obligations to Native tribes and Victor's connection to his late father, one problem with this reading is that it does not fully consider the historical consequences of extending the construction of the United States as a "parent" to Native nations. This symbolically familial relationship has pervaded Federal Indian policy and enabled a range of paternalistic legislation, including legislation and court rulings establishing U.S. wardship over not only Native governments but also the removal of Native children from their own parents.

Arnold Joseph's complex relationship to the United States and its master narratives of national history (for which fireworks are a visual symbol) encompasses both resistance and patriotism. Arnold is not a figure *for* the United States, but is rather a figure colonized *by* the United States. The fact that he is the vehicle for the destruction of Thomas's family through the toxic fire of a U.S. Independence celebration attests not to his symbolic embodiment of the United States but rather to the intimacy of the colonizer and the colonized. The visually spectacular aspects of the fire also resemble the totalizing vision of mainstream media — the film's emphasis upon Independence Day reveals that celebration to be not only a military reenactment but also a way of enforcing a collective story that aims to overwhelm individual Native voices and tribal counternarratives. The way that personal and familial losses are intertwined with formal international relationships in this image of the house fire emphasizes close-knit intergenerational relations, as when Arnold Joseph rescues baby Thomas from the fire, extending the Phoenix metaphor of regeneration from ashes. It is also, like other details in *Smoke Signals*, autobiographical: Sherman Alexie's sister died in a trailer fire when he was in his teens. This autobiographical event takes on the political dimensions of nation-to-nation discourse and reveals the 4th of July rituals (here further amplified because it celebrates the U.S. bicentennial, 1776–1976) to be a form of ongoing, recurring symbolic violence, a national celebration of Native dispossession.[4] Native history is filtered through the lens of personal pain.

10. The burning house.

The house fire as a manifestation of colonization by the U.S. government resonates intertextually with another, less publicized Native feature film screened at Sundance in 1998, which also culminates in a house fire. *Tushka*, directed by Ian Skorodin, tells the story of FBI persecution of Native activists through its COINTELPRO "antisubversive" agency in the 1960s and 1970s; it is a fictionalized account that hews closely to the actual story of John Trudell — the activist and actor who plays DJ Randy Peone in *Smoke Signals*, and who was the chairman of AIM in the 1970s. Trudell's family was killed in an arson fire at their home in Nevada only hours after Trudell burned a United States flag during a speech and rally in front of the FBI headquarters in Washington DC (see the extended discussion of casting Trudell in chapter 1). In Skorodin's film, a suspicious house fire destroys the family of a Choctaw activist.[5] Both *Smoke Signals* and *Tushka* connect devastating real events to their filmic worlds, intensifying the symbolic meaning of the house fire while emphasizing the human and emotional toll.

In taking an Independence Day celebration as the story's originary event, *Smoke Signals*'s filmmakers ask us to see its subsequent intertextual references in the context of tribal nations and their historical and ongoing relations to the United States. This thread is carried through the film quite consistently in frequent references to Westerns, military figures such as Custer, and dialogue such as Lucy's comment that Victor and Thomas should take their passports with them when they leave the reservation, since the United States "is as foreign as it gets."

Thomas's introductory voice-over description of the Independence Day celebration — "On the fourth of July, 1976, my parents celebrated white people's independence by holding the largest house party in tribal history" — brings normally obscured patterns into view. To say "white people's independence" rather than "American independence" or simply "Independence Day" is to highlight what Charles Mills calls the "racial contract" informing U.S. national origins. In Mills's example, the first three words of the Declaration of Independence, "We the people," do not refer to all people but rather only to white men, since African Americans, Native Americans, and other nonwhite peoples, as well as all women, were not enfranchised in the new nation.[6] Alexie is certainly not the first to point out the unspoken politics of possession and colonial violence embedded in a supposedly shared national holiday. In the 1852 speech "What to the Slave is the Fourth of July?" Frederick Douglass addresses the audience of the Rochester Ladies' Anti-Slavery Society as "fellow citizens" but goes on to say that the benefits of citizenship are not shared: "I am not included within the pale of glorious anniversary! . . . The rich inheritance of justice, liberty, prosperity and independence, bequeathed by your fathers, is shared by you, not by me. . . . This Fourth July is yours, not mine. You may rejoice, I must mourn."[7] Smoke Signals, too, rearticulates Independence Day as a day of mourning — but in a literal and familial sense as the anniversary of the death of Thomas's parents.

Thomas's narration makes whiteness visible as the term of national belonging while also making "independence" visible as a racial privilege and a historical and ongoing form of political domination. With this simple magnification, Thomas takes the fireworks that ritually mark U.S. independence out of an obfuscating race-blind abstraction and into an Indigenous world that is populated by families, families that become visible because the (normally invisible) practices of racial exclusion and inclusion have also been revealed. Arnold Joseph's devastating mistake in "celebrating white people's independence" with patriotic fireworks causes a genocidal fire that "rose up like General George Armstrong Custer," unleashing the enemy into Thomas's house and the reservation community. We see the aftermath of Arnold's fireworks in the burning house, suggesting that the toxic fire of U.S. nationhood inhabits the territory of the familial (particularly, the familial and tribal past).

As a manifestation and central symbol of the dominating presence and consuming appetite of the United States in Native lands, Arnold Joseph's fireworks inflect *Smoke Signals* with political issues of national identity and tribal sovereignty. Media studies scholar Mary Beth Haralovich has suggested that images of fireworks in film and television — like the illuminated screen itself — can function as a site of communal spectacle with overtly nationalist associations. Attending to film characters that turn away from "the pleasure of gazing at fireworks," Haralovich finds a range of disengagements from civic involvement as well as indications of isolation and critical dissent.[8] In *Smoke Signals* we don't see an impressive display of Independence Day fireworks, nor expressions of communal awe. Instead, scattered images allude to formal fireworks shows (which are themselves echoes of military display) and to fire: children watch outdoor fires or hold sparklers, and Suzy Song burns sage to purify and then burn Arnold Joseph's trailer home (a dwelling that suggests temporary residence) — but the idea of the civic is still present in the images.

Beyond the nationalist implications of the fireworks, the distress call implied by the "smoke signals" of the title invites us to see the film in these terms of U.S.-tribal relations. In this sense, the fireworks instantiate a colonial discourse, and even what Chadwick Allen calls "treaty discourse": "Since it operates within a paradigm of nation-to-nation status, the discourse of treaties, like the discourse of declarations of war or declarations of independence, provides one of the few interpretive frames within which contemporary Indigenous minority activists and writers can stage formal dialogue with dominant settler interests on (potentially) equitable terms."[9] By reminding us that the United States is a nation created by and for "white people's independence," Thomas implicitly also reminds us that the excluded Indigenous tribes exist independently of it, as separate nations.

The film's focus on issues of fatherhood, masculinity, and abandonment is equally freighted with national significance. Perhaps the most common and clichéd iteration of this cultural construction is the Great White Father figure and other tropes of paternalism. Nineteenth-century statesmen — Andrew Jackson in particular — used the language of paternalism to enact legislation dispossessing tribes from their lands. Michael Rogin argues that within this nineteenth-century discourse, "if Indians were 'red children,' whites thought of themselves as parents. . . . Whites could not imagine Indians outside the parent-child context."[10] The U.S. government in its self-appointed role as a guardian codified relationships of dependency with tribes as wards (defined by the Supreme Court in 1830 as "domestic dependent nations"). This paternalism, defining the United States' metaphorical and legal relationship with tribal nations, posited the U.S. president as the rhetorical "father," a construction that, if extended, frames the U.S. disavowal of those economic and treaty commitments as a paternal abandonment.[11]

The infantilizing aspects of U.S. paternalism emerge in popular culture representations of loyal Indian sidekicks such as Tonto, a figure dependent on the leadership of the heroic white colonizer (the Lone Ranger) as well as in hypermasculine media products such as Rambo (whose long hair and headband, bare chest, and choker pendant are all meant to symbolize Indian primitivism). The angry, traumatized, violent Indian veteran appears in *Powwow Highway* (Buddy Redbow, played by A. Martinez), drawing together both the nineteenth-century rhetoric of the Indian as a savage child and a romanticized warrior stereotype. Scholars such as Dana Nelson and Joane Nagel have argued that the construction of masculinity is at the heart of U.S. nationalism and imperialism. Nagel and David Anthony Tyeeme Clarke point out the way turn-of-the-century institutions encouraged "playing Indian," such as the American Boy Scouts' attempt to expropriate an imagined Indian masculine power: "In seemingly innocent acts of commodity exchange, white men restored their futures at the expense of Indigenous people by robbing them of their cultural capital, infusing it with new meaning, then using it to remake themselves as masters and masterful."[12]

While it is possible to see these symbolic discourses at work in *Smoke Signals*, the film also focuses on "the actual problems of father-son relationships among Native Americans" as well as "the internal conflicts Native Americans sometimes face when coming to terms with the legacies of their ancestors (or forefathers)," as Brian Klopotek points out.[13] Victor and Thomas's parallel journeys to understand Arnold as a father figure, and his role in the fire that destroyed Thomas's family, link them and their families while driving the film's narrative. Arnold Joseph's problem of self-destructive rage is shared by Victor. It is inwardly directed but stems from conditions of dispossession — poverty, domestic abuse, substance abuse, pervasive and oppressive media representations — and is countered by Thomas's more androgynous model of masculinity. In writing the screenplay, Alexie had in mind "the idea that in Indian cultures in particular, men have lost all their . . . traditional masculine roles. . . . I mean, driving a truck for the BIA is simply not going to fulfill all your spiritual needs, like fishing for salmon or hunting for deer once did, so in some sense Indian men are much more lost and much more clueless than Indian women."[14] At the same time, he notes that "in every ethnic or racial community . . . it's fathers who are missing."[15] Thus, in the context of Chris Eyre's characterization of his films as "home dramas," *Smoke Signals* bridges its Native and non-Native audiences through its focus on fathers and sons, making familiar by making familial the effects of colonization on Indigenous youth.

Making the emotional consequences of systemic social injustices feel more persuasive for audiences through stories that reveal the suffering of innocent victims and families is also the work of melodrama. We can see *Smoke Signals* as a form of male melodrama particularly in its fraught representations of Indigenous patriotism and in the visual spectacle of fireworks as a mark of emotional excess in the mise-en-scène — an image that conveys the characters' psychic crisis stemming from feelings of both loyalty and rage toward the United States as a colonizing power. Like fireworks, industrial cinema has functioned as a technology of imperialism, but in *Smoke Signals* both forms of popular spectacle are retrieved and "Indigenized," their race politics made visible through reflexive storytelling and subversive humor.

The quintessentially American national ideal of "independence," materialized in the Independence Day fireworks and fire that consumes Thomas's family, also suggests an attribute of mainstream white American masculinity that is equally destructive in Victor and Thomas's Indigenous context. Arnold Joseph achieves independence by leaving his family, or in Thomas's narration, "vanishing"; the equation of independence with vanishing intimates that the U.S. discourses of freedom and independence are a false and ultimately destructive model of citizenship for Native men. The fireworks/house fire and the image (described by Thomas Builds-the-Fire but not pictured in the film) of Arnold Joseph protesting the Vietnam War (with the caption "Make love, not war") stand for the contradictions emerging from definitions of Native patriotism, citizenship, and loyalty to the United States in the context of loss related to ongoing U.S. conquest and colonization of Native peoples. Thomas's lines come from Alexie's short story "Because My Father Always Said He Was the Only Indian Who Saw Jimi Hendrix Play 'The Star-Spangled Banner' at Woodstock," which addresses the problem of Indigenous participation in U.S. politics when Indianness is appropriated as a popular and publicly available sign of alterity, so that Arnold Joseph's protest inadvertently becomes a spectacle rather than the political action of a speaking subject: "During the sixties, my father was the perfect hippie, since all the hippies were trying to be Indians. Because of that, how could anyone recognize that my father was trying to make a social statement?"[16]

Arnold's desire to make a social statement represents not only his demand that the United States acknowledge the distinctiveness of Native nationhood but also his demand to be included in the United States *as an Indigenous person* (not an inclusion based on assimilation). The film's discourse about U.S. Independence, then, is also about claiming a stake in the nation that has excluded its Native people from participation in its legal, social, and economic processes and opportunities. In Thomas's story about the demonstration in the 1960s, Arnold wants his voice to be heard and recognized as his own by the American public. The fact that the distinctiveness of his Native voice is drowned out and obscured by masses of "wannabe-Indian" counterculture protesters, and the fact that his image is taken up and circulated beyond his control as part of a jingoistic news snippet for mass consumption, are allegories for the mediascape that *Smoke Signals* itself must contend with as a Native production fighting for public attention in a marketplace dominated by films like *Dances with Wolves*.

Smoke Signals very explicitly links popular representations, specifically the discourse of "Independence," with the trope of the "vanishing Indian" in Thomas Builds-the-Fire's voice-over description of Arnold Joseph early in the film: "He practiced vanishing" by drinking, and later "did vanish," acting out a script written in the confluence of popular culture and public policy. This "rehearsal" is interpreted in the film as a performance of Hollywood Indianness when the young Thomas, in a conversation with Victor, predicts, "Your dad ain't comin' back you know. When Indians leave, they don't come back — *Last of the Mohicans, Last of the Winnebago* . . ." The film's more subtle intertextual references extend the connection between Indian vanishing and Hollywood films in Arnold Joseph's Independence Day monologue early in the film, when he asserts that he can "make anything disappear": "Wave my hand and poof! The white people are gone, sent back to where they belong. Poof! . . . Wave my hand and the reservation is gone.

The trading post and the post office, the tribal school and the pine trees; the dogs and cats, the drunks and Catholics, and the drunk Catholics. Poof! And all the little Indian boys named Victor. . . . I'm so good, I can make myself disappear."

Denise Cummings and Dean Radar have identified the intertextual joke associated with Indian "vanishing": Gary Farmer, whose character Arnold Joseph "vanishes" by abandoning his family in *Smoke Signals*, is also cast as a character named "Nobody" in the Jim Jarmusch films *Dead Man* (1996) and *Ghost Dog* (1999). In *Smoke Signals*, the young Victor tells his parents that his "favorite Indian" is "nobody, nobody, nobody," referring at once to the triad of himself and his mother and father, and to his father's psychological absence from the family. His repetition of the word seems to give it a prophetic power as well. Significantly, a bottle of beer is in the foreground for much of Arnold Joseph's "disappearing" monologue. Arnold's speech and Victor's favorite Indian — "nobody" — suggest that his struggle against powerful and dominant stereotypes, in the context of a culturally and racially mixed community, has become self-hatred.

The allusion to "Nobody" also works as a Homeric reference to the *Odyssey* (the ur-plot of the road movie), because it is the name Odysseus used to trick the Cyclops, a "native" to an island who is blinded by newcomers. In the scene from *Dead Man* in which Gary Farmer explains why he prefers to be called Nobody, viewers see in flashback his experiences of being captured by whites and exhibited in Europe and later educated in European schools; upon returning to his tribe, his knowledge of Europe and settler culture is rejected, and he is called a liar. Like Odysseus, Farmer's character in *Dead Man* — and also in *Smoke Signals* — journeys away from home and returns (although in *Smoke Signals* his return is symbolic and noncorporeal: his physical ashes). The speech also refers subtly to the Ghost Dance religious movement and the belief of some followers that the dance could bring back tribal family members who had passed away, change the course of Euro-American settlement, and make the whites "disappear" (a point I explored in chapter 1).

Arnold Joseph's other (non)identity as "nobody" and his absence from his family and community function powerfully as metaphors for Euro-American colonizing strategies and disruption of Native identities and families, bringing together iconic instances of vanishing across continents.

Victor's loss of his father — through alcoholism, abandonment, then death — is linked repeatedly to pervasive stereotypes of Indians, especially in Hollywood Westerns. If Young Victor's exposure to Westerns on television is "answered" by Thomas's joke about Indians watching Indians on TV, the tension between the "real world" of the characters and the staged world of the TV Indian reveals the way the virtual world of popular images crosses over into lived social relations. Victor "watches" himself in other ways as well, seeming to catch a glimpse of his younger self in the mirror or from the corner of his eye out the window of the bus, while also seeming to vanish through tricks of editing. These cinematic transitions between past and present are almost completely visual, formally dramatizing both "rupture" and mediation between generations.[17] In light of the media saturation that infects Victor and Arnold with images of Indian absence, the name Nobody also suggests that Arnold Joseph has "no body"; like the virtual TV Indian, he is a figment of the airwaves. This is literally true in that he has been cremated and Victor is carrying his ashes, but it also figuratively describes Arnold's loss of identity as a disembodied subject, stripped of corporeal presence in the distorting mirror of the virtual Indians on the television screen. Describing Suzy Song's view through Arnold Joseph's trailer on the day she discovers his death, Alexie's screenplay envisioned the camera, adopting Suzy's POV, tilting up from a blank television screen to reveal Arnold's body.[18] The shot evokes the way that even as audience members, Indians are spectral — excluded from television's imagined viewing audience by the producers who create virtual worlds.

In *Smoke Signals*, television is a bad mirror for Native viewers and a distorting lens or filter through which non-Natives see Native people. Alexie claims to have always hated Tonto even when he loved other Indian movies such as *The Searchers* and *Billy Jack*. Like Tonto in the televised *Lone Ranger* series, Indians on TV can't speak well. All Tonto's lines are in English, but his speech is stilted and he is often reduced to agreeing with the (only slightly more articulate, but significantly more grammatical) Lone Ranger. Tonto was played on television by a Native actor, Jay Silverheels. As a version of what Michelle Raheja calls "redfacing," Tonto's structural positioning is always subordinate. Chadwick Allen has argued that *The Lone Ranger* represents a national narrative and treaty metaphor that joins "two bodies as one."[19] If *The Lone Ranger* translates the proto buddy pair of Chingachgook and Hawkeye in *The Last of the Mohicans* to the radio and pulp Western, *Smoke Signals* decisively breaks with the cross-racial buddy-film structure in which the racial other pledges allegiance to the white hero out of love or debt. Here, both "buddies" are Native; as Victor points out when he corrects the admiring comment of Holly (Perrey Reeves) that Victor and Thomas are heroes like the Lone Ranger and Tonto: "We're more like Tonto and Tonto." The reduplication of "Tonto and Tonto" here draws our attention to the mechanical reproduction of Indians on television and film, and thus to stereotyping — the practice of making copies (and making couples) — as a Hollywood staple. The line comes immediately before Victor and Thomas's encounter with the cowboy police chief (Tom Skerritt), further situating them in a scenario patterned and scripted by Westerns.

"John Wayne's Teeth": Sound and Speech

Smoke Signals engages with the history of Indian representations in the Western through sound bridges, the figure of John Wayne, and allusions to film and television Westerns. Returning to the bus scenes in which Victor and Thomas engage in a debate, heavily influenced by Hollywood images of Indians, about how to "be a real Indian" and "look like a warrior," I want to focus on the way that two sound bridges, drawn from specific folk music traditions, function as bounded motifs that can be attached and detached from the contextual images that contribute to their meaning. After Victor's assertion that "people won't respect you if you don't look mean," Thomas obliges by cultivating his warrior look during a rest stop — he unbraids his hair, removes his glasses, dons a "Fry Bread Power" T-shirt, and affects a scowl. After the rest stop, Victor and Thomas return to the bus to find that two white men, coded by their costumes as cowboys and "rednecks," have taken their seats. Told by the men to "find someplace else to have a powwow," Victor and Thomas move to the back of the bus, a move that not only recreates the bus as the segregated social space of the American South in the civil rights era, but also echoes the federal policies of Relocation and dislocation of Native tribes. (It is also a reversal of Victor's own actions in silencing the young gymnast, who moved from her seat to the rear of the bus to avoid him after he suggested that she "should just be quiet.")

The sound bridge that accompanies this "relocation" is nondiegetic music, an adaptation of the Irish song "Garry Owen" (sometimes spelled "Gary Owen") by the Native group Ulali. The tune is barely recognizable due to the changes in tempo, but according to screenwriter Sherman Alexie the choice was deliberate:

> I always wanted to include Ulali's version of "Gary Owen," a traditional folk song, in this scene. "Gary Owen" was George Armstrong Custer's favorite song. He had it playing when he attacked Indian camps. So, I thought its use during this scene would be very ironic. I also thought it was one of my brilliant, original ideas, but a few months later, I saw Peter Bratt's film *Follow Me Home* for the second time and realized that he had used "Gary Owen" in the same context. I told Peter I had unintentionally ripped him off, or "paid homage to his film," but he just smiled and said, "Well, that's okay, I ripped it off from *Little Big Man*."[20]

Indeed, John Ford made ironic use of the song's association with the cavalry even before Arthur Penn used it as contrapuntal sound to accompany the brutal massacre scene at the end of *Little Big*

Man in 1970. Ford turned to it frequently as a musical signifier for the military (much as he did with the bugle call), and in his most famous revisionist Western, *The Searchers* (1956), the song forms a sound bridge as the racist Civil War veteran Ethan Edwards (John Wayne) and his mixed-blood companion Martin Pawley (Jeffrey Hunter) encounter the Comanche survivors of a wintertime cavalry raid and massacre.[21] The music accompanies images of Indian women and children being marched through the snow by cavalry soldiers. The images recall the Trail of Tears and other forced marches, and clearly underline the association of the tune with relocation and removal. The allusions through music to the Western genre and to frontier history are paralleled in *Smoke Signals* by visual allusions in other parts of the film, as when Victor's mother and father fight in front of the television that is playing a black and white Western film.

The name "Garry Owen," meaning "Owen's Garden," refers to a place, Garryowen, a suburb of Limerick in Ireland, and the song is an Irish jig first documented in 1788 as "Auld Bessy." The Irish poet Thomas Moore wrote lyrics for the tune under the various titles "Daughter of Erin" and "We May Roam through This World."[22] The song was well known in the United States during the Civil War years through its publication in songsters, and after that war it became associated with General Custer's Seventh Cavalry. According to the legend, Custer heard his Irish troops (or in some versions a specific person, Captain Miles Geogh, an Irishman and former member of the Papal Guard) playing the "drinking song" and liked it so much that it became the unofficial marching song of the Seventh Cavalry. The tune is said to be the last song played by the regiment as it left the Terry column to begin the attack at Little Big Horn in June of 1876. The song and story signaled by the title "Garry Owen" continue to carry a powerful association with and within U.S. military culture, particularly in mapping a continuity between U.S. imperialism in Native American territories and in Southeast Asia and the Middle East. The Seventh Cavalry insignia now includes the words "Garry Owen," and the story of the song's association with Custer and the Indian Wars appears on many military websites, as the Internet is an important contemporary mode of transmission for the legend. The website for "Camp Garry Owen" (Fourth Squadron, Seventh Cavalry) in South Korea, for example, specifically identifies the unit with "the cavalry of the early days, who forged ahead on horseback to find the enemy," and the term is used to designate members of the Seventh Cavalry deployed in Iraq, as well.[23] The military rhetoric substituting Indians for Vietnamese, which circulated during the Vietnam War, here supports other U.S. imperialist efforts.

The "Garry Owen" musical sound bridge in *Smoke Signals* extends the characters' dialogue about pan-tribal Indigenous identity to the realm of song, a conversation that, significantly, takes place in the "imagined community" of a bus called the "Evergreen Stage." This vehicle links Westerns and road movies, genres that share the trope of traveling over Western American public land to find both authentication and transformation. These prized American images of travel are simultaneously fraught with irony, covering over histories in which Indigenous people's movements through the landscape were restricted or coerced during the nineteenth century and the reservation period. The "mobile homes" on the reservation, Lester FallsApart's trailer ("broken down at the crossroads"), Velma and Lucy's car that only runs in reverse, and Arnold Joseph's yellow pickup truck that helped him to "disappear" are all vehicular images that further complicate earlier cinematic desires — often frustrated desires — to see the West as a space of individual mobility and freedom (such as Hopper's *Easy Rider* [1969]).

The bus as a multivalent symbol — a modern stagecoach — acts as a microcosm of the social mix on the frontier, as it did in John Ford's *Stagecoach*. That film excluded Indians from the social relations of the "stage"; *Smoke Signals* depicts a continuing exclusion in this symbolic vehicle-as-performative-space when the Native characters are allowed inside but relegated to the rear seats. Who drives the "bus" of popular culture, and who gets the best seats? The film's director, Chris Eyre, has a cameo in the film as the first

11. The Evergreen Stage Lines.

12. A bird's-eye view of Arnold Joseph's yellow truck.

passenger to leave the bus at the end of this sequence, further underscoring with his physical presence on screen the reflexivity of the bus sequence and the symbolic resonance of the bus as a metaphor for the production of identity through cinema. The bus represents not only the contested space of the American West but also the space of popular culture, which is, as Stuart Hall observes, unfixed and historically contingent. Hall writes that popular culture symbols are the sites of cultural transformation and of a "double movement" or contradictory play of recognition and refusal, containment and mobility. What is at stake in such representations, Hall argues, is "the active destruction of particular ways of life, and their transformation into something new."[24] As a metaphor for the relations of production in Hollywood (especially Westerns), the bus also comes to signal the potential for Indigenous filmmaking to stage a vocal interruption from the margins of media systems, resignifying popular iconography and concomitant assumptions about the identity of film spectators.[25]

From their new seats in the back of the bus, Victor and Thomas resume their conversation about cowboys and Indians. Thomas asserts, "The cowboys always win," while Victor claims, "You know in all those movies you never saw John Wayne's teeth? Not once. I think there's something wrong when you don't see a guy's teeth." Tapping on the arm of the seat, Victor begins to sing:

> John Wayne's teeth, hey ya, John Wayne's teeth, hey ya, hey ya
> hey ya hey,
> John Wayne's teeth, hey ya, John Wayne's teeth, hey ya, hey ya
> hey ya hey,
> Are they false, are they real, are they plastic, are they steel,
> hey ya, hey ya, hey.

This second sound bridge, "John Wayne's Teeth," is then picked up by a professional drum group, the EagleBear Singers. The diegetic sound becomes nondiegetic sound as the shots of the interior of the bus cut to long shots of the bus moving through the Western desert landscape in the warm light of early evening. Like Thomas's voice-over narration in the opening and closing sequences of the film, this semi-diegetic sound emanates from the fictional world of the characters to address audiences more directly, thereby asking the film's audience to more powerfully identify with the characters at this moment and to acknowledge the real effects of Hollywood representations that also cross beyond the fictional spaces of film and into our world. Thus, the transition from diegetic to nondiegetic music bridges the film and its audience, and invites spectators to see the way the racial dynamics on the bus also operate in the world outside the screen.

The song itself resembles not so much powwow as "49" style singing, the informal drumming and singing at parties that take place on the margins of powwows in parking lots and campsites after the more formal events of the powwow are over.[26] In the two sound bridges of this final bus scene in *Smoke Signals*, an Irish folk tune that became associated with the imperialist campaigns of the U.S. military is appropriated by an Indigenous vocal group (Ulali), and the figure of John Wayne is deconstructed through music that, as Alexie asserts, "is a combination of English lyrics and Western musical rhythms along with Indian vocables and Indian traditional drums."[27] Told to "find yourselves someplace else to have a powwow," Victor and Thomas do exactly that, transforming the marginalized space of the rear seats into a platform for protest through powwow or "49" music; in the process, they gain the attention of the other bus riders and the driver with the power and volume of their voices.

This transition between scenes and within the sound bridge lends a broader, even cosmic dimension to the song's lyrics, a discourse that raises questions about the authenticity of the physical body of John Wayne/Marion Morrison, especially his mouth (and hence his speech). John Wayne — "the toughest cowboy of them all," according to Thomas — becomes vulnerable to analytical dismantling in the song, giving the characters of Victor and Thomas, as well as the film's audience, the pleasure of an oppositional gaze.[28] At the same time, the Hollywood style of "speaking" about Indians through the "teeth" or mouth of the figure of John Wayne, and the medium of film itself as a source of information and history, is rendered suspect (although, ironically, it is Evan Adams who is actually wearing a prosthetic tooth in this scene).[29] In its extensive engagement with the tropes of the Western, *Smoke Signals* enacts a strategy that Paul Willemen ascribes to Third Cinema, demonstrating "what can be done with a selective redeployment of the dominant cinema's generic elements while refusing to reduce films to, or to imprison them in, that 'varietal' relationship."[30]

Traces of a conversation about nationalism and tribal self-determination infuse the two sound bridges. "Garry Owen," detached from live performative contexts, represents an already-displaced Irish immigrant settler identity at the same time that it signals the U.S. military's nationalist claims to Indigenous land and the cavalry's appropriation of Irish identity as part of that effort. It is a signification that claims place (Indigenous lands/the American frontier) through the displacement of immigrant traditions. The hybridization of Indigenous and Western "traditional" musical forms, such as the contemporary Native American rendition of "Garry Owen" and the mixture of powwow/49 singing with Western elements, suggests the fluidity and availability of cultural signs of traditionality for reinterpretation and for interpenetration with popular culture. The figures of John Wayne and General Custer are defamiliarized, or made strange, through their reconstitution in Indigenous song forms.

This sound- and music-based intervention in Hollywood images of Indians is carried out through *Smoke Signals*'s road movie conventions, a film genre that inherited from the Western the feature of movement across the continental landscape. In *Smoke Signals* the trope of traveling on the road, with its antecedents in the theatrical conventions of the Western, also becomes a way of moving through time and transitioning between stories and perspectives in the film's prismatic narrative structure.

13. An imposing small-town Western sheriff.

14. Thomas, intimidated by the sheriff's office, with its display of badges and portrait of John Wayne in the background.

Flashbacks and Flashforwards

While Chris Eyre emphasizes the clarity of the dramatic arc as one of the attractions of the road/buddy movie genre (characters move "from point A to point B and back to point A"), Alexie stresses the film's departure from Hollywood's linear time frame and his desire to imitate "the way time works in Indian culture," which "is a lot more circular, so that the past, the present and the future are all the same thing."[31] In a sense, the filmmakers compel the formulaic dramatic structures of mainstream films to function in a parallel way to more traditional Native conceptions of time.

As we have seen, Victor and Thomas's social relationships are mediated by visual culture and visual technology (such as TV), and by the history of imperialist media infrastructure; the characters — and filmmakers — take visual pleasure in a range of intertextual references to such media while simultaneously employing and disrupting standard techniques of film language and tropes of popular culture. In particular, the film employs a nonlinear plot structure and disunified central characters through the use of flashbacks. These techniques raise issues of time and of the absence and presence of events in memory, issues that — although central to cinema in general — are especially significant here because of the fundamental importance of the past to the definition of Indigenous identity, and because temporally based metaphors and images (such as the vanishing Indian) have been so widely engaged in popular and political constructions of Indianness.

Making Victor and Thomas's road trip circular rather than linear revises the "dead end" in films about journeys like *Easy Rider*, *Midnight Cowboy* (dir. Schlessinger, 1969), *Thelma & Louise* (dir. Scott, 1991), and even *Butch Cassidy and the Sundance Kid* (dir. Hill, 1969), which all close with the protagonists' deaths and with cessation of cinematic movement (through freeze frame, for example). In contrast, *Smoke Signals begins* with a character's death, and its protagonists' literal journey and frequent flashbacks continually ask viewers to meditate not on the finality of death (or vanishing) but rather on the process and possibilities of memory, retrieval, and return. *Smoke Signals* also refers to *Powwow Highway* (1989) as an earlier Native road movie, one that Sherman Alexie once loved and now cringes to watch; it, too, is widely known in some Native communities, and like *Smoke Signals* it stars Gary Farmer. The genre of the road movie itself, then, can be seen as a bridge between Native film and a wider (non-Native) audience, along with (in the case of *Smoke Signals*) comedy and brief moments of melodrama. The road to and from the reservation is also a metaphor for "mental traveling," as Meredith K. James notes, and is a trope developed from Alexie's frequent references to the line "I'm in the reservation of my mind" from Adrian Louis's (Paiute) poem "Elegy for the Forgotten Oldsmobile."[32]

Alexie's homage to *Thelma & Louise* "as an anti-road movie which deconstructs the whole macho road/buddy movie" also incorporates a car driving in reverse (the transmission is out) as a visual metaphor for the film's play with time and its "seamless transitions from past to present." The characters of Velma and Lucy and their singular backward driving style also act as another manifestation of the film's address to multiple audiences through the Indigenization of mainstream media references. Time is made material as a technological, mass-produced, aging consumer object in the images of Lucy and Velma's car, a car that seems move in two directions at the same time and that forces the driver to look back in order to move forward. The run-down car suggests the film's broader strategy of genre revisionism and of gleaning and reshaping iconic elements from the field of dominant representations; genre becomes an inescapable past that can't be left behind — it's always in view through the "rear-view mirror" of flashbacks.[33] Alexie notes that "within that circular sense of time, I also wanted to have this car driving in reverse. The phrase that I always use is, 'Sometimes to go forward you have to drive in reverse.'"[34] Non-Native audiences might think the scene funny, but they are often puzzled by it, while "Indian audiences are really going to laugh . . . because they're going to completely understand it." He characterizes this address and strategic in-joke for Native audiences as one of his "Indian trap-doors" because "an Indian falls right in, while a white person would just keep on walking."[35] Native audiences recognize the car driving in reverse as a potential reality in reservation communities — Alexie goes on to say, "It's an Indian metaphor because our cars are always screwed up. There was a man who one summer drove his pickup all over the reservation in reverse because none of the forward gears worked." Significantly, the film's reference to "oral traditions" comes at this moment, suggesting that the car's movement backward parallels the film's narrative circling back through Thomas's repetitions — his stories about the past that move the narrative forward. Thus the car itself and the act of driving represent what Alexie (in the screenplay) calls the film's "magical transitions" from flashback to present-day action.

Smoke Signals's complex narrative pattern of flashbacks and story-visions involves a series of relations between past and present activated by a combination of continuity editing and disjunctive (or discontinuity) editing. The flashback structure is premised on shared memories triggered by interactions between Thomas and Victor, sometimes being narrated by Thomas. Their journey together involves a contest of wills over whose narratives will frame the memory of Arnold Joseph and define their linked family histories. Thomas's continued desire to speak about the past and about Arnold is met with Victor's desire to prevent him from speaking and to discredit his stories as lies. In the flashbacks, these individual and shared memories are negotiated specifically through Thomas's narration as a process that makes private histories into a public history. In her work on the flashback, film scholar Maureen Turim draws our attention to Christian Metz's assertion that the work of narrative is to "create one time in another time." Objecting to the bifurcation or "simply double" oppositionality of Metz's structural model, especially in films with voice-over or voice-off narration of flashback sequences, Turim invites us to "consider narrative as a weave of voices" that allows us to "see how temporality is multiply inscribed" rather than doubled in narrated flashback sequences.[36] Although mirrors in *Smoke Signals* offer characters a vision of themselves, and are important in the transitions to flashbacks (especially Victor's flashback to his angry smashing of his father's beer bottles while his parents sleep), they are, like televisions, ultimately inadequate portraits. Instead, characters are deepened with story flashbacks. In fact Suzy Song, creating a weave of voices, also narrates flashbacks of Arnold Joseph, telling stories that, like Thomas's, supplement and reshape Victor's memories of his father while mediating the relationship between Victor and Thomas.

Just as Lucy and Velma's car suggests that time can move in multiple directions, enabling the telling of multiple stories, the "magical transitions" to flashback sequences almost always occur through movement, including character movement (Victor running, for example), camera movement, and editing on movement. In this sense, the language and technological power of cinema itself is part of the "magic" that Alexie refers to in the screenplay when he describes the shift to flashback as the film's "magical transitions."[37] Victor often literally walks into these transitional moments. For example, when he exits the convenience store after rejecting Thomas's proposal to help fund his trip to Phoenix, Victor steps into his younger self. In the first shot, he opens the door and exits the store, and this action is carried through in the second shot with a match-on-action (a technique for maintaining continuity of movement over a cut by matching the visual action in two contiguous shots). However, we do not see Victor's present-day self exit the doorway, as we would in a normal match-on-action — in fact, he seems to have "vanished" in the reverse shot, and where Victor's body should have been we see a blurry Thomas, out of focus in the deep interior of the store. But Victor reappears as the camera then tilts down to his younger (and shorter) self, with Young Victor looking slightly confused. The adult Thomas and young Victor appear on screen in the same shot (although not in the same frame), blurring the boundaries between past and present and between the characters' reality and their memories.[38]

The idea to use cinematic language (match cuts, pans, and tilts) to create these magical transitions between past and present came in part from Alexie's viewing of an episode of the 1980s television show *St. Elsewhere* (MTM Productions and NBC, 1982–88) that incorporated flashbacks — "Any time someone walked through a door they went back into the past" — and the 1995 John Sayles film *Lone Star* "with the amazing pans and tilts that moved you from past to present."[39] It is easy to understand Alexie's attraction to *Lone Star* as a model. That film is also about history, memory, and storytelling, and in the tradition of the celebrated prismatic narrative structure of *Citizen Kane* (dir. Welles, 1941) — but without the use of dissolves — it pivots into flashbacks as characters narrate remembered episodes in the life of an absent central character, just as the characters do in *Smoke Signals*.

These magical transitions in time take place through movement in (cinematic) space in part because the characters' stories provide the literal action of the movie. Alexie describes Thomas's narration as, like the car and bus described earlier, "the vehicle by which everything happened," while crediting the screenplay for *All About Eve* (dir. Mankiewicz, 1950), with its expository voice-over by different characters in the first twenty minutes of the film, as a model that helped him allow Thomas's stories "to essentially be the action" of the film.[40] The flashbacks offer the past as a form of narrative action in the film that continues into the present, yet the characters' recollections amplify the film's adapted textuality and a sense of stasis in important ways. Thomas's memories are visualized in a stagy manner — we view the past as if on a soundstage (or screen), an effect that is amplified by Thomas's uttering of the characters' lines within the flashback, as when Arnold Joseph speaks to him on the bridge, or when Arlene Joseph makes fry bread for the feast. Thomas's voice-over functions as a form of diegetic dubbing; it is imperfectly synchronized in these scenes with the on-screen Young Thomas, Arnold Joseph, and Arlene Joseph, and of course his voice doesn't match our expectations for these characters' voices. This contrapuntal sound — the mismatch between Thomas's voice and these characters' regular speaking voices — is reflexively theatrical, commenting through sound technique on the way that performed storytelling shapes how we see and remember one another, and underscoring power of voice and ventriloquism in constructing audiovisual representations of individuals and their histories.

This emphasis on storytelling as a way of *performing* the past through narrative countermands the tendency to view film and photography as a direct index of reality and appears to complicate the film's claims to represent contemporary Native life. But rather than engaging in oppositions between reality and stereotype, Thomas's narrated flashbacks augment the film's stylized, somewhat allegorical expression, and its reflexive attention to the ways that we all create ourselves and others through our imaginations. In this sense, the stagy feel of the flashbacks results in a flattening but not a simplification of the character portrayals; rather, the flashbacks take on an intricately self-aware and declamatory form, like that of political theater, which is oratorical in its formal, dramatic mode of public speech. The emphasis on the way our perception of characters can only come through the filter of Thomas's stories recalls N. Scott Momaday's influential assertion that Indigenous identity resides as much in the imagination as in the blood — that "an Indian is an idea a man has of himself."[41] Instead of focusing on issues of blood quantum, the filmmakers explore Indigeneity in the context of contested stories and acts of storytelling.

In addition to the performative creation of Native characters in Thomas's voice-overs, the Native characters are revealed to be partly creations of popular culture. *Smoke Signals* connects the well-established cinematic flashback structure, emphasizing subjective memory, with Indigenous speech and storymaking through the voice-over. Alexie's script returns our attention to storytelling as a primary site of Indigenous political resurgence and decolonization; Thomas's story flashbacks make *Smoke Signals*'s mediated communication a narrative basis for collective historical knowledge. Thomas's voice, as well as the radio host Randy Peone, can be seen as stand-ins for the filmmakers, and Thomas's voice in particular seems to be Alexie's (as noted in chapter 2, Alexie has characterized actor Evan Adams as his "Injun-ue").

The road movie as a genre structured around linear, forward movement in space and time also positions characters outside of regular space and time, and the flashbacks extend this sense of time-within-time, which asks audiences to understand the characters as having complex relationships to their personal and national histories. In contrast to the deadline structure of many action films and other forms of male melodrama organized around cross-cutting between parallel lines of action, in *Smoke Signals* it is already "too late" for rescue to occur. Arnold Joseph's death has already happened and the film's "action" is organized by telling a story about the past rather than building tension through anticipation. It is a revision perfectly suited to the road movie genre: like Velma and Lucy, viewers are asked to look back in order to go forward.

"Ghosts of Salmon": Bridges and Rivers

If *Smoke Signals* begins with an image of intersecting highways — Lester FallsApart's trailer "broken down at the crossroads" — it ends with a different kind of intersection, as Victor stands on the bridge over Spokane Falls, scattering his father's ashes into the water. This crossing — of the bridge across the river — is a symbolically freighted place in a number of ways, and the filmmakers' treatment of the location subtly underscores its importance. Screen images represent places that are also, of course, nonplaces, fictions attesting to the cinema's power of illusion (and allusion) through representational verisimilitude. *Smoke Signals* creates a storied landscape by fictionalizing real places (like Phoenix, Arizona) while at the same time making one place seem to be another (Eyre followed the common production practice when, for example, he shot the Arizona scenes in a desert area around Soap Lake in eastern Washington). Yet while some of *Smoke Signals*'s settings are entirely conjured using such substitutions, the scenes over Spokane Falls were shot on the actual location of a bridge over the Spokane

River Falls in downtown Spokane. The materiality of this site, and the environmental and economic issues in Spokane and Coeur d'Alene tribal history that become visible there, powerfully inform the film's repeated return to this specific place. The stakes of this representational strategy are high because they suggest not only that the locations themselves — and their histories — are meaningful in a symbolic way, but also that the relationship between Native cinema and Native lands can imbue fictionalizations of places with an underlying context of realism in production. *Smoke Signals's* depictions of the bridge and river are images crucial to its closing scenes and to its thematic emphasis on the directionality of roads and rivers in acts of leaving and returning; the historical context of the locations gives this place further meaning for inland Salish tribes.

We first see the bridge over the falls early on in the film, midway through the bus trip to Phoenix, in a flashback. Thomas tells Victor the story of another trip away from the reservation — his journey on foot to the Spokane Falls:

> That was the summer he left. You and I were twelve, enit? Yeah, I had this dream, you know? And the dream told me to go to Spokane, to stand by the Falls, you know those ones by the YMCA? Yeah, so I walked there, you know? I mean, I didn't have no car. I didn't have no license. I was twelve years old! It took me all day, but I walked there, and stood on this bridge over the Falls, waiting for a sign. I must have been waiting there for a couple hours. But I just watched the water. It was beautiful. I kept hoping I'd see some salmon, but there ain't any salmon in that river no more. Then I hear this voice: "Hey, what the hell you doing here?" It was your dad yelling at me. He keeps yelling: "I asked you what the hell you're doing here?" So I told him I was waiting for a vision and he just laughed. He said: "All you're going to get around here is mugged!" Then he took me to Denny's. It was afternoon, you know? But I still had the Grand Slam Breakfast. Two eggs, two sausages, two pieces of bacon, and two pancakes. And some orange juice. And some

milk. Sometimes it's a good day to die. Sometimes, it's a good day to have breakfast.

Thomas's story, which he tells with his eyes closed, becomes the voice-over narration for the scene in flashback. In shot/reverse-shot, we see Arnold Joseph speaking to Young Thomas (Simon Baker, Cree), Young Thomas looking up at Arnold, and Arnold reaching down to grasp Young Thomas's hand and help him up. As Jhon Warren Gilroy points out in his perceptive article on the film, this exact low-angle, point-of-view shot of Arnold Joseph — representing a child's-eye view of Arnold's massive and, at this moment, benevolent presence — is also inserted in the scene when Victor has collapsed while running for help through the Arizona desert after finding the victims of an auto accident. Gilroy points out that Victor, who has resisted Thomas's stories throughout the film, finally "literally 'sees' his father through Thomas's eyes" and is able to internalize and identify with Thomas's more idealistic vision of Arnold. Victor's adoption of Thomas's narrated vision of Arnold demonstrates his new ability to listen to Thomas's stories, internalizing this vision rather than the mass-marketed visions of Indian masculinity propagated by mainstream films. This moment, central to Victor's growth and transformation in the film, suggests that he may find other truths and strengths in Thomas's stories as well (and it is significant in this context that when the young Victor turns his house lights on and off to "signal" an sos to his father using Morse code — a way of calling him home — it is Thomas who sees and responds to the signal). Gilroy argues further that Victor's "paradigm change" is a metaphor for the work of the film itself in "opening a new era of filmic self-representation" for Native artists and audiences.[42] Thomas's vision of Arnold is precisely a cinematic one, consisting of a repeated shot that sutures Victor, as Thomas's listener/viewing audience, to this filmic mental image. The filmic nature of Thomas's narrated image of Arnold supports a reading of the characters as acting out the filmmaker's intended intervention in the larger arena of mass media representation.

15. Arnold Joseph finds Young Thomas at the bridge.

With his vision at the bridge, Thomas offers Victor a way to forgive his father by balancing the pain of Arnold's abandonment with his good intentions, focusing not just on what has been lost but also on what has been saved and retrieved; like the "old-time Indians" that Evan Adams tried to evoke in his performance, Thomas models a way of "staying loving" in the midst of loss. The symbolic location of the bridge over the river is an intersection that extends the film's metaphor of the road as a contested public space, while at the same time signaling a very old, very specific Spokane meeting place, a place where Victor and Thomas reconcile their visions of Arnold Joseph and mourn his death. In this sense the bridge carries overt significations of crossing over, both spiritually to an afterlife, and in terms of generational transition. The loss of traditional sustenance and lifeways, here, can be seen in familial terms as related to both lineage and assimilation. Far from a clichéd trope, the "water under the bridge" here is not just a metaphor but also a material Spokane birthright and heavily contested natural resource in the arid West. Finally, the bridge carries a certain emblematic freight as a place of interracial (and intertribal) gathering; like the road (and like the repeated aerial shots of Arnold's pickup truck that narrate his leaving and Victor's returning to the reservation) it is a shared public space that is re-Indigenized in its cinematic representation, similar, in a way, to the work of the film itself as a media product that brings different peoples into the same physical space.

But the bridge is the most significant location in the film for another reason: Spokane Falls was a traditional tribal site for harvesting salmon. Thomas's hoped-for vision of salmon comes in the form of Arnold Joseph, who provides for him the sustenance that salmon once did for the Spokane tribe. And Thomas's seemingly casual comment about the absence of salmon in the river alludes directly to the intertwined histories of the Spokane tribe, river, and city.

This contemporary urban bridge, arching over an ancient site of intertribal rendezvous and immense harvests of fish, also stands for relationships between peoples. Both a border and a space of encounter, the bridge has facilitated meetings not only between Native tribes and whites, but also between tribes before European contact and between contemporary Native people and generations from the past.[43] The closing sequences of the film focus less on the bridge than on the river itself, emphasizing visually its directional movement downstream in order to underscore the Spokane relationship with salmon, the significance of leaving and returning to Spokane land, and the characters' relationships to memory and time. The film's closing, then, brings audiences into an audiovisual field with a complex history linking the Spokane river, city, and tribe.

The bridge also alludes to larger, downriver dam projects on the Columbia, such as the Grand Coulee, that contributed to the decline of salmon runs on the Spokane. In an interview Sherman Alexie emphasizes both his tribes' relation to the salmon and the effect of the 1930s construction of the Grand Coulee: "We're a Salmon people. Our religions, our culture, our dancing, our singing-had everything to do with the salmon. We were devastated by the Grand Coulee Dam. It took away 7,000 miles of salmon spawning beds from the interior Indians in Washington, Idaho and Montana. We've had to create a religion for many years. We had fish hatcheries so

16. The Spokane River.

17. Victor Joseph on the bridge in the film's closing sequence.

now our salmon are homegrown. People often ask me, 'Why didn't they build a fish ladder?' I say, 'You haven't seen the Grand Coulee Dam, have you?'"⁴⁴

The Spokane River flows from headwaters in the mountains of Idaho westward into Washington to meet the Columbia, a downstream movement followed by the camera in the final sequence of *Smoke Signals*. Alexie's original ending for the film, as written in the screenplay, describes Victor throwing his father's ashes over the bridge just as a salmon leaps from the water through the ashes. The camera was to shoot the river as a mature salmon would travel it, moving upstream; as the forks in the creek become smaller, many Indians would appear on the banks, until "we see a group of people standing ahead at the very source of the river" including Young Victor and Young Thomas, the adult Victor and Thomas, and their families, as Arnold Joseph rises from the water, his back to the camera, and walks toward the shore. This magical reemergence from the river's source makes Arnold's symbolic alignment with salmon in the rest of the film more literal (although historically salmon may not have spawned upriver of the Spokane Falls). But this ending was not shot for various reasons, including lack of funds for casting and for digital effects. Eyre shot a version with just Young Victor and Young Thomas at the river's edge, which Alexie insisted on reshooting as written. Dissatisfied with both endings, Alexie and Eyre, with editor Brian Berdan, reversed their original footage of the river's directionality from a movement upstream, footage that would have emphasized circular or cyclical movement backward in time and echoed the film's narrated flashbacks. The cinematic technicality of this reversal functions as both a visual solution and a signifier of memory; the manipulation of footage to move upstream or downstream suggests a flexibility with time that is also enacted by the flashbacks (which Alexie, following Waldo Salt, the screenwriter for *Midnight Cowboy*, calls flashforwards, because although they move backward in time, they move the viewer forward through the story). As with Lucy and Velma's car that moves backward to go forward, the filmmakers resignify temporal direction to create an ending that Alexie calls "more poetic, much more emotional, much more unpredictable and open-ended." This directional choice — following the river downstream — amplifies the significance of the bridge as the moving camera's destination, connecting the route salmon travel downstream away from spawning grounds to the bridge as a place of passing and generational mourning. Also, as noted earlier, the bridge is like the screen itself in its historical constitution of a racialized space of colonization. In *Smoke Signals* the bridge is made to encompass encounter and reconciliation with lost relatives and with the legacies of previous generations through its connection to an open-ended conception of time, memory, and emotion.

In shifting the scene away from Alexie's initial vision of the reemergence of Arnold Joseph's human form at the river's source, the filmmakers further develop the motif of Arnold's simultaneous absence and presence. At the bridge, Arnold is only present in a noncorporeal way as an idea or act of imagination, first through Thomas's story-image and, later, as ash scattered over the water. He is present in memory but literally has no body, fulfilling Young Victor's earlier claim to love "nobody." In this way the image of Arnold mirrors the physical absence and yet defining historical and spiritual presence of salmon at the "center place," the old fishing site of the falls below the bridge.[45] As in the scene in which Young Thomas says, "When Indians leave, they don't come back," and the scene in which Thomas narrates the way Arnold Joseph "practiced vanishing" and then "did vanish," the scene on the bridge asks viewers to think again about Indian vanishing, about what vanishing looks like on screen, and about the screen itself as a place where what has vanished can resurface in the virtual space of a Native cinematic imaginary.

Spokane Falls, River, Reservation

By shooting the conclusion of *Smoke Signals* on the bridge over the Spokane Falls (and by shooting much of the film on Alexie's father's Coeur d'Alene reservation in DeSmet, Idaho), the filmmakers align the production of the film with its content. The history of Spokane Falls as a "center place" for Spokane people informs *Smoke Signals*'s allusions to Spokane relationships with salmon and with the settler city of Spokane.

Like Arnold Joseph, salmon leave and then return to the place where they were born.[46] Thousands of salmon once migrated up the Columbia River and the Spokane tributary to spawn each year and were stopped by the Spokane Falls, making this a place where many inland tribes gathered for annual harvests of fish. Of the prime fishing sites on the Spokane River, Alex Sherwood, former chairman of the Spokane Tribal Council, identified Spokane Falls as the most important — "a kind of center fishing place" and a dividing line between Spokane and Coeur d'Alene territories, although harvests were considered a communal resource and shared with other tribes (Kalispel, Colville, Palouse, San Poil, and Columbia).[47] Standing above the Spokane Falls after a meeting in 1973, Sherwood described the scene of the annual harvest: "I remember this river so well as it was before the dams. My father and grandfather used to tell me how it was before the white man came when, right below where we are standing, Indians from all over would gather every year for the annual salmon fishery. . . . It was beautiful then, thousands coming for many miles. You could hear the shouting welcomes as they arrived, the dancing, the singing, the trading, the games, the races — always the hearty hugs — and the fish! The fish sometimes so thick it seemed that they filled the river."[48]

While the inland tribes also harvested camas roots and a variety of berries, and hunted game, salmon (as well as steelhead, an anadromous trout) were the mainstay of all the Columbia River basin tribes.[49] The name "Spokane" itself, often translated as "children of the sun" and "children of the rainbow," has also been described as "derived from an Indian word that refers to an important or great salmon fishing place";[50] linguist Grant Smith argues that the most accurate translation is "children of the refracted light," referring to the experience of fishing in the mist of sunlit spray in the river falls.[51]

The river and falls were also the engines of white settlement. Settlers saw the river's resources with an imperial vision — the entire region was commonly referred to as "the Inland Empire" at the end of the nineteenth century — and anticipated prosperity in the form of waterpower for manufacturing and for flour mills supporting regional agriculture. Letters and news articles at the time reveal the broad-based assumption on the part of settlers that control and commodification of the river's power represented its highest use.[52] The early and relentless emphasis on electricity for industry reflects the Euro-American settlers' underlying ideologies about technological development and profit as the twin emblems of progress — Spokane had electric streetlights only three years after New York City, and before San Francisco or Portland.[53]

In developing the city of Spokane Falls (as it was originally called), white settlers displaced the Spokane and Coeur d'Alene nations from the area of the river's falls; this period of early urban and industrial development, then, is important also as the story of diminishing salmon harvests and the expropriation of key portions of the Spokane tribe's land base. President Rutherford B. Hayes had established the Spokane reservation in 1881, and through the early 1880s there were many conflicts over fishing sites as Indian agents tried to force the Spokanes and Coeur d'Alenes to move to the Indian reservations by destroying salmon traps on the river, and settlers began to claim and homestead favorite tribal camping and fishing sites.[54] The falls was also the site of the 1887 agreement in which "the bands of Spokane Indians in council deeded to the United States all right, title and claim which they had, or ever would have, to any and all lands lying outside the reservation."[55]

The intertribal Salishan relationship with salmon, ongoing for thousands of years, was abruptly interrupted by private and government hydropower projects between the 1880s and the 1930s.[56] Spokane Falls was a major rail center by 1890, with bridges crossing the river and train tracks running alongside it. The river yielded power from a dam and hydroelectric plants for streetlights, streetcars, and elevators; "Falls" was dropped from the city name in 1891, dissociating the city from the falls as a defining natural feature at the same moment that the river and its falls powered its urban development during an intense period of dam building.

Settlers organized possession and management of the falls very differently from the Salishan tribes. In 1889 companies competing for claims to the water organized the Washington Water Power Company in order to "consolidate rights to the river current" and "control the hydro-electric potential" through a series of dams that would eventually provide energy not only for Spokane but for the entire region, including its developing mining industries.[57] Each new dam lessened or closed off the salmon runs up the river to the traditional fisheries. In his 1973 speech, Alex Sherwood remembered the history of the dams this way: "The salmon came up to the river in full force up to the time . . . when the Washington Water Power Company built Little Falls Dam. . . . When Little Falls Dam went in, it stopped the salmon from migrating up river when it was finished in 1911. The salmon carried on for quite a few years after that below the dam . . . until Grand Coulee went in and that was the end of it."[58]

During the early twentieth century, when dams proliferated on the Columbia River and its tributaries, public discussion and government statements often elided the effect on salmon runs even as the Army Corps of Engineers created a new river environment, one essentially hostile to salmon. Fish are not mentioned at all in the pamphlet on the Grand Coulee Dam published by the U.S. Department of the Interior in 1938, which emphasizes the "reclamation" of land for irrigated farming and the regulation of river flow for power plants and navigation. The pamphlet opens with a quotation from President Franklin D. Roosevelt, speaking in 1937: "I look forward to the day when the valley is dammed up to give the first opportunity to these American families who need some good farm land in place of their present farms. They are a splendid class of people, and it is up to us as a Nation to help them to live better than they are living now. So . . . it is a national undertaking and doing a national good."[59] The narrow view of resources evident in the speech acknowledges only farming as a source of abundance; fish and other wild harvests do not appear as possibilities for helping families to "live better." Roosevelt's words manifest but do not acknowledge the "racial contract" underlying economic development in the West; the Salish-speaking tribes — especially the Coleville and Spokane — are excluded from the benefits of this "national undertaking" for "national good." The Grand Coulee Dam, built partially on Coleville reservation land, not only destroyed the salmon runs that were the center of Native subsistence economies and spiritual life, but also flooded towns, burial grounds, and the best farming lands.

Almost no wild salmon remain in the Columbia River system. Most salmon are now born in hatcheries, barged downstream to the sea, and caught before maturity by oceangoing vessels; sports fishermen, commercial fishing operations, and tribes compete for the rest.[60] Given the inefficiencies of current industrial management of fish on the Columbia River — the costs of hatcheries and barging far exceed the economic return of the harvest — the continued investment in the fisheries demonstrates that salmon are clearly important to Pacific Northwest Native tribes, regional identity, sport fishers, environmentalists, and others for reasons beyond economics. Historian Richard White writes that the Columbia River is "no longer particularly suitable for salmon. What was once cool water has become warm; what was fast water has become stilled; what was clean has become fouled; what was reasonably free of predators of young salmon has become full of them. . . . Fewer and fewer salmon pass up the river; the vast majority of smolts never reach the sea."[61] Currently, the Spokane riverbed is dry for parts of the year due to upstream aquifer pumping that feeds increasing regional demands for water and due to water diverted for power generation in upstream dams. It is also polluted — the Spokane Regional Health District has posted riverside signs warning of PCB- and lead-contaminated fish.[62] When Chris Eyre scouted the location before shooting the bridge scenes in *Smoke Signals*, there was strong runoff from spring snowmelt and rainfall, and the volume of water was high, but when he returned to the location later, the river was dry — the flow had been diverted elsewhere. Fortunately for the filming, the water was scheduled to flow on the day the bridge scenes were to be shot, but the near miss illustrates the complex relationship between real places and cinematic fictions. At the same time, filming at this site makes Victor and Thomas's experiences of dispossession and hunger literal and historical, rather than purely metaphorical, when they stand at the water. Yet *Smoke Signals* also depicts a lush reservation environment, one that seems less a site of loss than the desolate and seemingly empty landscape meant to represent Phoenix, Arizona.

The images of rushing water at the falls, the lush landscape, and the relationship of the river with food are deliberately opposed to the fiery story of regeneration associated with the desert city of Phoenix, itself an abstractly symbolic space of encounter with Arnold Joseph.[63] Alexie has suggested that the desert scenes deliberately call up the Western genre's panoramic long shots over arid landscapes: "In fact, the film is very self-conscious about the history of Indians in cinema. Some of the way Chris shot the film recalls certain Indian cinematic images. There are these gorgeous landscape vista shots of these two Indian guys walking along, and some of them are very western looking shots — very John Ford-ish — and you'd expect these guys to be on horseback. But no, it's these two Indians in western shirts and JansSport backpacks. So even how they dress totally contradicts all perceived information about Indians."[64]

Furthermore, the "Phoenix, Arizona" where Arnold Joseph lives appears to be an isolated circle of run-down trailer homes accessed by dirt road; it bears no resemblance to the sixth-largest city in the United States. As Victor and Thomas walk from the Phoenix bus depot to Arnold's trailer over dusty roads, it is as if they've walked into an arid Western, far removed from their verdant reservation or, for that matter, from any actual place. Their argument about whether Arnold Joseph really resembles Charles Bronson in *Death Wish V* (he doesn't) further distances the place from representational verisimilitude, locating them rather in a cinematic virtual space, an imagined place where Arnold seems to live in seclusion except for his neighbor Suzy Song.

Near the end of *Smoke Signals* Thomas predicts that Arnold Joseph will "rise like a salmon" from the river, but like Arnold, salmon are a defining absence in the film, the thing for which other things are substituted — movies about buffalo-hunting Plains Indians, images of fathers, and fast-food restaurant feasts. Like a palimpsest written upon many times over, the falls represents multiple layers of time united by a single place. The bridge, as the film's final symbolic location, brings the cinematic landscape together with the film's investment in land and treaty rights located in the history of tribal use of the falls and in its current incorporation into the urban landscape of Spokane.

"I Have a Way to Feed You All": Fast Food and Jesus Fry Bread

The legacy of colonization visualized through the city bridge arching over an ancient river fishing site emptied of salmon also informs Young Thomas's actual hunger while he waits at the bridge for a vision. The material and spiritual (and now metaphorical) nourishment of salmon and the literal concern for children in poverty come together at the place where fishing once happened. Unlike fast-food and chain restaurants, which are meant to seem the same no matter where you are, the bridge over the falls is not a place that is interchangeable with other places; the specificity of the river responds to the placelessness of its substitutions. Thomas's vision of Arnold Joseph at the bridge — a vision that, in the fictional story on which the script is based, he interprets as a message to "take care of each other"[65] — is a vision of sustenance: Arnold finds Young Thomas and brings him to Denny's for breakfast, in a narrative of rescue. Like the bridge, Denny's restaurant is Indigenized in Thomas's story as a public space that takes on a particular meaning in the context of Native history and of colonization. Thomas's lovingly detailed memory of exactly what he ate at Denny's infuses the story with his fantasy of abundant food, a fast-food bounty for a child who may have gone hungry in the past, and who certainly craves satiety for his emotional hunger. Thomas's hope for a vision of salmon is answered not only by Arnold's nurturing of him but also by food — two eggs, two sausages, two slices of bacon. The doubled breakfast, typically served this way at Denny's, suggests plenitude, and further gestures to the ways that Thomas and Victor are twinned in their need for Arnold Joseph's fathering. Eating breakfast and feeling full — a feeling also present at the end of one of the short stories that Alexie took as the basis for the screenplay ("Because My Father Always Said He Was the Only Indian Who Saw Jimi Hendrix Play 'The Star-Spangled Banner' at Woodstock") — here signals the characters' survival of poverty, of colonization, of the night, to see another morning. It also signals the power of storytelling to support not just survival, but also a more active *survivance*, through Thomas's buoyant, resilient visions of finding satiety.

In Alexie's screenplay, Victor accuses Thomas of frequently changing details in this story, such as the restaurant where Arnold Joseph took him: "You've told me that Denny's story a few hundred times, Thomas. Except, sometimes, it's Taco Bell. Sometimes, it's KFC. And once, just once, it was Pizza Hut."[66] The foods that replace salmon in Thomas's vision of plenty are fast foods and commodity foods, and his stories also include frequent mentions of fry bread and Coca-Cola. Sherman Alexie's stories in *The Lone Ranger and Tonto Fistfight in Heaven*, such as "Witnesses, Secret and Not," link fast-food meals with empty pantries at home and with the high rates of diabetes on the reservation.[67] At the same time that salmon have become increasingly scarce, commodity foods have become widely available; as nature writer and conservation biologist Gary Nabhan writes, "Because their income levels are so low, many Native American families are eligible for government surplus commodity foods, nearly all of which are nutritionally inferior to their native counterparts."[68] But making use of commodity foods has also been a survival skill. In *Smoke Signals*, characters take pride in preparing fry bread. "Fry bread is a commodity," says actor Irene Bedard, who played Suzy Song. "Basically, we had flour, water, and some lard. So we were put on a reserve and weren't allowed to do the things we normally did for food, and fry bread became traditional."[69]

While Arnold Joseph is associated with salmon and with fast food in *Smoke Signals*, Arlene Joseph is associated with fry bread, as are Suzy Song and Thomas Builds-the-Fire. Arlene's fry bread is emblematic of the power to make white foods functional and meaningful in an Indigenous context, just as *Smoke Signals* itself repurposes popular media to nourish a Native audience. Fry bread is associated with women and with Thomas in *Smoke Signals*, and with an almost magical power to make something out of nothing; Arlene and Suzy make fry bread on screen (in fact, part of Suzy's "magic" is her ability to make good fry bread, just like Arlene). Thomas, with his kitchen apron and his "Fry Bread Power" T-shirt, models for the audience a different kind of masculinity than Victor does, one that is less embedded in conventional American media images of stoicism and aggression. Instead, Thomas's cooking (including fry bread) for his grandmother connects his character's habitual story-telling to the fry bread–making survival skill of "taking care of one another." Scholar Angelica Lawson (Arapaho) has pointed out the powerful influence of the female characters in *Smoke Signals*, who provide key elements of knowledge catalyzing Victor and Thomas's emergent self-knowledge. Arlene Joseph even takes the metaphorical place of a deity in Thomas's story of her wondrous ability to create a sense of abundance within circumstances of scarcity.[70]

Thomas's story-vision of Arnold Joseph at the bridge ("Take care of each other") is matched by his vision of Arlene miraculously providing fry bread for everyone at an Indian feast ("I have a way to feed you all!" she says). Arlene's magical act — dividing large pieces of fry bread in half so that one hundred people could share the fifty pieces of fry bread — is of course also a reference to the biblical story of Jesus's miracle of the loaves and fishes, an allusion underscored by Thomas's characterization of Arlene's "Jesus fry

18. Arlene Joseph divides a piece of fry bread.

bread" that is "so good they use it for Communion back home. Arlene Joseph makes some Jesus fry bread, enit? Fry bread that can walk across water. Fry bread rising from the dead." The biblical connection of Jesus with fish or ichthys also gives a Christian connotation to Thomas's prediction that Arnold Joseph will "rise like a salmon." "Salmon is very Jesus," Alexie noted in an interview.[71]

> It's funny, I don't get talked about much in these terms, but I'm very Catholic: grew up Catholic, Catholic father, still am vaguely Catholic (I'm not very good at it anymore). So I think Catholicism and forgiveness and that aspect of Christianity is a really strong influence on me. And then once you place Catholicism in the context of me being tribal and the ways in which the church horrendously oppressed Indians, there is a serious amount of guilt. So, I think it's a combination of guilt and irony and contradiction and forgiveness that mix up together and become a dominant theme in everything I do.[72]

In Thomas's narrated flashback to the Indian feast, Arlene's "magic" synthesizes Christian references to miracles and fry bread as an Indigenization of commodity flour to solve the problem of scarcity through what is, in the end, a very simple act of sharing. The principle of division into two parts also aligns this story with other matched pairs in the film — the metaphorical brotherhood of Victor and Thomas, and their equal division of Arnold's ashes at the end of the film — a symbolism that Lawson suggests resembles the "hero-twin" brother figures who are featured in oral narrative traditions across many Western Native American tribes.[73] Sharing, taking care of one another, and forgiveness are the survival tools that Thomas's idealized stories about Victor's parents convey to the confused and angry Victor. The materialization of these values in and around Native and non-Native foods — as well as foods, like fry bread, that are products of syncretism — underscore their physical importance for Native resilience; Smoke Signals answers the "independence" of "vanishing Indians" with the substantiation of familial and community ties in the form of food, and in the memories of food in Thomas's storied feasts. At the same time, fry bread, basketball, and pickup trucks are, like the movies, things of Euro-American origin that have become Indigenized through the process of Native appropriation and narration.

"Nobody, Nobody, Nobody": Arnold Joseph's Body

Smoke Signals's images of Indians are at once tribally specific — all the Native characters except Suzy Song are Coeur d'Alene — and pan-Indian in its references to things like fry bread and powwows that are intertribal. Suzy Song's tribe isn't revealed in the film itself, because some of her expository dialogue was cut from the final version; in the screenplay she talks about her mixed-blood heritage — Mohawk and Chinese — and how her parents met in an Indian bar in Brooklyn, New York. The omission of this story of Suzy's tribe was disappointing to Alexie ("I mean, we wanted her to be mysterious, but not that mysterious," he wrote in the notes to the published screenplay),[74] and also functions to simplify the film's presentation of Indigenous identity. The debates in the film about "how to be a real Indian" take place overwhelmingly with relation to popular culture images, excluding any mention of issues that affect legal or tribal recognition of Native American status, such as blood quantum and intermarriage with non-Indians.

Contemporary policies for determining Native American identity require certain quotas of "Indian blood" for a person to be listed as an enrolled tribal member, a practice that (unlike the "one-drop rule" that determined African American identity throughout much of the nineteenth and twentieth centuries) means intermarriage can result in fewer and fewer people qualifying for federally recognized Native status and the treaty rights that accompany that recognition of identity. Further, questions about Indigenous identity in general — who is a Native American, how Native identity is determined, who makes the determination, and what kinds of treaty-based promises and responsibilities accompany that identification — often hinge on the concept of "blood quantum" or even on visually identifiable "Indian" qualities, including physical appearance. Indigenous identity itself is contested as an unstable category because of questions about how Indianness is constructed legally, cases of ethnic fraud by "wannabe Indians," blood quotas, federal vs. tribal rights to determine tribal membership, and other issues. The location of these debates in the public sphere influences popular images of Indigenous population decline and the long-standing Western practice of treating Native artifacts and remains as public property, so that fantasies of Native vanishing have occurred simultaneously with the theft of actual Native remains by museums and private collectors.

This history informs *Smoke Signals*'s story of the repatriation of Arnold Joseph's ashes to his family. The story of Victor's journey to Arizona to retrieve Arnold's ashes and bring them home to his reservation comes in the shadow of the 1990 passage of the Native American Graves Protection and Repatriation Act (25 USC 32), a law that recognizes tribal ownership of Native ancestral remains and cultural artifacts and mandates that federally funded institutions (such as the Smithsonian) facilitate tribal recovery of cultural patrimony. The issue of tribal recovery of human remains is present in a Kafka-esque sequence in "This Is What It Means to Say Phoenix, Arizona," the short story upon which *Smoke Signals* is based, when Victor turns to his tribal council for financial help. Tribal government is mocked as paternal bureaucracy in Victor's dialogue with a condescending tribal council that speaks in one voice: "'I thought the council had special funds set aside for stuff like this.' 'Now Victor, we do have some money available for the proper return of tribal members' bodies. But I don't think we have enough to bring your father all the way back from Phoenix.'"[75] But through Victor's retrieval—and then division—of his father's ashes, *Smoke Signals* suggests both the possibilities of recovery and the limitations of what can be repatriated.

Significantly, three films released after *Smoke Signals*—Chris Eyre's second feature film, *Skins* (2002), Sherman Alexie's second feature film, *The Business of Fancydancing* (2002), and Creek director Sterlin Harjo's first feature film *Four Sheets to the Wind* (2007)—all follow *Smoke Signals* in depicting funeral rituals following the deaths of central male characters, continuing *Smoke Signals*'s work of measuring and altering relationships between media stereotypes of "disappearing" Indians and contemporary conditions on reservations. Arthur Tulee, a family friend of Alexie's who played Junior Two in *The Business of Fancydancing*, characterized his role this way: "For the whole of my character's screen time I am a mourner. . . . Being Indian in touch with life, mourning is not far from my thoughts or feelings. It is a dam of turbulent water held back by daily strength, daily rituals. I mourn the loss of all my people's freedoms, the great majority of our ancestral lands and rights, the many sharp hardships of colonialism, disease, poverty, alcoholism, diabetes, postcolonialism, and racism we have struggled with as individuals and as a people. It was not difficult to mourn."[76]

The funerals in *The Business of Fancydancing*, *Skins*, and *Four Sheets to the Wind*, like the one in *Smoke Signals*, are not just rituals of mourning, however—they are also acts of physical retrieval and return in which the living and the dead who have left the reservation return home. In that sense these filmmakers resist tropes of what critic David Moore calls "colonial closure," as well as media vanishing; instead, they make visible the re-anchoring of the films' Native protagonists in their family and reservation homes, and dramatize the revision of mainstream media discourses.

In *Smoke Signals*, because Arnold Joseph has been cremated, his body and identity are defined by absence, like Hollywood's movie Indians; his noncorporeal self is remembered in images of his movement away from home, disembodied as a figure of memory in flashbacks. But while Arnold is absent in the film's frame narrative, he has a continuing material presence (or body) in the form of his pickup truck and his basketball, both of which Victor also claims, along with his photograph of the family with the caption "Home." Arnold's basketball comes to Victor through a trick of cinematic editing, a temporal transition from a nested flashback in which Arnold Joseph tells a story about Victor's triumph in a basketball game against some imposing Jesuit priests. As Arnold, in flashback, lets the ball roll away at the end of his story, Victor catches it in the present moment as Suzy Song ends her recounting of Arnold's story. The "passing" of the basketball from flashback to frame story, from past to present, and from father to son dramatizes transmission of stories as a specifically intergenerational exchange. Arnold's story is a lovingly crafted lie (Victor actually lost the game), but the gift of the basketball along with the story answers the film's first introduction of Victor, playing basketball with his friends: as they argue about whether Geronimo, an Apache, could be the greatest basketball player ever, Thomas asks Victor, "What about your Dad?" Victor, with a studied blankness, returns the question: "What about him?" thus inviting the further unfolding of the film's narrative about Arnold.

Basketball — the game, the ball itself, and the practice of telling epic stories about past games — connects Victor and his father. When, late in the film, the police chief questions Victor and Thomas after their car wreck, he focuses his attention on two things he found in Victor's pickup truck — the basketball and the tin containing Arnold's ashes. In the next scene, as Victor lets go of the first of these objects by kicking the ball out of the frame, he also prepares to let go of his closely held beliefs about his father in a subsequent scene, when he gives Thomas half of the ashes. This repetition of Arlene's division of the fry bread at the feast also responds to the bureaucratic fragmentation of bodies in calculations of Indian identity by blood, a literalization of blood "quantum" that also posits Arnold Joseph as a magically divisible being. It does so by offering a different construction of physical partition that simultaneously addresses Thomas's need of parental nourishment and Victor's need to take up the values of sharing, taking care of others and forgiveness that he has begun to learn from Thomas's stories. Dividing his father's ashes is Victor's magical act, because the literal sharing of his parents maintains human ties in face of the scarcity and loss of colonization (the house fire) by extending the sustenance of Victor's family.

Arnold Joseph's presence is a figment of memory, a box of ashes — he is both immaterial and physical. His "disappearing" monologue, quoted earlier in this chapter, also includes lines about magic: "I'm feeling extra magical today, Victor. Like I could make anything disappear. Houdini with braids, you know?"[77] Arnold's stories and magic tricks share some of the charismatic qualities of Thomas's storytelling performances, and indeed the performance of story *is* magic in this film — it can connect us to the past, and it can change the world by changing our interpretation of it, which is the work of the film itself.

Throughout *Smoke Signals*'s eighty-nine-minute running time, the filmmakers appropriate already-circulating commodified symbols (Superman, Denny's, John Wayne, Independence Day) to make them "mean something different" in an Indigenous context. It is a crucial shift in perspective, one that the filmmakers hoped would pave the way for a concomitant shift in relations of power in the film industry. Close analysis of *Smoke Signals* as a cinematic text demonstrates the centrality of genre and popular culture appropriation as an Indigenizing strategy that reorients the images, sounds, symbols and visual language of American cinema. *Smoke Signals* is successful in part because of its open and porous aesthetic; rather than sealing its boundaries against outside influence, it is a film that finds connections. Perhaps the film's most successful strategy in this regard is its focus on moments and spaces of conjuncture: its bridges, crossroads, and the old-time "center fishing place." Attending to the film's textual architecture — particularly its editing, sound bridges, temporal shifts, and other forms of transition — and its condensed references to historical moments (the U.S. bicentennial) and to actual places (Spokane Falls), reveals elements that formally echo the film's larger purpose of becoming that "center place" where viewers are given ways "to sit at the same table."

The film seems to insist on its right to combine and recombine ubiquitous and available symbols in a process of innovation that continually negotiates Indigenous nationhood and American nationhood, Native inclusion and exclusion from American popular culture. This nationalist symbolism is important to the film's audiovisual discourse of sovereignty, its contestation over nationhood in the representational field of mass culture. The location shooting layers the materiality of expropriated Spokane waters and the Coeur d'Alene reservation lands across this dematerialized rhetorical landscape of pop nationalist symbolism. Ultimately the film's open framework seeks to Indigenize the commonplaces of popular culture through an expansive mode of accretion. As a revolutionary mainstream film, *Smoke Signals* captures and repurposes American pop in service of an Indigenous agenda.

CHAPTER FOUR

"Take Your Dad's Pickup"
Smoke Signals's *Reception*

In a 1998 interview for a *Los Angeles Times* article on
Smoke Signals, Alexie described his expansive ambitions for the
film's impact: "I want to change the world. . . . I want to change the
world's perceptions of Indians." Because *Smoke Signals* was conceived
and marketed as an intervention in media representations — a film
that could change the world by changing its mediascape — the
stories of its production and reception became an important part
of the critical response to the film in reviews and interviews. This
discourse tends to reproduce, in its contextual framing of *Smoke
Signals* as a Native cinema phenomenon, the formal elements of
the film itself that make claims about generational exchange, Native
spectatorship, media intertextuality, and the positioning of Indigeneity in mainstream popular culture. *Smoke Signals* speaks to its
audiences about changing the way films speak to their audiences,
a metacommunicative strategy taken up vigorously in interviews
that focus on predictions that the film would initiate an industry
embrace of Native filmmaking. In scholar Houston Wood's view,
"few films have entered theaters carrying greater burdens of expectation than did *Smoke Signals*."[1]

In making *Smoke Signals*, Chris Eyre and Sherman Alexie entered into an ambitious and complicated relationship with their
film audiences. We can measure the film's reception in a number
of related ways: in terms of paying audiences; in terms of the Hollywood film industry's facilitation or hindering of future Native
filmmaking projects; and in terms of the film's influence upon a
continuing Native media movement. In a televised interview at the
University of California San Diego, Alexie observed that *Smoke
Signals* "changed radically depending on the audience":

We screened it in Minnesota at the university, and the crowd was about 75% Indian, and sound on the film kept breaking down, but there were enough Indians in the crowd who had seen the movie enough times that they started filling in the dialogue, so it was like Rocky Horror Indian Picture Show, and you know it was amazing. And yet I've also been in theaters where it was screened for 100% white audiences, on the East Coast, where nobody laughed through the entire movie. Not one joke was understood or interpreted as a joke. And I screened it on my reservation, and we had to play it immediately a second time because the people laughed so much in the first screening that they missed out on the story — you know, everybody yelling "Ah, there's my cousin," and cameo appearances. And so, that's the joy of storytelling, and the pain and agony and magic and loss of it, that it changes all the time, and it's kinetic.[2]

Alexie's story about the wide range of audience responses to *Smoke Signals* highlights the way relations of speaking and listening embedded in the film's content suffused its public reception as well. The failure of sound at the Minnesota screening, and the synchronization of audience and screen sound as people spoke the lines from memory, reveal audiences' embrace of and physical alignment with *Smoke Signals*'s literal scripting of Native speech. The largely Native audience's identification with the characters becomes a way of claiming the film through performative vocalization from their positions as viewers, echoing the configuration of Victor and Thomas when they speak back to images of John Wayne on the Evergreen Stage. Thus, the event illustrates the way *Smoke Signals*'s off-screen relationship with its Native audiences mimics its on-screen countermand of the Western's silencing effects.

We've seen how *Smoke Signals* speaks to its audiences with a range of cinematic strategies; this chapter considers how the film was heard — its impact when it was released and in the years since. If many Indigenous audiences take possession of *Smoke Signals* through their intimacy with its content and references and see themselves and their family members in the screen images (Alexie's "Indian trap-doors"), other viewers engage with the images as entertainment, education, personal counsel, cult object, or profitable investment. Non-Native audience members have reacted strongly to the film, but with varying degrees of comprehension. At the Sundance festival, one white woman brought sage to the director after a screening ("which is the equivalent of someone coming up and handing us Communion wafers," says Alexie),[3] while after another screening a woman told Alexie that she was planning to call her father, whom she had not spoken to in twelve years.

Alexie describes screening the film for a test audience in an upstate New York shopping mall in which "one of the more racist, homophobic, sexist guys in the focus group loved the movie." In the same interview, he anticipates the reaction of another target audience: "There are 7- and 8-year-old boys and girls out there who are going to see this film, who are going to see publicity about it, who are going to see themselves on screen, who are going to know that Chris and I directed and wrote it, who are going to know that Irene and all the actors in it were Indians playing Indians, and it's going to change their lives, it's going to hand them dreams."[4] The film's young Indian viewers are, as discussed earlier, envisioned in the film itself, modeled by Victor and Thomas, who are versed in the "last-of" image of Indians in Hollywood movies and comfortably aware of themselves as examples of "Indians watching Indians on TV." To some extent, Alexie's vision has come to pass. Filmmaker Nanobah Becker (Navajo), then an intern at the National Museum of the American Indian (NMAI), notes in an interview with actor Evan Adams that "I've worked with Indian youth a lot and every Indian child I know has seen that movie, owns the movie, and probably has it memorized."[5] Sherman Alexie said in a 2001 interview that "by now, at least ninety percent of Indians have seen *Smoke Signals*, and there's something powerful in that. . . . What is tribal? Appealing to your tribe."[6] Chris Eyre, speaking of the film's continuing reception, says:

Ten years later, I'm happy that people still love it. Every year, I screen it to people and get responses. I screened it for the Oregon Indian boarding school, Chemawa, last fall — four hundred Indian school student kids. . . . They're sitting there reciting lines back to me on stage. That's the kind of reception where you're like, wow! It's an anthem, I think, for Indian country, a filmic anthem that people seem to really love. . . . I've screened it at Leavenworth Federal Penitentiary for Indian inmates and seen them think about the forgiveness of their own fathers or mothers, or cry, or come up to me at the end and say stuff like, "I'm gonna write a screenplay."[7]

The film's envisioning of Native spectatorship has meaning for Native and non-Native audiences in educational contexts; it has been picked up in mainstream classroom education for high school and university classes, and the NMAI, among other institutions, has facilitated and documented Native youth mediamaking through, for example, their Teen Video Program and Native Youth Video Production Workshop.[8]

Initial Reception and Reviews

When *Smoke Signals* premiered at the Sundance Film Festival in 1998 it won two prestigious awards — the Audience Award and the Filmmakers' Trophy. Eyre and Alexie were both at the festival, but unlike many other first-time feature filmmakers, they didn't need to find a distributor — they had already screened the film for several companies, including Sony and Miramax, which won an early bidding war for the film.[9] And *Smoke Signals* continued to pick up awards: Best Film at the American Indian Film Festival (1998); Outstanding Achievement in Writing (Alexie), Outstanding Achievement in Directing (Eyre), and Outstanding Performance by an Actor in a Film (Adams) awards from First Americans in the Arts (1998); Special Recognition for Excellence in Filmmaking from the National Board of Review (1998); the Christopher

Award (1998); Best American Independent Feature, Best Screenplay (Alexie), Best Actor (Beach), Best Director (Eyre) at the San Diego World Film Festival (1998); Taos Land Grant Award (Eyre) at the Taos Talking Picture Festival (1998); Best Artistic Contribution (Eyre) at the Tokyo International Film Festival (1998); Best Newcomer (Eyre/Alexie) at the Florida Film Critics Circle Awards (1999); and Best Debut Performance (Adams) at the Independent Spirit Awards (1999).

Trade publications praised the film but were not optimistic about its commercial viability because, as Chris Eyre notes, "the only commodity in making a movie with Indians is making a movie from 1860–1890 about the Indian Wars."[10] *Variety* predicted that "Miramax will have to use all of its ingenuity and muscle to raise anything more than a core paying public for this eminently accessible work, due to perceived lack of interest among urban auds in stories about the modern West in general and contempo Indians in particular."[11] But Miramax distributed the film very successfully, using a slow platform release pattern, starting on 5 screens with an opening-weekend gross of $48,574 on June 28, and working up to 66 theaters by its fourth weekend, and 353 theaters before Labor Day weekend, 1998.[12] By mid-October of 1998, *Smoke Signals* had grossed $6,719,300, a significant return for an independent film with a budget of under $2 million. VHS and now DVD sales have significantly expanded the film's profitability since 1998, but these numbers are harder to track than box office tallies, since producers and distributors generally guard DVD sales figures.[13] The film played in theaters internationally through 1999, though probably not on very many screens; film scholar Kerstin Knopf notes that the film's Canadian distribution as "rather meager" in cities like Calgary and Regina, with few copies in circulation.[14]

While not in the same financial league as the major studio hits of the year such as Spielberg's *Saving Private Ryan* (which grossed over $216 million), *Smoke Signals*'s box office take was quite respectable, especially compared to films like New Line Cinema's *American History X* (dir. Kaye), which grossed only slightly less at the box office but was made for a much higher budget of $10 million. *The Big Lebowski* (dir. Joel and Ethan Coen), also released that year, remains a cult favorite but began with a slimmer profit margin than *Smoke Signals*, with a box office gross of $17,439,160 on a $15 million budget.[15] *Smoke Signals*'s profits remain far lower, however, than Hollywood's major studio films about Indian characters from the 1990s production cycle: *Dances with Wolves* earned $184.21 million in 1990, *The Last of the Mohicans* made $72.46 million in 1992, and *Pocahontas* made $141.60 million in 1995.[16]

Alexie's public name recognition along with overwhelmingly enthusiastic reviews helped sell the film. This sense of collective excitement upon the release of *Smoke Signals* is palpable in reviews like Roger Ebert's for the *Chicago Sun-Times*, in which he enthusiastically characterizes Victor and Thomas as "the next generation." Gerald Leary of the *Boston Phoenix* called the film "a Native American masterpiece," and Janet Maslin wrote for the *New York Times* that the film "needs no dispensation for novelty; it stands beautifully on its own merits." Peter Stack of the *San Francisco Chronicle* praised it as "well-acted, well-written, with spare, beautiful imagery." The *Austin Chronicle*'s Marc Savlov praised the cast as "uniformly excellent in their roles" and noted that Eyre's "persistent use of long, trailing shots reinforces the story's elegiac tone." "Simple and elegant," he writes, "*Smoke Signals* is a delicious, heady debut that lingers long after the tale is told."[17] The film was also positively reviewed in major publications such as the *Chicago Reader, Entertainment Weekly*, the *LA Weekly*, the *Los Angeles Times, The Onion, Reelviews, Rolling Stone*, and *Time*.

A few reviewers panned the film. Scott Kelton Jones of the *Dallas Observer* called it "ham-fisted" as well as "too obvious, too calculated, too forced" in his review "Smoke Gets in Your Eyes." Michael O'Sullivan of the *Washington Post* didn't care for the film's "conventional story" and "pictorial prosaicness," finding it to be "more of a literary than a cinematic success," but in the same paper his colleague Stephen Hunter gave the film a glowing review, reserving special praise for Gary Farmer's "great performance" as Arnold

Joseph. Chris Eyre remembers that "Martin Scorsese wrote me an unsolicited letter about how much he liked the movie. . . . President Clinton screened it at the White House."[18] Many reviewers — and the filmmakers themselves — compared the film to Spike Lee's early features *She's Gotta Have It* (1986) and *Do the Right Thing* (1989) as a milestone film that contemporized minority characters in leading roles. Some pointed out similarities in the opening shots between *Smoke Signals* and *Do the Right Thing*, both of which feature radio DJs who function as voices and arbiters of the communities as well as figures for the films' conscious intervention in the media's representational field.[19] Even more important than the positive tenor of the reviews, however, was the sheer number of them; the film was widely reviewed, featured in major publications (*Rolling Stone*, *Time* magazine) and selected for special attention in other venues, such as Gene Siskel and Roger Ebert's popular television show *At the Movies*.

Smoke Signals proved that a feature-length drama with a contemporary setting and a Native writer, director, and cast could draw an audience, make money, command attention from critics, and win awards. For Eyre and Alexie, media attention pressured their shifting relationship with their film and with each other. The *LA Times* has reported that the two were "bombarded with offers to work together again" but parted ways instead to work on separate projects.[20] They fell out in part over sharing the public spotlight in the wake of *Smoke Signals*, with each staking a claim to the film's authorship and reviewers focusing primarily on Alexie because of his literary celebrity and charismatic, outspoken style.[21] But the filmmakers' intentions had been to create a stepping stone for a Native New Wave at the height of the American indie film boom.

Smoke Signals was a strategic production — a film made, in part, with the purpose of enabling other films to be made. In this sense we can see the film as an event or an occasion, and ask what its impact has been on Native American filmmaking and Native presence in the film industry infrastructure. Eyre and Alexie's deliberate positioning of *Smoke Signals* as the first in an expected wave of feature films — a Native New Wave — clearly circulated as a buzz in the press when the film was first released. Eyre spoke directly to this promise in an interview with @sk Hollywood shortly after the film's release: "This movie opens the door to a lot of things. It opens the door to other Indian filmmakers. It opens the door to contemporary Indian material." In a 1998 interview with the *Los Angeles Times*, Alexie claimed that *Smoke Signals* was, for Native cinema, a point of origin, "our 'Great Train Robbery.'" In a 1999 interview, Alexie projected his hopes for the film: "It's the beginning. We proved it can be done. The real effect is that in ten years the idea of an Indian filmmaker isn't going to be strange. There will be three or four of them a year, maybe. You'll be interviewing somebody and asking them what their first, formative experience was. And they'll say, *Smoke Signals*. Hopefully."[22]

Ten years later, asked by Matthew Fleischer at the *LA Weekly* what has happened in Native cinema since *Smoke Signals*, Alexie was equally categorical: "Absolutely nothing."[23] Pointing out that productions and roles for Native actors are still sparse, the article suggested that *Smoke Signals* remains a singular phenomenon in its commercial success and in the breadth of its popular influence on American audiences. Alexie is right that Native films continue to be underfinanced and excluded from major distribution, but if we see this as a partial failure to change the media landscape, we can also see *Smoke Signals* as a crucial precursor for some of the accomplishments in Native filmmaking that have come after it. The field of independent Indigenous film production is clearly richer ten years after *Smoke Signals*, as evidenced by the increasing number of Native film festivals, the new prominence of actors like Adam Beach, and the recent emergence of many young Native filmmakers just now releasing their first short and feature films. A wave of Indigenous feature filmmaking is in fact underway, although not at the level of funding, distribution, or Hollywood production that Alexie and Eyre had hoped for.

Smoke Signals's intervention in romanticized representations of Indians has not diminished the Hollywood trade in expensive, faux-historical Indian epics and contact narratives like Mel Gibson's *Apocalypto* (2006) and Terrence Malick's *The New World* (2005), yet even as the distribution market has contracted economically, the range of independent low-budget filmmaking has expanded to include young Native filmmakers producing their first features, including Shirley Cheechoo's *Bearwalker* and *Johnny Tootall* (2000 and 2005), Randy Redroad's *The Doe Boy* (2001), Larry Blackhorse Lowe's *5th World* (2005), and Sterlin Harjo's *Four Sheets to the Wind* (2007) and *Barking Water* (2009). The worldwide success of the Inuit film *Atanarjuat/The Fast Runner*, which won the Camera d'Or prize at the 2001 Cannes film festival, is a brilliant example of a growing Indigenous media movement internationally. By aggressively constructing and marketing *Smoke Signals* as a Native cinema "first," the filmmakers positioned it as a kind of parent film, and to some extent it has been generationally influential for emerging Native filmmakers regardless of Hollywood studios' continued assumptions about the lack of commercial viability for representations of contemporary Native characters. Educational courses for Native youth like the NMAI programs have helped familiarize a new generation with media technology, and increasing options for off-Hollywood filmmaking — including less expensive equipment and digital video as well as diversifying distribution venues such as the internet, Netflix, DVD sales, cable, and an explosion of new film festivals — have put filmmaking within reach for Native artists. Eyre notes, "There's a whole generation of Native filmmakers right now that didn't exist ten years ago. When I was in graduate film school in 1992 at NYU, the horizon was a handful of documentary Native American filmmakers, maybe a couple of narrative filmmakers that hadn't broken out in any way. The number of film festivals has totally spiked and generationally, a lot of people want to be in entertainment now. There's . . . Native American people wanting to be actresses and actors and directors and musicians."[24]

However, Eyre also echoes Alexie's pessimism about the difficulty of making Native voices heard. Finding distributors for independent films has become far more challenging, and even straight-to-DVD deals, which have significantly lower acquisition prices, can be difficult to accomplish. "Right now the whole hard part is getting the movie seen. . . . If *Smoke Signals* were to come out today, it may not have a theatrical release like it did ten years ago. . . . *Smoke Signals* had an effect and it had good timing, and I like to think that people were inspired by it, and I think that there's a whole wave of Native filmmakers that will find their way, myself included, to new ways of being seen and heard. Really what it's about is being heard."[25]

Eyre and Alexie each premiered new feature films at the 2002 Sundance Festival: Eyre's film *Skins*, based on Adrian Louis's novel about two Lakota brothers fighting social dysfunction and alcoholism on the Pine Ridge reservation; and Alexie's film *The Business of Fancydancing*, about a young, gay, successful Spokane Indian poet returning to the reservation for a funeral (producer Scott Rosenfelt calls the story "a comedy about an Indian wake").[26] Alexie had several projects in development after *Smoke Signals*, including screen adaptations of his novels *Indian Killer* and *Reservation Blues*, the latter envisioned as a sequel to *Smoke Signals* with Evan Adams continuing his role as Thomas Builds-the-Fire. But after a frustrating experience developing the film with Miramax, Alexie instead made *The Business of Fancydancing* on his own, using digital video and location shooting to keep costs low.[27] By taking on much of the financial risk of the filmmaking (Alexie went into debt to produce the film and was its second-largest financier) he was able to control the production process to a great degree, steering the film away from mainstream accessibility and exploring alternative modes of production and circulation.[28] Actor Evan Adams worked closely with Alexie after *Smoke Signals*, playing the lead, Seymour Polatkin, in *The Business of Fancydancing*, and is currently the voice of Raven in the Canadian animated television series *Raven Tales*, one of the first Native-produced animated children's programs.

Chris Eyre's subsequent films continued to target a wider viewing audience, and he has since worked for cable and public television, and as a director and producer of independent features, with the express aim of establishing greater Native presence across film and television production. He notes that "there's no room in Hollywood for new directors — there's only room for new voices. A new voice is about cultivating an audience. . . . Slowly, once you've built an audience and you develop a marquee Indian actor, you're able to say more things that you want to say."[29] Eyre's other projects include two films made for the PBS *Mystery!* series — *Skinwalkers* (2002) and *The Thief of Time* (2004), both produced by Robert Redford and adapted from the popular Tony Hillerman novels about Navajo detectives Jim Chee and Joe Leaphorn, played on screen by Adam Beach and Wes Studi, respectively. His third feature film, *Edge of America*, was selected to open the 2004 Sundance Film Festival, and he directed the signature film for the NMAI, titled *A Thousand Roads* (2005). He has also used his industry experience to produce and market films from other directors, including Randy Redroad's *The Doe Boy* and Michael Linn's *Imprint* (2006). His new historical documentaries — episodes from the *We Shall Remain* series on Native American history for the PBS *American Experience* program — reach out to a wider audience through publicly funded television channels, a crucial source of funding for documentary production in lieu of a federal film office of the kind that Canada established long ago with its National Film Board (NFB).

The most visible impact of *Smoke Signals* on American screens may be the studio and television industry embrace of actor Adam Beach, who went on to co-star with Nicholas Cage in John Woo's *Windtalkers* (2002) about Navajo Code Talkers during World War II, in addition to many other film and television roles, including the Hillerman adaptations directed by Eyre. Beach has crossed over into mainstream film and television as the closest thing to a "marquee Indian actor" in the Native cinema world, with parts as Native detectives and war heroes. After Beach's role as Ira Hayes in Clint Eastwood's *Flags of Our Fathers* (2006), Paramount and Warner Brothers lobbied for an Oscar nomination for Best Supporting Actor for him, an effort that suggests the studios' strong interest in him as a bankable star, as does his subsequent role as Mohawk detective Chester Lake on the high-visibility television franchise *Law and Order svu*.[30]

Sherman Alexie's disappointment in the aftermath of *Smoke Signals* stems in part from his general frustration with the American film industry's business structure, driven by investment, profit, and anxious obsession with box-office outcomes:

> There's no getting it or not getting it, that's not even the issue. The issue is, is this going to make enough money for us to make this movie. It has nothing to do with whether they get it or not. ... According to their definitions and their pie charts and their graphs and formulas, no, *Smoke Signals* wasn't enough of a success. And moreover I think that even though it was one of the most successful independent movies of 1998 — in the top five, moneywise, and for gross compared to budget one of the most successful movies of the year, period — but because it is filmed with Indians and is an Indian story it does have a ceiling. It does have an economic ceiling. ... I mean, I guarantee that there's no movie [by] Indians ever going to break out and make 50 or 100 million dollars — there's no movie going to win that lottery. I'd be amazed if one did. I'd be so happy. But it's not going to happen, and they know that.[31]

Smoke Signals is a film and a story that exposes, questions, and resists the film industry practice by which images of vanishing Indians — especially in the 1860–90 time period — are sold as media commodities. Given that media commodification of Indian images has historically functioned as an act of colonization, and that Hollywood systems of production and distribution extend and continue that colonization by co-opting voices of resistance, Alexie's disillusionment with Hollywood illustrates the problems Native filmmakers face in seeking to be the authors and marketers of their own images. And in order to be effective in changing public perceptions, that resistance to commodification must itself also sell, thus profiting the mass culture industries generated by and for consumer culture.[32]

This foregrounding of a story's potential market value over other measures of value can be debilitating to its production, as Alexie describes in an essay on his first experience with writer's block, which he attributes to his work writing screenplays for Hollywood studios — a process that involves writing "by committee" and responding to requested changes that "always, always, always have something to do with making the screenplay more 'accessible.' I've always lived my life and written my books outside of the power structure. In order to be accessible, I'd have to work within the power structure. And yes, while writing screenplays, I have been working within that power structure, right in the damn middle of that power structure. And yes, the contradiction is killing me. Yes, this is my brain, a cute little egg, and this is my brain on screenplays, an egg sizzling in a frying pan with ten hypodermic needles, six vials of crack, and a copy of Syd Field's *Screenplay*."[33]

The silencing effect of hearing Hollywood industry "voices" in his mind is reminiscent of the dynamics of mediation revealed in *Smoke Signals* when Victor and Thomas debate the efficacy of performing Hollywood's images of Indians and find that the versions of themselves "spoken" by the movies are ultimately hostile to their own expression. Alexie phrased his frustration with Hollywood-style film production more directly in the introduction to his screenplay for *The Business of Fancydancing*, the film that marked his departure from accessible filmmaking: "Fuck resolutions, fuck closure, fuck the idea of the story arc."[34] His emphatic rejection of commercial screenplay fundamentals may reflect not only the writer's individual chafing at corporate writing but also the embedded politics of such aesthetics. Narrative "arcs" ending neatly in resolution and closure can be structurally inappropriate for representing ongoing conditions of colonization and may instead recapitulate mainstream audiences' expectations that the story of Indians is not just aesthetically but also historically ended, or "closed." As David L. Moore has pointed out regarding Alexie's statement above, "Colonial closure means tragedy for Indians."[35] Yet Alexie also maintains the contrary goal of making films and writing books that are accessible for tribal youth, who are immersed in standard media structures.

The mark of Indigenous authenticity in *Smoke Signals* (and that authenticity is, in an important way, what Eyre and Alexie used to market the film) is not its freedom from mediation and commodification, but rather its very immersion in and reflection upon these practices from an Indigenous perspective. Its authenticity resides in its measure of liberatory "control over the process and proceeds of marketization," and its powerful message that we are all already living in a mediated world. There is really no question about whether "to commodify or not to commodify,"[36] or to mediate or not to mediate; rather, the question is how to most effectively speak counter to the din of "their voices, those Hollywood voices" that so dominate the grounds of popular culture without having self-representations appropriated by that very power structure.[37]

Smoke Signals's Cinematic Influence

Relationships between Native filmmakers and Hollywood production systems are far more complex than can be accounted for with a simply oppositional model, particularly when the goal of much Native feature filmmaking is to be picked up for theatrical distribution, as *Smoke Signals* was. Alexie's articulation of the contradictory position of Native filmmaking in debates about accessibility works against tendencies (both critical and industrial) toward the polarization of accommodation and resistance in the mainstream media marketplace. Beverly Singer approves Eyre and Alexie's "demonstration that American Indians can make a good commercial product," because "for too long, Native Americans have been viewed as activists and positioned as opponents of mainstream white filmmakers."[38] Thomas Elsaesser, seeking to theorize alternative cinemas beyond overdetermined binaries of "identification and antagonism," suggests that the relationship between major and minor cinemas can "be thought of as a series of palimpsests, a sequence of texts, each rewriting other cinematic and pre-cinematic spectacles in the form of intertextual narratives."[39] Elsaesser's formulation facilitates a consideration of *Smoke Signals'*s impact as an extension of its intertextual content. One gauge of the film's afterlife in the public memory of the mainstream popular mediascape, as well as its continuing influence on Native filmmaking, is the way it has, in turn, been taken up in intertextual references in both Hollywood features and Native independent films. The David Spade vehicle *Joe Dirt* (dir. Gordon, 2001), for example, is certainly not Native cinema, yet it still offers a further translation of *Smoke Signals* into the purview of mainstream audiences through the comic reflexivity of stereotypes that are extended and intensified into parody. In contrast, *Four Sheets to the Wind* (2007), by Seminole and Creek director Sterlin Harjo, refers more obliquely — and more powerfully — to *Smoke Signals* by continuing its focus on sons who have lost their fathers, on storytelling across generations, and on the assimilationist pressures that accompany movement between cities and reservation homes.

Joe Dirt contains an extended parodic quotation from *Smoke Signals*, including crossover casting — Adam Beach plays Kicking Wing, who runs a roadside fireworks stand on an unnamed reservation.[40] *Joe Dirt* amalgamates the "buddies" in *Smoke Signals* by making Adam Beach's character resemble Thomas Builds-the-Fire, not Victor Joseph. According to Alexie, this was not deliberate on the part of the filmmakers but rather the result of a mistaken phone call inviting Adam Beach rather than Evan Adams to perform the role. Kicking Wing wears nerdy glasses and braids, and maintains a mild-mannered, gentle optimism that resembles the innocent Thomas. This compound character continues the work of *Smoke Signals* in flouting stereotypes about Indian masculinity. Kicking Wing only likes, and so only stocks, sparklers; Joe offers him an education in "real" (meaning hazardous) fireworks as the scene unfolds. The parody amplifies the film's plot about a character's road trip in search of his lost parents, who abandoned him in the Grand

Canyon as a baby. In its continuing return to issues and indicators of social class, the film incorporates *Smoke Signals*'s humorous subversion of Indian stereotypes into its comic recalibration of kitschy Americana and "white trash" stereotypes. The reference to *Smoke Signals* is also significant to the film's underlying thematic exploration of the mediation of public images in the film's closing: Joe Dirt wins over a radio-show audience after having been a janitor at the Los Angeles radio station. The image of physical marginalization in media industries is immediately resonant to the production and circulation of Native films because it points to the class differences that undergird racialized, differential access to media production.

The economic conditions that originally nourished American independent cinema and *Smoke Signals*'s production and distribution have changed since the late 1990s, and Native filmmakers are currently facing a very different climate for independent production. Films are cheaper to make, but harder to sell. In October 2009, the *New York Times* reported that Miramax Films, the company that bought and distributed *Smoke Signals*, would pare its staff to only twenty employees in a "pilot-light" strategy to avoid shutting the operation down completely. Under the leadership of its founders, Harvey and Bob Weinstein, Miramax had at one point employed five hundred people and played a major role in the independent film movement of the 1980s and 1990s.[41] With the shrinking of companies like Miramax or their absorption into large corporations (Disney, in the case of Miramax), slowing DVD sales, and economic recession, financing for independent films has subsided. "The glory days of independent film" are "now barely a speck in the rearview mirror," as Michael Cieply wrote for the *New York Times* in August 2009. Independent filmmakers are largely "doing it themselves — paying for their own distribution" in hopes of recovering enough through a limited theater run (a "guerilla release") and DVD sales to recoup production costs.[42]

Sterlin Harjo's *Four Sheets to the Wind* continues the cinematic conversation about Native intergenerational relationships and movement between reservation and urban spaces initiated by *Smoke Signals*. In fact, we can see the film as *Smoke Signals*'s successor in its themes and crossover casting. A quiet and powerfully acted story about a Creek and Seminole family in Oklahoma, its most resonant moment of intertextual allusion comes early in the film, when actor Cody Lightning, playing the lead character Cufe Smallhill, informs his mother (Jeri Arredondo, Mescalero Apache) of his father's suicide. She tells him to fetch his cousin Jim (Jon Proudstar, Yaqui) — who drives a hearse for a funeral home — for a family meeting about burial arrangements, instructing Cufe to "take your dad's pickup." In the next sequence, Cufe exits the house, with the cab of the big black pickup truck in the foreground, followed by a shot of Cufe sitting in the truck and a reverse shot of his fathers' belongings in the passenger seat. In this and later scenes, Cufe takes up the empty places his father once occupied (the driver's seat of the pickup, his father's easy chair, his father's suit) and encounters things associated with him.[43]

Four Sheets to the Wind was not picked up for theatrical distribution but was immediately available on DVD, and it was very well received at the 2008 Sundance festival. Tamara Podemski, an Ojibway/Israeli singer and actress raised in Toronto, won the prestigious Special Jury Prize for acting at the Sundance Film Festival for her role as Miri Smallhill in *Four Sheets to the Wind*. Cody Lightning, the Cree actor from Edmonton who was nominated for a Young Artist Award for Best Performance in a Feature Film — Best Supporting Young Actor for his role as the twelve-year-old Young Victor Joseph in *Smoke Signals*, won the American Indian Movie Award for Best Actor at the American Indian Film Festival for his portrayal of Cufe. Lightning's physical maturation since his role as twelve-year-old Young Victor Joseph, and the similarity between the characters of Young Victor and the nearly grown Cufe in their reserve, their loss of their fathers, and their desire to explore the world beyond their reservation towns all seem to take the measure of the time elapsed between the two films. Like Gary Farmer's performances in *Smoke Signals* and *Dead Man*, which bring those films into a relationship that progressively redefines the possibilities for representing Indians in the 1990s away from romantic vanishing in *Dances with Wolves*, here the choices in production and casting of Lightning frame *Smoke Signals* as a media progenitor by setting up a reflexive relationship with its images and filmmaking practices.

For Cufe, as for Victor in *Smoke Signals*, seeing to his father's physical remains poses a problem and sets in motion a story about coping with emotional turbulence following parental abandonment and loss. Like Arnold Joseph, Frankie Smallhill's absence is manifested by his having "no body" — Cufe having sunk the body in their fishing pond according to his father's wishes — so Cufe and his mother and cousin fake the funeral, an act that complicates the film's representation of grief and remembrance. The fabricated, yet also very real funeral is beautifully shot and takes seriously the characters' work of mourning, despite the comic absurdity of the loudly decorated coffin (a gift from a family friend and wannabe-Indian) that actually contains watermelons. The theatricality and humor of the funeral's pretense (as well as earlier preparations for the subterfuge) pivots emotionally, midway through the sequence, to a more emphatically realist mode as the grieving character Miri Smallhill arrives and longer takes of the male chorus singing hymns in the Muskokee Creek language lend an aural and visual sense of gravitas to the ceremonial commemoration.

Like *Smoke Signals*, *Four Sheets to the Wind* begins and ends with a voice-over that refers explicitly to storytelling across generations. Instead of visualizing an absent father figure in flashbacks, Harjo frequently relies on long takes and eyeline matches as well as sparse descriptions by the characters. The duration of the shots and the slow, steady rhythm of the editing invite the audience to identify with Cufe's reticent interiority, becoming the visual equivalent of the contemplation and listening that were defining qualities of Cufe's father. Like Arnold Joseph, then, Cufe's absent father is evoked in the very structure of the film, and this cinematic ghosting becomes even more ethereal when we discover, at the film's end, that the Muskogee-language voice-over is his. That Frankie

19. Young Thomas and Young Victor examine a sparkler.

20. Cufe in his father's pickup truck. From *Four Sheets to the Wind*.

Smallhill's voice-over is in Muskogee and not English suggests that his silence during his life might have been related to a disinclination to communicate in English, although in the end he says simply that despite his grandmother's encouraging him to "exaggerate and tell stories" in order to effectively teach his children, he "just always liked listening." This voice-over, with its metacommnicative commentary about the techniques of hyperbole and performance, pedagogical utility, interactive dynamics, and essential role of listening to the practice of storytelling, is synchronized with footage of Cufe's departure from the reservation in his father's pickup truck, casting the film's story of Cufe's decision to travel away from home within a framework of intergenerational communication.

Thus, the film's construction makes visible and audible the way the two generations of the Smallhill family tell stories differently than they heard them from their parents, and this emphasis on shifting modes of transmission and teaching calls our attention to Sterlin Harjo's own filmmaking as a generational form of storytelling. Frankie Smallhill's pickup truck remains as a lingering stand-in for his physical presence and legacy; that Cufe leaves the reservation at the film's end in his father's pickup (having brought his sister home from the city) extends *Smoke Signals*'s symbolic vehicle of mobility and familial retrieval, including its allusions to road movies about leaving and returning to the reservation.

In *Smoke Signals*, Victor's acquisition of his father's pickup truck gives him new powers of mobility that accompany his new powers of apprehension and self-knowledge, and part of the film's message involves his use of that power to return home and repatriate his father's remains rather than to sever ties in the name of independence or to remain suspended, as Arnold did, in an invented place. Victor uses his father's pickup truck to reunite his family, a point underscored by the parallel bird's-eye-view shots of the road and the river at various points during the film. The pickup truck's association with all-American masculinity, with the road movie, and with rural Americana becomes, like movies themselves, a tool of Indigenous expression in *Smoke Signals*, and a way of reconnecting with ancestors in the face of cinematic efforts to dissociate tribes from their histories. The American icon of the pickup truck is transformed into an intertextual cinematic metaphor for the shared work of intergenerational storytelling in Native media and for the Indigenizing of public media space.

Smoke Signals on YouTube

Smoke Signals has reverberated not only as an established film text and a temporally bounded cinematic event, but also as an ongoing phenomenon that has migrated to the virtual space of new media. The film is widely taught in high school and college classrooms, and is a sufficiently prominent cinematic presence to make it a target for absorption by YouTube's remix culture, a venue that offers us an up-to-the-minute snapshot of some viewers' continued relationships with the film. YouTube videos based on *Smoke Signals* extend the film's initial intervention in American popular culture, an intervention that, as I have argued in this book, focuses on issues of voice, speech, and mediated transmission. The uptake and active reproduction of *Smoke Signals* in the new media "arenas" of participatory online culture make visible and audible the collective consumption of this Indigenous public address. YouTube video quotations and parodies also expand upon the film's textualized countermand of the Western's silencing effects. The expansive emphasis on speaking and listening in the film itself — the ubiquitous storytelling performances, voice-over narration, prominent radio DJ and flashbacks, for example — is magnified by the context of YouTube's generative framework, a platform that accentuates the replication and transmission of media through users' performativity. Native and non-Native audiences lay claim to the film by vocal imitation, acting out their identification with the film's characters. Speaking the film's lines from memory in amateur videos, like the audiences that supplied lines for the film in the Minnesota screening described at the beginning of this chapter, reveals youth audiences' physical alignment with *Smoke Signals*'s characters and the film's power to rewrite the public script for Native dramatic speech. The curatorial aspects of YouTube, in which users extract clips from films to spotlight and share, bring into focus the intersection of Native cinema and broader public reception. Media scholar Henry Jenkins suggests that new media platforms like YouTube provide "a resource through which we make sense of our everyday lives,"[44] and creating YouTube videos requires users' close textual attention and analysis, especially in remixes.

The videos described below don't generally achieve wide viewership, because as media theorist Michael Wesch points out, YouTube is emphatically not mass media: most YouTube videos are viewed by fewer than one hundred people, and 88 percent of uploaded videos are new, original, largely amateur content — far different from network television. With a few exceptions, YouTube videos about *Smoke Signals* fall into the categories of curated excerpts of the film itself, school projects, amateur reenactments or parodies, and home-made music videos, the latter including bands covering songs as well as the appropriation of songs to accompany home videos or remixed pop-culture image montages.

Most of the clips are extracted directly from the film, curated by users to highlight one element of the film separately from its other varied tonal elements. These quotations are a form of veneration-through-transmission, expanding the film's reach and longevity. But the emphasis on individual curation of excerpts and their recontextualization in relation to users' own lives also has the capacity to minimize *Smoke Signals*'s more overtly political content. Some of the parodies and reenactments of *Smoke Signals* clearly originate in educational contexts as high school or college class assignments. The eighteen to twenty-four, college-age demographic group, which comprises the majority of YouTube users (over 50 percent, according to Wesch), matches the age at which many students are first exposed to this film (users aged twenty-five to thirty-four make up the second-highest number accessing YouTube). This classroom viewing context is illustrated in "fry bread," a twenty-second video shot from the back of a classroom. Students rest their feet on their desks and watch the screen showing the scene from *Smoke Signals* when Thomas describes Arlene's magical fry bread.[45] Another video set in a classroom, the three-minute "smoke signals rap," is described by the user as "a rap about our English group smoke signals, it was a project and they chise [*sic*] to do it in song."[46] The two men rap the story of *Smoke Signals* from Victor's perspective, focusing on the relationship between Victor and Thomas. In a five-minute video, "smoke signals school rap," three students recite rhyming, descriptive monologues in the voices of Arnold, Victor, and Arlene in front of a pickup truck and a trailer, and reenact fragments of dialogue between Arnold and Young Victor.[47] A seven-and-one-third-minute video, "Interviews on Smoke Signals," is accompanied by the description "Made this for school." In the video, an unseen interviewer wielding a salt-shaker "microphone" interviews "viewers" who have just seen *Smoke Signals* in a movie theater and a mall. The viewers, played by other students, act out exaggerated stereotypes announced by intertitles: Little Boy, Native American, Crazy White People, Rich Lady, Intellectual Person, Rich Guy, Cool Guy, Sixth-Grade Cool Kids, and Some Random Guy.[48]

YouTube's platform facilitates the individual exercise of public voice, mediating public and private forms of address; it both masks and foregrounds the boundaries of identity in the juncture of mass-media, small-group circulation and individual speech. Jay David Bolter and Richard Grusin characterize new media's refashioning of prior media forms (painting, photography, film, television) as "remediation," arguing that remediation ultimately affects users' own identification through digital processes of self-reformation. In its self-reforming function, YouTube intersects with the vexed and nebulous realm of identity politics; it can be a platform — a new stage — for the very old American performative tradition of redface, or playing Indian. What happens to "race" as a social system based on "visible difference" in YouTube's space of encounter, a space that exaggerates both visibility and invisibility? The broad-spectrum twin emphases in studies of YouTube on issues of imitation and authenticity are at least partly the result of the heightened sense of speaking to an unseen audience, a sense of being in the presence of everyone and no one, which Michael Wesch calls "context collapse."[49]

Both because of its engagement with identity politics and in spite of that engagement, YouTube videos that excerpt, remix, parody, and otherwise reproduce *Smoke Signals* on YouTube amplify the film's emphasis on speaking and listening, on the interracial politics of encounter in the public arena of mass culture. The videos represent a collective "speaking back" to *Smoke Signals*'s initial spoken intervention, self-consciously echoing its most stylized performative moments. As one of the largest online archives of film clips, YouTube, for all its youthfulness as a digital platform first made public in 2005, depends on a basic, though sometimes temporally shallow, historical sensibility. The users who curate clips and upload remixes require prior footage, or "originals" from which to make copies or reproductions. The reproduction of *Smoke Signals* on YouTube returns us to longstanding historical problems of Indigenous visibility and invisibility (Native absence and presence) in popular visual media. For although YouTube has given rise to new forms of representation, the strategies of curating, remixing, and imitating that characterize many YouTube videos related to *Smoke Signals* are often familiar derivations from popular representations of Indians. Imitative performances of Indianness, and Hollywood-style remixing in the form of location shooting intercut with footage taken on studio soundstages, have been ongoing in an industry that has historically exerted enormous power over images of Indians in the stream of popular culture. In the case of *Smoke Signals*, the film's discourses about Indigeneity as politically "original" or "first" on the land — a discourse that encompasses specific legal and political rights connected to that identity as first inhabitants of the continent — deepens the seemingly casual remediative aesthetic activity of remixing. Remixing is often both historically archival and analytic in showcasing the creator's appropriation of prior footage, encoding tensions between originality and reproduction in the context of First People's cinema.

Video quotations from *Smoke Signals* function as limited-circulation pop-culture sound bites, providing a Native-made alternative common lexicon to replace the "How" and "Ugh" of Hollywood Westerns. In those films, the formal, stilted greeting imagined an interracial frontier encounter in which only one party had the power of legitimate (or grammatical) speech.[50] For the Native actors in *Smoke Signals*, as Sherman Alexie recalls, "it was rare . . . to even get those many lines. In the entertainment industry, it's all about monosyllables, even in contemporary film . . . it's never about language. So in writing all that stuff and allowing everybody to talk in poetry and be funny and be smart and have a wide range of emotions and verbal moments — that was the big thing, just the sheer size of their vocabulary."[51]

One of the most widely emulated of these "verbal moments" from *Smoke Signals* is Thomas Builds-the-Fire's enthusiastic hailing of Victor: "Hey, Victor!" The YouTube video appropriately titled "Clips of people saying 'Hey Victor' from the movie Smoke Signals" consists simply of a remix compilation of these "Hey, Victor" salutations. Sherman Alexie has said that "over the last ten years I've met ninety guys named Victor who cursed at me because they spend their entire lives getting 'Hey, Victor' from every Indian they know." Director Chris Eyre says that even now at screenings of the film, "mothers still come up to me and say, 'How do you get your son or daughter to stop coming up to me saying, "Hey, Victor!"'"[52]

In *Smoke Signals*, this greeting is directed toward the film's focal character of Victor Joseph, and the speaker is most often Thomas Builds-the-Fire. Thus the greeting alludes to the friendship between these two men that is the engine of the film's emotional trajectory. Taking up Thomas's accented voice also draws our attention to one of *Smoke Signals*'s important contributions to popular culture: the figure of the Indian nerd. Thomas's facility with language and extensive knowledge of esoteric aspects of pop culture (he casually sprinkles references to Tom Mix and Charles Bronson in his conversations) attest to his intellectual prowess and his ability to know things by naming them. Thomas is smart, verbose, idiosyncratic, and curious about the aesthetics of the popular media in which he is so well versed; he's the precise opposite of the mute and stoic Indian of Hollywood movies. At the same time that his signature call-out and his relentless storytelling project a sociable and outgoing nature, both his and Victor's personality traits also signal their complex inner lives, giving them three-dimensional qualities that mainstream cinema's stereotyped Indian characters rarely (if ever) seem to have.

More than a decade after the film's release, YouTube users are still posting parodic imitations of Thomas's nasal, nerdy, accented greeting. Unlike the forms of "playing Indian" that are temporally and spatially limited to images of the Plains cultures in the mid- to late nineteenth century, or that are emotionally limited to a romantic stoicism or savagery, non-Native performers appropriate a present-day, regionally Northwest, energetically youthful English-language nerdy salutation. Their YouTube quotations exemplify new media's proclivities for disguise and revelation (e.g., the avatar), but depart from previous occasions of redfacing by taking a contemporary Native-authored movie as their "original." While some videos focus exclusively on the greeting, in others the easily replicated contemporary setting imagined for *Smoke Signals* is key to the humor. In the video "Thomas from Smoke Signals . . . wait, that's Matt Salazar!!!" Salazar paraphrases Thomas Builds-the-Fire's breakfast cornucopia at Denny's, while sitting at Denny's.[53] In another sequence, fifteen very short (five- to fifteen-second) filmed segments, three students read a short analysis of *Smoke Signals's* commentary about stereotypes of Indians. But instead of quoting from the book *The Lone Ranger and Tonto Fistfight in Heaven* or from *Smoke Signals* the students act out scenes using a ping-pong table as a stage for Barbie doll actors. Thomas becomes a blond Barbie with braids that are dramatically unbraided on camera (Thomas's transformation in *Smoke Signals* takes place off screen). In another quotation, Velma and Lucy's car (again driven by Barbies) drives in reverse perilously close to the edge of the ping-pong table, inadvertently reenacting the ending of *Thelma & Louise* that is quoted in *Smoke Signals*.[54]

If the Western genre film's stock Indian stereotypes function as a kind of Althusserian "hailing" — an interpellation of Indigenous spectators into a schema in which they are already named and already destined to vanish — we can also see the ubiquitous naming going on in *Smoke Signals* as a crucial occasion of its contrapuntal relationship to the genre. Film Studies scholar Hamid Naficy has suggested that in addition to cinematic "'hailing' there is much 'haggling' in cinematic spectatorship."[55] Naficy's expansion of the Althusserian model of interpellation to account for the sometimes raucous ways that audiences speak back to the screen is also particularly suited to YouTube's multidirectional space of encounter, a crowded exchange consisting of countless videos addressing disembodied, invisible, sometimes hazily defined recipients. When *Smoke Signals*'s Indian characters (especially Thomas) address Victor, they revise previous Western-genre interpellation of spectators while moving the performance of greeting out of the trope of Indian/white encounter and into a sphere of Indigenous interaction. With their imitative appropriations of "Hey, Victor," YouTube participants synthesize the emphasis in *Smoke Signals* upon the politics and possibilities of public address with new media's intensified capacities for haggling.

Many of the YouTube remixes engage *Smoke Signals*'s own haggling commentary on Westerns — summed up in Thomas's joke that "the only thing more pathetic than Indians on TV is Indians watching Indians on TV" — using the song "John Wayne's Teeth," written by Sherman Alexie and performed by the EagleBear Singers. In one video the song accompanies photos from an activist march. Some videos actualize the song by adding stills and footage from John Wayne movies, or cartoonish drawings, while others depict bands or single performers covering the song, or the EagleBear Singers themselves performing it. The first category of videos acknowledges *Smoke Signals*'s intertextual relationship with the Western, foregrounding the artifice of the popular construction of John Wayne as the Western film genre's mouthpiece. The remix video "John Wayne's Teeth" by user "twinmonsterslayer," for example, assembles a montage of cinematic and caricatured portraits of John Wayne's face, fragmenting what seems to be a unified image into its many constituent parts. The video has been widely seen compared with most YouTube videos, with nearly 143,000 views and 361 text comments by viewers. These comments present a further, even more active and plural site of haggling, as the viewers carry on a heated debate about whether John Wayne was racist, about ongoing Indigenous land rights, and about textbooks that limit Native presence to origin myths. Covers of the song "John Wayne's Teeth" on YouTube exemplify the way the film has spoken to multiple audiences. With these performances, the film's soundtrack hovers close to home, as in a performance by a man at the Yakama Nation Path of Healing event in 2008, and crosses international boundaries, as in a performance of the song by the Czech youth band Moury Z Roury.

Much of the recent scholarly work on YouTube explores the impact of the proliferation and interaction of new media delivery platforms on the relationships between audiences and corporate media producers. The very ownership of industrial storytelling becomes contested in the wake of the new curatorial and remix capabilities of online fan and spoiler communities.[56] YouTube, in particular, facilitates forms of critical engagement and interactive storytelling; users excerpt, curate, recontextualize, and archive film clips; edit and remix film sounds and images; and generate amateur reenactments and parodies. As an online venue celebrated for its leveling capacities, and for its "double function as both a 'top-down' platform for distribution of popular culture and a 'bottom-up' platform for vernacular creativity," YouTube instantiates a digital form of Stuart Hall's class-based articulation of popular culture as a political "arena of consent and resistance." It is "one of the sites where this struggle for and against a culture of the powerful is engaged: it is also the stake to be won or lost in that struggle."[57] In fact, this visible, mediated contestation of popular culture has been the particular project of *Smoke Signals*, from its inception in Sherman Alexie's short story collection (and Alexie's dream about the Lone Ranger and Tonto in a boxing arena) to its cinematic adaptation and successful theatrical run.

A YouTube video post entitled "Smoke signals our version" re-enacts *Smoke Signals* by reproducing the opening sequences. Two young women (username NativeRockers, on-screen credits Marisa and Jonisha) paraphrase, amid riotous laughter, the radio announcements, traffic reports, and initial voice-over from the film's first few minutes.[58] They use a computerized sketch of a burning house while paraphrasing Thomas's voice-over describing the Fourth of July fire, and then toss a bundle across the room while narrating Thomas's assertion that "I flew." As they act out Grandma Builds-the-Fire and Arnold Joseph's lines when the baby is rescued, they are laughing so hard that their father comes in to tell them to "go to bed, now." The video is exuberantly amateur, including a very shaky camera, many skips in the filming and sound, poor lighting and lots of giggles and missed lines. The youth of these reenactors (still subject to parental bedtime warnings), and their embrace of the opening credit sequences and radio voice-off (arguably the film's strongest assertion of the importance of Native voices in mass media) powerfully counterhail the naming of Indian absence and vanishing in the Western. Opening credits are, after all, where the film's title and players are named, assigning the ownership and authorship of its story. By substituting their own names on screen, "NativeRockers" honor *Smoke Signals*'s writer, director, and actors by displacing them, laying claim to the film as a "first" story that modeled Indigenous ownership in the public sphere. They show us how *Smoke Signals* created a wave of possibilities for Native youth in the popular mediascape by mapping a place for new Native names in movie credits.

There are many variegated strands that make up a film's reception: the encounter of the film and the audience in the theater; the emergence of fans; the financial measure of the film's theatrical run and box office gross; its formal recognition with awards on the festival circuit and its assessment by professional reviewers in the press; intertextual references to the film in Hollywood and independent productions; and its twenty-first-century uptake in the new media arena of YouTube, a powerful indicator of the way the film is actually used or appropriated by viewers. *Smoke Signals*'s position as a Native cinema first has affected each of these elements of reception because the film took on additional burdens of expectation. Too often, the discourses of commodification — profitability as reflected in box office receipts — become the most widely deployed assessment of a film's successful address to a real audience. Yet *Smoke Signals*, as I have argued throughout this book, had other ambitions as well. In particular, it embeds an address to imagined spectators — both Native and non-Native — and makes the politics of that Indigenous address a primary trope in figures like the K-REZ Radio DJ and the storyteller Thomas Builds-the-Fire. The moment when these imagined spectators and the actual audiences align most precisely may be in the active reenactments of the film, as in the Minnesota screening (with sound supplied by viewers) witnessed by Sherman Alexie, or the YouTube parodies. Unlike the mainstream media's gauge of the film's release as an industry event or product, YouTube videos indicate the film's ongoing impact at the same time that the videos, because they are messier and more populist than professional press reviews, massively complicate the film's political significations beyond issues of oppositionality or commodification. What is revealed in these convergences of spectator and audience is *Smoke Signals*'s embeddedness in an American popular imaginary. In light of its continuing presence across these shifting venues of popular culture, *Smoke Signals* does more than measure or correct past media disconnections and stereotypes. It radically repositions Indigenous peoples as its central and most important speakers and listeners, writers and readers, and directors and viewers — and that shift in cinematic address may be its most important legacy.

Conclusion — "Be a Crazy Horse of Filmmaking"

*Smoke Signals and the Ongoing Production
and Reception of Native Cinema*

Smoke Signals was introduced to the public in 1998 as a Native cinema "first": the first feature film written, directed, and acted by Native Americans to receive national distribution. By marketing *Smoke Signals* this way upon its initial release, the filmmakers and their distributor, Miramax, positioned the film as a historic intervention in mainstream images of Indians. While other Native-controlled documentary and feature films came before *Smoke Signals*, the film has been taken up, here and elsewhere, as one identifiable origin point in the unfolding history of Native media. It has remained a touchstone for discussions of Native film in educational contexts as well as in film industry and other media production circles such as festivals. Looking back on the film, Sherman Alexie maintains that it is still "the only film that ever went even remotely mainstream."[1] This book has situated *Smoke Signals* both in terms of its extensive engagement with mainstream Hollywood film and in the context of the ongoing rise of Native American cinema; it has both honored and interrogated the film's complex self-positioning as a cinema "first." Other Native directors have marketed their films as firsts, including Valerie Red-Horse and Georgina Lightning, who have presented their feature films (Red-Horse's *Naturally Native* and Lightning's *Older than America*) as the first feature films to be directed by Native women. Describing these films as firsts constructs Native cinema as a category with a certain kind of history, oppositional to Hollywood yet also significant for its mainstream appeal and potential for national distribution. This category also provides a productive framework for describing the tensions that continue to energize viewings of *Smoke Signals* and other Native films because it foregrounds their status as simultaneously new and old, original and originary.

On Novelty and Primacy

What kind of freight is carried by *Smoke Signals*'s claim to be a Native cinema "first," and what do we mean when we say "Native cinema"? How do critical views of *Smoke Signals* as both an intervention and a popular success — both revolutionary and mainstream — construct Native cinema history in particular ways? *Smoke Signals*'s intertextuality expands the purview of what some critics have called an "Indigenous aesthetic," but perhaps it reveals more about Native use of established cinematic languages and genres to access a wide audience, an interplay of resistance and accommodation to dominant film production and forms.[2] In its address to multiple audiences, the film successfully appropriates the archives and legacies of mainstream filmmaking. At the same time, it takes aim at the real phenomenon and ongoing power imbalance represented by Hollywood's domination of American and global screens. This quality of subversive intervention is one of the things that makes *Smoke Signals* innovative, but the claim to be first is more nuanced and complicated than just innovation.

Being a cinematic first is a claim commonly made by a number of Hollywood films, too. Studios market films this way to advertise advances in mimetic realism or technological spectacle, offering audiences both the comfort of a genre film and the excitement of revisionism in the film's promise of a newly immersive viewing experience. Revisionist Westerns, for example, are familiar genre products sold as novelties. Audiences often respond to such invitations to witness these amplified representations of the past — to see the "real" frontier on screen for the first time. Production values are an important part of this appeal.[3] For example, in a 1991 article on *Dances with Wolves*, *Entertainment Weekly* reported that director Kevin Costner "took charge of 3,500 buffalo, 300 horses, two wolves, 42 wagons, 36 tepees, 130 crew members, and 500 extras" in the course of shooting the film. The emphasis on epic scale and authentic detail in production is intended to heighten viewers' sense of the film's innovative verisimilitude, yet the story of a white man "going native" is an old one. Similarly, the science fiction film *Avatar* tells a story about colonization that is drawn largely from the plotlines of frontier adventure films like *Dances with Wolves, Last of the Mohicans, Pocahontas,* and *Apocalypto,* while clothing those older fictions about frontier race relations in a new technology of immersive display. The industrial and financial resources marshaled in service of these formulaic adventure fantasies — *Avatar,* notoriously, cost nearly $500 million to make and market — attest to the commodity value of cinematic products that link generic storytelling with novel presentation.[4]

In an Indigenous activist context, however, invoking the claim to be first has the opposite signification and goes far beyond straightforward innovation. Unlike the film industry's emphasis on novelty, this claim is connected instead to legal and ethical discourses of sovereignty and to claims about the past. Indigeneity is defined in part through primacy on ancestral lands; Indigenous peoples are "First Peoples" and (in Canada) "First Nations." Thus, in Native cinema, "first" indicates both novelty and history; film industry innovation brushes up against fundamental historical precedence. These competing realms of signification give *Smoke Signals*'s claim to be a cinema first a sense of temporal depth and political gravity.

Smoke Signals's self-positioning as the first Native-made feature film to achieve national distribution is a way of making history and also of writing history that depends on this other inherent, fundamental status of Indigenous priority. The film's release created an intersitial space, Indigenizing the novelty claims of Hollywood's genre-film marketing and consciously refusing audience expectations of genre revisionism and mimetic novelty. Eyre and Alexie appropriated the machine of cinematic commodification in order to "make audiences comfortable" with an Indigenous perspective about nationhood. This perspective comes from the filmmakers' ownership of the production process and their investment in the film's storytelling voice. Hollywood's genre films usually keep white narrators in control of the story (e.g., *Little Big Man, Dances with Wolves, Geronimo, Avatar*), and *Smoke Signals*'s aesthetic innovation is in large part not its increased verisimilitude but rather focalization and voice — in a word, its storytelling. *Smoke Signals*'s "firstness," then, is about not only newness but also oldness, not only originality but also origins. The film was able to be both new and old because of who is telling the story. *Smoke Signals* is successful as a Native cinema first not because it represents Indians accurately for the first time, but rather because of the creative control Native artists wielded over its authorship.

Definitions of Native Cinema

Native cinema, as a relatively new film category, powerfully links cinematic storytelling with Native authorship and control in production. *Smoke Signals*, in particular, emphasizes this element, but in fact Native films are organized and presented differently by studio producers, scholars, reviewers, tribes, producers, distributors, institutional infrastructures (e.g., the Sundance Institute), networks of festivals (Sundance, the American Indian Film Festival, the NMAI festival, the ImagiNATIVE festival, the National Geographic All Roads festival), and of course a community of individual filmmakers and actors.

Despite its capacity to invite viewers in, *Smoke Signals*'s refusal to conform to the anticipation of traditionalism sometimes challenges that broader viewing audience. Some audiences expect Native cinematic interventions to take the form of ethnographically accurate representations of traditional or historical tribal cultures. Chris Eyre emphatically distinguishes such a project from *Smoke Signals* even as he supports something like this definition of what a "real Indian movie" might look like in its ideal form. In a 2000 interview with Michael Sheyahshe-Lell, Eyre maintained that *Smoke Signals* is "the tip of the iceberg . . . like an Indian 'Cosby Show' — it's what the audiences will tolerate," arguing that "it's not an 'Indian movie' in the true sense. An Indian movie deals at least with culture, at least with religion, or at least with language. *Smoke Signals* doesn't do any of those things, culturally."[5] He elaborates on this idea in another interview:

In cinema we haven't scratched the surface, especially in terms of spoken language. There is also the visual "language" of cinema. The way that we have it now is totally different from what I think an Indian movie would be. It wouldn't follow the same convention, shot structure or story structure. And it probably wouldn't be palatable for a commercial audience. . . . Film is a language that you watch — you expect an establishing shot, and then a medium shot, and close-ups, reverses and inserts. There are conventions, and a true Indian movie wouldn't have the same conventions. . . . But one day yet, there may be a real Indian movie.[6]

Eyre's comments demarcate the established visual conventions of English-language mainstream cinema from a hypothetical category of Indian film based on cultural traditionalism (as expressed especially in Native languages). But this kind of distinction raises questions about how Native audiovisual media can or should be categorized. Does a "real Indian movie" translate traditional tribal aesthetics to film language, advocate for political sovereignty, envision a broad range of contemporary Native experiences in urban and rural communities, or all of the above? Can mainstream film language transmit traditional tribal aesthetics? How should critics account for the variety of Native film forms — genre films, experimental films, features, documentaries, and shorts? What kind of Native participation in production defines a film as Native cinema? An authorial or auteurist definition, based on the presence or control of a Native director, obscures the level of collaboration necessary to make films. And what some viewers' desire — a culturally "pure" film product — is based more in fantasy than in the contemporary dynamism of an interconnected, postcontact world. Feature films, especially, are usually the result of efforts carried out by many people and are thus very rarely culturally singular products, even when produced in remote areas. Houston Wood makes this point in *Native Features*, arguing that a continuum of Native productions (with, for example, a broad middle range between a film like

Dances with Wolves at one end and *Smoke Signals* at another) offers a better definitional paradigm than rigid categories of Native and non-Native film.

Smoke Signals, Eyre contends, is "a 'pan-Indian' movie that . . . was intended for a white, liberal audience. It is a movie that makes the audience comfortable."[7] It is also a movie that, for the first time, made many Native audiences comfortable by telling a story about contemporary young people, full of references to reservation life directed specifically at Native viewers. The implications of its politics reach beyond the limits of the film text to speak to people's lived sense of their nation and their citizenship, their emotional allegiance to certain kinds of stories about history. This deliberate strategy of inviting multiple audiences to participate in a Native cinematic story complicates conversations about which films can be called Native American cinema and which films cannot. The issue of what constitutes Native cinema is not easily resolved, because the category is applied across a range of situations and discourses, including producers, filmmakers, and scholars. In fact, the unanswerability of the idea of a "real Indian movie" suggests that this category must be conditional. *Smoke Signals* rests at the intersection of Indigenous and mainstream filmmaking (in its conventions and road/buddy genre structure), thus "making audiences comfortable" enough to stay in their seats while the film tackles less comfortable issues. If Hollywood film forms and Native cinema can be seen as two overlapping sets, *Smoke Signals* occupies the area of intersection as a product of their interrelation.

Native actors and filmmakers have expressed both appreciation of and ambivalence toward Native cinema as a category that overlaps with mainstream film but is also distinct from it. In fact, the category of Native cinema can burden films with unwieldy expectations; Houston Wood has remarked that "audiences tend to see Victor and Thomas in *Smoke Signals* as typical of not just Coeur d'Alene men but of all contemporary Indian men associated with hundreds of diverse tribes across North America."[8]

Native viewers make up less than 1 percent of the total audience that studios profit from, and Native cinema isn't highly visible on Hollywood industry radars.[9] In this market-based industry context, Native cinema is a miniscule category that can create disadvantages for Native actors and directors if it is too rigidly construed in terms of a narrowly delineated representational range. Of the few roles for Native actors in Hollywood, most are in period films or what actors sometimes derisively call "leathers and feathers" or "loincloth roles." For example, actor and filmmaker Georgina Lightning describes her frustration with industry categorization. As a graduate of the prestigious Academy of Dramatic Arts in Los Angeles, she had trained for and played a wide range of leading roles in Academy Repertoire Company stage productions. But when auditioning for Hollywood films, casting directors filed her portfolio under "Native American," refusing to consider her for other parts.[10]

The problems that Native cinema poses for actors and filmmakers come from external perceptions of its limitations as an industry category, imposed by executive decision-makers preoccupied with risk and profit in the entertainment market. But Native cinema can be more productively viewed as a heterogeneous rather than tightly unified phenomenon; it is perhaps best defined by its practitioners, who are less prescriptive than reviewers, scholars, executives, and marketers. In a 2009 interview, filmmaker Sterlin Harjo described his ambivalence about the label "Native filmmaker," yet at the same time expressed his appreciation for the community of filmmakers that this category has enabled:

> The only reason I say "Native cinema" is because there's nothing else to really call it, except there's a bunch of Indigenous people making films and all of a sudden it's like something new is happening. *And* we have a lot fresher stories. Right now, it feels like Hollywood is scrambling for stories. We have our pockets full of stories we can tell. The other side of it, too, is that we're influenced by all these filmmakers . . . or we can make films that don't have a Native person in them at all. When I first wanted

to be a filmmaker and an artist, I didn't ever say, "I want to be a Native filmmaker" — I just wanted to make film.[11]

Changing Film Worlds

There are many ways to think about movies. In this book, my close attention to *Smoke Signals* has taken the form of an extended critical analysis using the lens of visual sovereignty as it's been developed by scholars such as Jolene Rickard, Beverly Singer, Randolph Lewis, and Michelle Raheja. The concept of visual sovereignty is a valuable framework for thinking about *Smoke Signals* (and for defining Native cinema more broadly) because it reveals intellectual and artistic diversity in film production to be the result of politicized aesthetic choices. Visual sovereignty acknowledges Native cinema as a heterogeneous category, providing an intellectual counterpoint to market-based models that limit Native cinema's representational range to particular subject matters, film genres, character types, or target audiences. A sovereigntist approach creates a critical space for recognizing the power of strategy and self-determination in Native filmmaking — the choice to have a wide audience in mind or to follow individual or community visions; to access established cinematic languages or to innovate; to appropriate techniques from other filmmakers and film traditions or to hew closely to a traditional tribal aesthetic; to be activist or not; to make documentaries or features or experimental films or music videos; to make films about Native people or other people or all people. Rather than solving the "problem" of defining Native cinema as a category, visual sovereignty recognizes this plurality and complexity as its salient contribution.

But sovereignty is just one way of looking at *Smoke Signals*. Sherman Alexie wishes now that filmmakers would stop filming political subjects: "One of the great issues of Native American films is that we're still obsessed with our politics and we work in a very narrow aesthetic range. . . . Everything in some sense always goes back to . . . sovereignty. And I wish that an Indian filmmaker would make a movie that would center around the notion of getting laid."[12] Filmmakers like Sterlin Harjo — whose film *Four Sheets to the Wind* is in part a love story — have talked about *Smoke Signals* as a model for making small, personal films about where they're from, films that critics might best approach by thinking about reception studies, tribal epistemologies, and industry-based perspectives.

Native control over the production of *Smoke Signals* was dependent upon a fragile web of institutional training, independent financing, festival support, diversity in film distribution, and industry risk-taking. The fragmentation and atomization of audiences that affects the rest of the film industry has affected Native filmmaking as well. *Smoke Signals*'s crossover audience is much harder to reach in 2010 than it was in 1998, even though new Native feature films come out every year. "They're making the movies," Sherman Alexie says, "but nobody's seeing them." Alexie advises aspiring filmmakers to "completely give up the idea of theatrical distribution. . . . You have to go utterly independent. . . . Don't even pursue the traditional route. Stay away. Don't be a Hangs around the Fort. Be a Crazy Horse of filmmaking."[13] In this new world of cheaper equipment, lower-budget productions, and self-distribution, there are more young filmmakers but smaller audiences for their work, more Native film festivals but fewer theatrical releases. This phenomenon contributes to the diversity of Native cinema as a category even as it makes financing and distributing films much more difficult.[14]

Smoke Signals has functioned as a visible touchpoint for these diverging paths of Native film, from industry-based genre productions to micro-budget independent films for small audiences. The film's artistic, critical, and financial success, as well as its political assertion of visual sovereignty, focused the attention of diverse audiences on the aesthetic and political power of Native media storytelling. Chris Eyre calls *Smoke Signals* "an anthem for Indian country" — a song that celebrates a particular people; a definitive, galvanizing performance. It is precisely *Smoke Signals*'s ability to stake national claims, narrate Native history, and keep audiences in mind that has made it a Native cinema classic.

Appendix — Remembering *Smoke Signals*

Interviews with Chris Eyre and Sherman Alexie

The interviews that follow took place by telephone in the summer of 2008 and winter of 2009, and I have edited the transcripts for length and readability. I asked Eyre and Alexie to talk in some detail about the production and postproduction of *Smoke Signals* — including scripting, casting, and location scouting — and about their choices in visual style including shots, costuming choices, and editing. I also invited each of them to discuss *Smoke Signals*'s continuing impact on audiences and its influence on Native filmmaking. Both noted the changed landscape for independent filmmakers; the film industry's trend away from small productions powerfully limits the distribution potential of Native and other minority filmmakers. And importantly, the filmmakers also agreed on *Smoke Signals*'s lasting contribution to the cinematic landscape and to pan-Indian culture: "Every Indian has seen that movie — *every* Indian," says Alexie, while Eyre calls the film "an anthem for Indian country." Their emphasis upon the film's reception among Native audiences continues *Smoke Signals*'s original work of honoring Native presence in the viewing audience and on both sides of the camera.

Interview with Chris Eyre
Columbia, Missouri, and New York, New York, July 4, 2008

JOANNA HEARNE: First of all, thank you for making *Smoke Signals*. You haven't talked much about the story of the film's production after the Sundance Institute, so I just want to start out by inviting you to tell that story.

CHRIS EYRE: You know, in the '90s there was this whole movement of independent film that was coming to its height through the vision of the Sundance Institute. And it spawned *Clerks* and *Brothers McMullen*, and we were lucky enough to be part of that whole crescendo of independent film that . . . was a national catchphrase and piece of social consciousness. I remember my parents, you know, wanted to go see an independent film in the '90s, and nowadays you don't find people that say, "I want to go see an independent film tonight." So it was just cresting, and we were lucky enough to be part of it. I found Sherman's short story "This Is What It Means to Say Phoenix, Arizona" in the 1994, I think it was the 1993 anthology *The Lone Ranger and Tonto*. When I read this story, I said to myself, "Wow, I think that's a movie." The reason that I thought it was a movie was because it had a point A to point B back to point A chronology, you know basically it was a road movie.

And the other thing that really hit me was that when I read about Thomas Builds-the-Fire in the short story and Victor gives half of his father's cremated remains to Thomas, it really struck me that . . . he actually gifts his father to his best friend, which filmically was something I'd never seen. And that was the thing that struck me in the twelve pages of short story — the Indianness of it and the giving part of it. I mean, this is a guy who has nothing to give except a thank you, and in this Indian way he wants to give him a gift and the only thing that's available are the essence of what he's been looking for, which is his father. And that's what inspired me to say this as a movie, because of the impact that that scene had. So that was the genesis of me calling Sherman and saying, "Hey, I'd like to make this short story into a movie." And he said to himself, "Oh, here's this guy and he has no money and he wants to make a feature out of my story." But at the time, that was before *Reservation Blues*, I don't think Sherman had a novel out, it was before *Indian Killer*, so he didn't have a novel at the time. So being young guys, we thought, hey, we could do this. I was in graduate film school at NYU and we started talking about it. And I think I incited Sherman to turn to screenwriting by trying to write the first draft of the screenplay. I think that it infuriated him so much that he said, "That's not how you do it, let me show you how to do it," and he literally commandeered the screenplay and whipped out forty-four pages in like two weeks. He called himself a binge writer, and he definitely was a binge writer in creating that screenplay.

I'd submitted the year earlier to the Sundance Labs, Robert Redford's institute, and been denied. And then when we had the screenplay for *Smoke Signals*, they were inviting directors to participate in the filmmaking lab, and I submitted the screenplay *Smoke Signals*, and they accepted it and brought me to Park City, or brought me to Sundance, Utah, the institute. One of eight filmmakers that was invited to stay for the month, and work with people like Robert Redford and Denzel Washington to learn the craft. And so I spent the month up there and worked with all these amazing mentors, and that's what really gave it another push — people seeing this as a viable commodity in a world of independent film that was booming. And so even with that, it took a year and a half to find the money, even with the help of the Sundance Institute and the exposure that Sherman had and my winning best short film at NYU in the film department and independent film going the way it was going. It was before digital, we were shooting film at the time, and still the budget on the movie was two million dollars, which is a lot of money. To find somebody who wants to invest two million dollars still took a year and a half with all those things going for it.

JH: And you were pitching it pretty constantly?

CE: Yeah, we took it to several people. All of us — the institute helped, Sherman took it to some people, I took it to some people. And in the year and a half, you have people that kind of come and go and deals that aren't as attractive as you want them to be. I mean we had deal breakers in that year and a half. We had two other investors that we couldn't make terms of agreement with because Sherman and I wanted to own part of the movie. We wanted to be producers on the movie. We knew we had something that was special. John Sayles said it best when he said, "Financing a movie is like hitchhiking: just because the car stops doesn't mean you get in." And it's the same thing with financing a movie. As desperate as you are to make your movie, just because the car stops doesn't mean that you should get in. This is that part that people don't ever really talk about or recognize, the difficulty of getting a small movie financed, a personal movie financed. We had a couple of deal breakers that went on for six months at a time, and then they end up dying because we can't come to terms with the financier. We did that a few times, and finally took it to a financier that was from the Pacific Northwest, and there were producers that were involved, Scott Rosenfelt and Larry Estes. We all met, and it just kept working and working. And the money was real. And David Skinner, who's the executive producer of the movie, ended up financing the whole movie with his family, and Larry Estes and Scott Rosenfelt were the producers, and we all came to terms and got married. And thankfully it was a good marriage and we made a great baby, but it's . . . The difficulty of getting any independent film made is still the same — it's just an endeavor of love. The Sundance Institute spurred people into believing that their stories were important and personal vision was important and I was right in the thick of that, being in New York in the '90s and then going to the Sundance Labs and reading Sherman's work. So that's pretty daunting after three or four years of developing something, to say, "Okay, now the hardest part is here, now I've got to make a great movie."

JH: What happened next?

CE: We did a lot of conference calls and got agreements all signed with our attorneys, and the money started to flow so we could start hiring location people and we actually went on a location scout in the Pacific Northwest. Sherman had said that he wanted to shoot it on his reservation, which he was reluctant to do unless the producers were somebody that he wanted to stand next to on his reservation. And that was another issue, you know, who are the people you're inviting to your home, basically? So we went on location scouts on the Coeur d'Alene reservation, one of Sherman's reservations. We found locations we liked. We found a DP [director of photography] we liked, found an editor we liked. David Skinner kept allowing us to make the movie. And finally we had a schedule to shoot the movie in, must have been April of 1997. And I'll never forget after all these years of wanting to get up this great big hill, and doing a month of preproduction on location—I'd never stayed in a hotel for a month before in my life. After staying a month in a hotel in Coeur d'Alene, Idaho, I'll never forget waking up one morning and looking out my curtains and seeing semi-trucks in the parking lot, and thinking to myself, "Huh, that's strange, wonder whose those are?" And then it dawns upon you that these are our trucks for our show and it's all equipment and it's all camera packages, it's all props, it's all grip equipment. You sit there thinking it's honey wagons, it's trailers, all this stuff, and you say, "What have I got myself into?" You dream that it comes one day and then you're like, "Wow, now I have to perform." So I think we had a twenty-three-day shooting schedule. And having gone to film school, I understood it all. I understood the process and it's just a matter of having the bravery to own it. So day by day we went out and started chipping away at it. Sherman wrote a screenplay that is a beautiful screenplay and the producers were helpful and I was the only one besides the director of photography that was there for every single shot of the movie. And so we shot the movie in twenty-three days and it's kind of like fishing—you never know what you're going to catch. Even though you've made a movie, you go back to the edit room and you're like, "Okay, what the hell did we do, or what have we caught here?" And Brian Berdan, who's an amazing editor, started putting it together and then you don't have any sense of well, how much are people going to really enjoy it? Is it just us that are enjoying it? Tom Skerritt came into the edit room and I remember he left in tears. We edited for about six months and Ulali did an amazing job on the score, and it's just those symbiotic things that kind of come together.

JH: When you were going through this process, were you envisioning the different audiences for the film? Very different groups of people respond to it.

CE: I wasn't thinking of an audience. I was literally as an artist thinking that I wanted to see Thomas Builds-the-Fire and this whole near miss, which is Victor trying to find his estranged father. I mean one of the things that spoke so deeply is that I was adopted, and I never met my biological mother until I was twenty-five. So I'd missed my own parents in that sense for twenty-five years, and as an artist, I could empathize and relate to Victor so deeply. That's what it was about for me, it wasn't about thinking of the audience. It was literally about being an artist and investigating through the actors and the emotions this thing that I was really close to. I mean Sherman was very close to it, because he wrote it, but I was close to it in a different way — I understood and I empathized with the pain of the subject. I met my biological mother about two years before I made this movie, and I understood that genetic pain and memory and that's what I wanted to see in Victor. It was the best of both worlds, because Sherman and I had different ideas. At one point we were asked in the Sundance Labs what is this movie about. Sherman said it's about Victor and his estranged father. I said no, it's about Thomas Builds-the-Fire being a storyteller that helps his friend realize what it is he needs. I don't think that at any one point we could truly articulate the one thing it did for us — it did a lot of different things for both of us. I think we covered all the bases, because if you really look at the story, it's not about Thomas Builds-the-Fire, and it's not totally about Victor; they both work in this harmonious way that is balanced. Sherman and I both had a deep desire personally for this material — and you could tell because we developed it for four years.

JH: I've noticed in several of your films, *Smoke Signals* but also *Skins* and *Edge of America*, characters drive to and from reservations. You have a lot of shots of from a moving car of the landscape outside, and it's so important for *Smoke Signals*, but it's something that appears in your other films. What are the advantages of that kind of shot for you?

CE: I didn't grow up in an urban area, so my whole repertoire of seeing things is not from an urban standpoint. I grew up in southern Oregon, and I got into filmmaking through photography, through taking pictures of landscapes — a nerd taking landscape pictures.

And that's the way that I love to see my environment — patiently, calmingly out a car window as you drive and you watch the landscape change. I love the West and I love looking out the windows and I love taking drives and I love framing the shots that way, and so for me it was just about looking at the area and getting a sense of it. All reservations are different. They all look different. For me, there's a whole context that you have to place a story in filmically. My biggest high is to look at the landscape and try and incorporate that into the volume of the sensibility and feel of the movie.

I'm doing something right now in Massachusetts. It's called *The People of the First Light*, and it's part of a PBS miniseries. It's on the Wampanoag Indians, and they lived on the coast down here in Massachusetts. So you go down to the coast now and you see industrialized steeples and power plants, and you see houses and boats, and it's very colonized for four hundred years. And so to imagine that landscape without the houses and the boats and the industrialized buildings, that's kind of shooting in landscapes. So we're trying to find that piece of coastline that speaks to a time before there was a lot here. We've been scouting for this beach and we finally found a parcel of beach that's probably only half a mile long. It's reminiscent of a landscape that I can conjure for being this place.

I love the landscapes and taking the photographs of landscapes. I have one shot that I love to do out of a car and when you take a shot of two characters sitting across from each other, one on the left and one on the right, they're facing each other, there's a term that you say, you know, give me a 50–50, and the DP says, "Okay, I got ya." It means that it's balanced, it's 50 percent of this character, 50 percent of that character and in *Skinwalkers* and I think in *Skins* and some other projects, I have a 50–50 shot that's a landscape and a character. You put the camera on the hood, you frame up the character, and you say, "Now I want to pan more to the right." And the DP says, "Well, there's nothing out there." That's the point — that you have 50 percent of the frame on the character driving and you have 50 percent of the frame on the landscape and the background.

Hopefully you won't see too much of the road depending on how you frame it. It's almost like a split screen, imagining the landscape. And that shot speaks to me as a photographer.

JH: In *Smoke Signals*, did you shoot the scenes on the bridge, the Spokane Bridge, on the actual bridge over the actual Spokane Falls in downtown Spokane or did you shoot it elsewhere?

CE: Yeah, that was actually on the bridge there in Spokane. We went out and scouted it and the runoff was pretty great in the spring and we thought, wow, these falls look beautiful. And we went back a week later and they had turned the falls off at the dam, and the falls were dried up. We checked to make sure they would be on the day we were shooting, they were, or they got them turned on. We went back and got that shot. Luckily we'd realized that at some point they go off and somebody governs that and not to show up on that day.

JH: I was reading in the screenplay that the footage that you originally shot, the footage that leads up to the bridge, was shot upstream.

CE: It was scripted where it started with a small creek and it went all the way back to a large river. It was scripted very differently. And it was shot and the editor, Brian Berdan, found a way to constitute the material in a way that we hadn't thought of and it turned out really nice. There was also a scripted scene — I don't know if you have the screenplay — where Victor's father comes out of the water. And that's what inspired the reversal of the order. So the way it was scripted was different from the way it ended up in the movie. And we shot it the way it was scripted and then just in the editing process it became better doing it in a reverse chronology. And it's because we had to lose Gary Farmer coming out of the water at the end of the movie. What happens is after he dies he comes out of the water and he greets young Victor and then you follow the ashes all the way downstream to Arnold Joseph coming out of the water to a young Victor. And the scene just didn't work as well as we wanted it to, so we reversed all the material.

JH: Yeah, it's beautiful. Did he physically reverse the footage or reverse the chronology of the editing?

CE: He reversed the chronology of the editing.

JH: I'm sorry I have to ask, but why does Adam Beach wear a wig? Did he not want to cut his hair because of another film role?

CE: Well, there's an unspoken rule with Native American actors that you really can't ask them to cut their hair, because this is something that they live by. Because every year there are period pieces that come out that people want roles in. For the sake of doing a movie, it's a burden to ask a Native American actor to cut their hair.

JH: So both professional reasons and personal reasons.

CE: Yeah, it's a cultural principle. So we didn't ask Adam to cut his hair. We used a wig, and the wig probably wasn't as expensive as it should have been [laughter], it probably needed to be a better quality wig. And the way that worked was that for years I wouldn't admit that he had a bad wig, because it was too close. But no, it's a bad wig. I can say that ten years later. And so the way that it worked was that we were about nineteen days into twenty-three days of shooting and I'd approved the wig, and when it showed up on set, it was much worse than what I remembered it to be. We had two wigs, because they're so expensive, one to cut and one to wear, just because of budget. And on the nineteenth day when he showed up, Adam looked at me and said, "How do I look, dude?" I looked at him and I said, "You look great." I said, "Give me just a minute." I turned around, I walked behind a trailer, and I thought to myself, I think I've just ruined my movie. Because at the time I knew there was nothing else to shoot except his scenes with the wig, and I knew that we weren't going to take a day at a cost of $75,000 and not shoot, and I knew that in order to get a wig, a new wig, it would take two days. There was no way we were going to do anything but shoot. So in fact, we did keep shooting. And when Harvey Weinstein bought the movie, he said, "The wig's fine." Because we did entertain doing a reshoot, and Harvey Weinstein, who owned the movie then, said, "The wig's fine, the wig stays, we're not going to reshoot it." So for years I deflected the comment, but now I can be honest about yeah it was a bad wig but a beloved movie.

JH: Where did you shoot the scenes in Phoenix, Arizona — obviously they weren't shot in Phoenix —

CE: They were shot around Soap Lake, Washington. In the arid desert of Washington, they were shot. We found a couple canyons with cliffs and of those couple canyons, we said okay this is Arizona. And actually we found one specific area near Soap Lake that actually looks somewhat like Arizona. So we used that one little escarpment or whatever that is, outcropping of cliff and rock, and I think it worked really well.

JH: The film was a huge success at Sundance, clearly. I'm sure that then you went on to experience different reactions in different communities, and probably for the last ten years ongoing continuing reactions and responses from people.

CE: I don't have anything to compare it to, and my biggest fear is that it will be the movie that I'm best known for. [laughter] It was the second-highest grossing independent film of the year. Martin Scorsese wrote me an unsolicited letter about how much he liked the movie. It just showed up in my mailbox. It was a big to do at the time. President Clinton screened it at the White House. I was getting calls from stars, movie stars, and doing major development with a lot of people.

Ten years later, I'm happy that people still love it. Every year, I screen it to people and get responses. And I screened it for the Oregon Indian boarding school, Chemawa, last fall — four hundred Indian school student kids that are sixteen or fifteen, fourteen, seventeen. They're sitting there reciting lines back to me on stage. That's the kind of reception where you're like, wow! It's an anthem, I think, for Indian country, a filmic anthem that people seem to really love. Mothers still come up to me and say, "How do you get your son or daughter to stop coming up to me saying, 'Hey, Victor!'" I've screened it at Leavenworth Federal Penitentiary for Indian inmates and seen them think about the forgiveness of their own fathers or mothers, or cry, or come up to me at the end and say stuff like, "I'm gonna write a screenplay." And they ask me really technical questions like, "Does the act break between two and three come on 178 or 197?" Leonard Peltier saw the movie at Leavenworth.

We had a ten-year reunion, and Sherman and myself and Evan were there. It was nice after ten years that the Agua Calientes had a big gala, I think there were a thousand people there, and we got to answer questions. I remember screening in Japan and Germany. In Japan, there was just such a lukewarm reception, and it's because it becomes very anthropological because it's about Indians. In Japan there was more of a quiet politeness over what they were supposed to be understanding. Year after year, I still get a lot of people commenting on it. I get it every month.

JH: Do you see *Smoke Signals* as having had an impact on Native filmmaking?

CE: I absolutely think it has. I know that there's a whole generation of Native filmmakers right now that didn't exist ten years ago. When I was in graduate film school in 1992 at NYU, the horizon was a handful of documentary Native American filmmakers, maybe a couple of narrative filmmakers that hadn't broken out in any way. The number of film festivals has totally spiked and generationally, a lot of people want to be in entertainment now. There's more actors, Native American people wanting to be actresses and actors and directors and musicians. I think that right now the whole hard part is getting the movie seen, because I know a lot of these independent Native movies are being made, but I'm in the same boat — to get the movie seen is a whole different trick. I've said this before — if *Smoke Signals* were to come out today, it might not have a theatrical release like it did ten years ago. It's more difficult to place an independent film than it's ever been. So all these people making independent films now don't necessarily have a place to get them released, except straight to video, and acquisition prices for those are not very high, and even to get a straight to video deal is still work. I think *Smoke Signals* had an effect and it had good timing, and I like to think that people were inspired by it, and I think that there's a whole wave of Native filmmakers that will find their way, myself included, to new ways of being seen and heard. Really what it's about is being heard. I happen to be an Indian person, but it's really just about being heard as an individual.

JH: How does that put pressure on your filmmaking and the filmmaking you see in other Native films in terms of representing Indigenous issues?

CE: I think the representation of Indigenous issues is an endeavor that all of us participate in — all the movies that get made every year by Indian people. I mean, Sherman made a movie, Randy Redroad — I produced a movie for him years ago — my friend Georgina Lightning has a movie called *Older than America*. We made a movie called *Imprint* that Michael Lynn directed. For me, I don't feel a need to make culturally relevant films. I feel the need to make films that are personal and that nourish and entertain. They might have cultural elements to them. I mean one of the biggest misnomers is that *Smoke Signals* is a cultural movie. It's not a cultural movie at all. I mean the most Native, the most Indigenous movie ever made for a commercial audience, that was absorbed by a commercial audience, is probably *The Fast Runner*. I don't feel the need personally to try to carry a cultural flag as I do to carry a human flag that happens to be connected to a culture.

JH: Thank you so much for talking to me. I appreciate it so much.

Interview with Sherman Alexie
Columbia, Missouri, and Seattle, Washington, February 10, 2009

JOANNA HEARNE: Thank you for doing this interview. I've been thinking about [*Smoke Signals*] for the past year and for years before that.

SHERMAN ALEXIE: Sorry about that. [laughter]

JH: You know, I liked it when it first came out but it's continued to grow on me. How does this industry or independent film landscape look different now for Native filmmakers than it did before or right after *Smoke Signals*?

SA: *Smoke Signals* remains the only film ever written and directed by Native Americans that received national and international distribution. It's the only film that ever went even remotely mainstream.

JH: What about young people making *Four Sheets to the Wind* and *Fifth World?*

SA: They're making the movies, but nobody's seeing them.

JH: So it's a distribution problem.

SA: And still, Sterlin as well. You know he's the big name now among the young guys, filmmakers. I think what has happened is that some of the business has changed. The studios are only making big movies, and the smaller movies they used to make are now being made by the smaller studios and the independents. *Taxi Driver* wouldn't be made by a studio now; it'd be made by some independent producers, by one of the independent companies. So what has happened is all these white independent films which used to be made by the studios are now being made by the independents that at one point might have made brown-skinned films. So the change in Hollywood has put minority filmmakers even farther into the margins.

JH: Do you see a generational influence of *Smoke Signals* on younger Native filmmakers and Native artists?

SA: I don't see those films, so I don't know. I know culturally speaking, every Indian has seen that movie. Every Indian. Over the last ten years I've met ninety guys named Victor who cursed at me because they spend their entire lives getting "Hey, Victor" from every Indian they know. So it has entered into the Native American pop cultural lexicon. I hear about it and from it all the time. And pretty much every reading I do in Indian country, two or three people come dressed in Fry Bread Power T-shirts. It has enormous cultural value in our world. . . . More than anything I think what *Smoke Signals* captured was the way that Indians relate to each other and that sense of magical realism and cultural stuff, you know, the 49s and the songs and the in-jokes. We artistically represented that but that's who we are as Indian people, so hopefully it influenced people in their films to present more of themselves than to have some specific political aim. I think I said in the *LA Weekly* article that one of the great issues of Native American films is that we're still obsessed with our politics and we work in a very narrow aesthetic range. You could say the same about our literature — that everything in some sense always goes back to the issue of sovereignty. And I wish that an Indian filmmaker would make a movie that would center around the notion of getting laid.

JH: That doesn't seem to be the powerful motivating journey in *Smoke Signals*.

SA: Exactly. Well, for Victor . . . well, there's a novel coming, my new novel, about Thomas and Victor ten years later.

JH: That's very exciting. Will you make a movie out of it?

SA: We'll try. It's called *Fire with Fire*. It's Thomas, there's a conceit in it, a sort of metaphysical conceit, that Thomas has seen the movie . . . but he points out all the lies in the movie.

JH: So when you're writing this book *Fire with Fire* and reimagining Thomas, how do you go back into this character?

SA: The thing is that Evan's Thomas is gone for me now. That was the only way it was possible for me to write this. He's gone. I mean, that's one of the reasons it took ten years was because he had to be erased. And one of the ways I dealt with it was to make *Smoke Signals* a part of the novel's world.

JH: So how did you then begin to think about Thomas as a character who's seen himself on screen. He's received, he's sort of watching himself.

SA: Well, Thomas says it in the movie, right, "The only thing sadder than Indians on TV is Indians watching Indians on TV."

JH: That's my favorite line.

SA: Evan improvised that. That's Evan's line.

JH: When did he improvise it?

SA: On the spot. I wish it was my line, but it's not.

JH: Were they improvising a lot on set?

SA: No, no. There were a couple moments but that was the big one. I tried to do that with *Fancydancing* but the ability of Indian actors to do that varies widely, because they haven't been trained to do, they haven't been expected to do it. But where were we?

JH: I was asking about reconstructing the character of Thomas as someone who is immersed not just in popular culture but also in himself.

SA: Well, it was actually fairly simple, because I have become famous. I am a pop-culture figure. That identity, that part of me, I can easily step away from and look at — and the reactions to me, how my life is, the ways in which I have to conduct myself and the things I have to be aware of. So perhaps other people who get more famous or who deal with whatever kind of level of fame get all drowned in it and lost in it. But I've always been able to keep separate from it. So it was easy to write about Thomas looking at himself, because I'm always stepping back and looking at myself, too, and finding it vastly amusing.

JH: One of the things that made *Smoke Signals* successful with so many audiences is this powerful engagement with popular culture.

SA: Well, that's always the thing that's curious to me, when people look at my work they always say I'm wrestling with popular culture. I mean I guess in some sense I am but I'm engaged with it, we all are. I think there's always sort of this mode of academic discourse, I'm recalling specific reviews or interviews especially by Indian scholars that sort of treat my engagement with popular culture as some sort of betrayal. I'm remembering the phrase that I can't remember who wrote it, was it Gloria Bird who wrote that I had failed to interrogate pop culture. That whole line of thinking always assumes that we Indians are outside of it. It also assumes that pop culture is somehow less than other parts of our culture. You know Shakespeare was pop culture. The *Iliad* and the *Odyssey* were pop culture. You can make arguments about maybe their pop culture was better, but I don't know, I would put *The Sopranos* up against *King Lear*.

JH: What did you think of the way *Smoke Signals* was taken up? I mean it was parodied in *Joe Dirt*.

SA: Oh it's hilarious! I was so happy!

JH: People parody it all the time and engage in its language and characters with one another but also it's been taken up and parodied and imitated and owned in a way.

SA: I'm incredibly happy.

JH: Do you think that a really broad audience picks up those references? Do the people who watch *Joe Dirt* get that?

SA: Of course not. No. I mean, in fact, I remember when the producers of *Joe Dirt*, they hired Adam to be in it, but they actually wanted Evan. They got the actors mixed up.

JH: You were talking about the in-jokes. A lot of your humor is so ironic.

SA: Well, I always refer to those moments in my books or my movies as trap doors. Indians and those really familiar with Indian culture will fall in, everyone else will keep walking. I guess the prime example of that is when Lucy and Velma are driving the Malibu backward, in *Smoke Signals*. When they first pop up and people realize they're driving in reverse, the whole theater laughs, but after a bit you can feel the non-Indians stop laughing, you can feel their collective, "Now what the hell?" But the Indians keep laughing.

JH: And is that recognition?

SA: Yeah, the state of our automobiles. I can imagine if I was in an audience of that movie in a really poor white community, let's say, they played it in Appalachia or northern Michigan among white folks or wherever, or I suppose any poor community in the world of any color, I think that would get a bigger laugh from poor folks in the audience, so I think that was cultural but also a class-based issue. . . . There's also more stuff, too, going on in that scene. Their names are Velma and Lucy, making fun of *Thelma & Louise*. That's actually my car.

JH: That's your car?

SA: Yeah, I was conceived in that automobile.

JH: That changes that scene for me. [laughter] One of the things I wanted to ask you was about shooting the film on the Coeur d'Alene reservation. You write in the screenplay about the first day of shooting being very close to where your father was born. What was your role in organizing the locations? What was the reaction of the people there to the shooting?

SA: Well, I missed a bunch of it, because my son was actually born during the shooting. So my son is the same age as the movie. I was on the rez for the shooting but I was not there at the bridge that day, so everything I know about that shooting is second hand. But the books were so well received on the rez and in Spokane at that point. You know I didn't have the kind of national reputation that I have now, but people gathered to watch. And on the Coeur d'Alene rez, of course, all the relationships, the ambassadors, all the people on the movie from the rez, helping out, the catering and that stuff, was done by my cousins. So the professionals on [the] film set did their job, but the people they were working with on the reservation were my cousins, so that just made it all much easier.

JH: And did you organize a lot of that?

SA: Yeah, I made all the introductions.

JH: And was there an economic impact on the reservation and the surrounding community?

SA: Well, yeah. The hotels were in Coeur d'Alene and all, but it was still a tiny film. A million and a half dollars? The Coeur d'Alenes are pretty successful — that's not a whole lot of money to the Coeur d'Alene. I mean it was more a cultural event. In fact, the reason we didn't shoot on the Spokane rez was because they wouldn't let us, the council voted not to let us do it . . . let's just call it tribal stuff. And it actually became a campaign issue in the next election. People were very angry that Adam Beach and Gary Farmer and Tantoo Cardinal had been wandering around the Coeur d'Alene rez and not the Spokane rez. So to this day, I still hear about it, people are still mad. "We could have had Clark Gable and Scarlett O'Hara here."

JH: How did you participate in the casting, finding Evan Adams?

SA: Evan Adams. You know . . . Chris shot a short film based on the screenplay. And a friend of mine played Suzy in that short film. She . . . actually knew Evan, and Evan was willing to do it for nothing for a student film and had his schedule open, so he came to do it. They shot it in New York somewhere. And Chris was actually calling me when he was shooting his film and saying how amazing Evan was and then he sent me a VHS copy of some scenes. The student film, it's the same scene when Evan and Adam are walking to the trailer and Evan is doing that Death Wish monologue.

JH: Yeah, yeah.

SA: Evan is doing it, and even at that point, very early on in the process, he had it. So just seeing Evan walking, we knew it. I knew it. So he was cast previously. Adam was cast without audition. Gary. Tantoo. Indians work tiny. We knew all these folks.

JH: So did you and Chris just communicate back and forth to do the casting, how about this person, how about this person, I'm in touch with this person . . .

SA: Yeah, for the main people, and then there were casting sessions in Vancouver, Los Angeles and Seattle. So some of the secondary roles, some of the smaller roles, we did do the casting process.

JH: Did you coach the actors in their roles at all? Or converse with them?

SA: Evan actually was the only one I had anything to do with. You know Chris did all the other stuff, but since Evan knew that Thomas was in large part me, we talked a lot about it. He would call me from set and talk about scenes and talk about what happened. But part of that was simply that Evan and I really connected as people. We're both Salish, and both had similar histories, so we just connected in all sorts of ways, and then he just borrowed my eccentricities.

JH: I love his performance. When you were scripting, how did you think about performance? Particularly at that early point when you were forming the movie as a movie in your mind and actualizing it in the script.

SA: Well, I didn't know shit. It was my first screenplay. So I didn't know anything about that. That was all Chris's job. That was the producer's job, not mine. I was just trying to make a believable character and make the story he was telling and all of that. Well I guess the thing is . . . it was rare for them to even get those many lines. In the entertainment industry, it's all about monosyllables, even in contemporary film . . . it's never about language. So in writing all that stuff and allowing everybody to talk in poetry and be funny and be smart and have a wide range of emotions and verbal moments — that was the big thing, just the sheer size of their vocabulary.

JH: When you were writing the script as your first screenplay, were you aware of the need to make it financially successful? Were you balancing that with the other work you were doing in terms of language and representations of these characters that were really a first in terms of their language and their poetry?

SA: If you actually film my books as they are written, they would be RS or NC-17s. So you know it was purposely written to be a PG, PG-13 movie. I knew that had to be the case. One of the issues I do have with the movie ten years later is it's far tamer than my work is. It's far tamer than the book it's based on. So there's a gentler tone at all sorts of moments than I would otherwise have had. But of course, film is a collaboration, too, so Chris has a more mainstream aesthetic than I do. . . . Generally in the movie, if it's weird, I'm probably more responsible for it.

JH: How did that work when you began to make the script into a movie?

SA: Well, Chris just shot. In writing the screenplay, the producers and Chris had notes by and large, but mostly they wound up just shooting what I wrote. So I had freedom in that — discretion. It never happened again.

JH: How did the work and the feeling of making film change for you over Smoke Signals, The Business of Fancydancing, and I know you've written about writing Hollywood —

SA: Well, with Smoke Signals I was utterly spoiled. After the Sundance workshop, Chris and I worked with a couple sets of producers that didn't work out for various reasons. Then Shadowcatcher here in Seattle called, and I'd met with them many years earlier. And they called and asked what I was up to, and I went and met with them, and they asked me what I'd been working on. And I said, this screenplay. And they said, well do you have a copy of it. And of course I had a copy of it in my bag with me, and I gave it to them. And that was on a Friday and they came back Monday wanting to do it, and two weeks later we were in preproduction. It was so quick and everybody was so excited and we just ended up shooting what I wrote, and in the editing room we had to fix a lot of shit, because I wrote poorly, structurally screwed things up, budgetwise scenes didn't pan out the way they should have. There were all sorts of editing decisions that we needed to correct other decisions. But in the end, it ended up being very much a collaborative creation that I was pleased with and the whole process was very respectful and in fact deferential to me as a screenwriter and originator of the whole story. But since then? I mean, *Fancydancing* was all me, so I had absolute control, but in the process of trying to get anything else made, even working with Shadowcatcher after that, working with Miramax trying to get something made, working on scripts for Hollywood, other studios. . . . I mean I understand the process, I understand why everybody gets to have an opinion, but in the end the screenwriter, the originator of the materials, is by far the least important person and has the least amount of power and influence over the process, and is the one most easily replaced.

JH: Have you done any work with Hollywood productions since that time?

SA: Only in development, only writing for hire. And you know, it's funny, I always thought of myself as such a failure, because nothing ever got made, but I never really paid attention to my screenwriters' guild pension. I'd get the paperwork and file it and file it and never thought about it, and then I looked at it one day, because we were meeting with our money guy. . . . I'd always talked about the pension but I just never thought it was going to be like it is. And when I retire from screenwriting, or when I hit the mandatory age of fifty-five when you can start collecting, I'll be making about $2,800 a month on my pension. So if it all goes to hell, I can be living on the rez.

JH: Writing screenplays?

SA: I worked on twenty, twenty-five screenplays in the years after *Smoke Signals*. And I worked with some incredible directors, you know. Big names, big dudes. I worked with every studio. I worked with HBO. I worked with the networks. I had two TV series almost go to pilot. I had a great run. . . . If it was the only business I was in, I could live with the compromises, because that would be my job and we all have to do that. But in the writing world, in the book world, I am fricking Fidel Castro. I am Stalin. There's no Obama thing going on. There's no democracy going on in the book world. I have absolute control over my career. Absolute. Absolute. I just can't live with that contract.

JH: So when did you stop doing the screen work?

SA: The last thing I actually got paid for in Hollywood was four years ago now.

JH: Now you've just been producer for *The Exiles*.

SA: I'm helping it get out into the world.

JH: Do you see that as sort of a continuation of the work you've done in film?

SA: Well, you know, *The Exiles* is such an interesting movie. I hope by associating with it I not only bring this great filmmaker, his work to greater visibility, but by doing it, I hope I inspire Native filmmakers, young filmmakers who see and realize that this nearly fifty-year-old film is far more interesting and revolutionary than any of the films we've made about ourselves. So get your asses in gear, Indians. I do not need to see another documentary about fishing rights. Nobody needs to see another documentary about fishing rights. Your fishing rights are just like my fishing rights. I know it, they broke the treaties, we're trying to get them back. There's court cases. I know. Now where's that movie about you trying to get laid?

JH: You're talking about releasing the film as an address to young Native filmmakers. Have you seen reactions to *Smoke Signals* in young people change from when it was first released and over the past years?

SA: I suppose one thing that has happened is there's of course more kids who haven't seen it — when you're talking about teenagers now or who were just toddlers when it came out, or college students. Some of them haven't seen it. Or they've seen it, and it's so new to them, I guess that's what I like too. It's not everybody seeing it for the first time, but you run into people seeing it for the first time and they feel like it's so new, and then you have to explain to them, no, we shot this thing twelve years ago. It was released ten years ago. It's not new. It's sad. It's not new. It should be new. There should be more. This is just it. I guess there's that same combination of loving the excitement of somebody seeing it for the first time, an Indian kid, but also the sadness of having to tell them that this is still it. And then non-Indians, it's been great. Two weeks ago I met a man who kept in his wallet, in one of those baseball card protectors for collectors . . . in that little plastic thing was his ticket for seeing *Smoke Signals* in Spokane at its premiere in 1998, which was amazing.

JH: That's a fan.

SA: A white guy. Yeah, and then in Philadelphia on book tour in 2007, I met a couple whose first date was a blind date and they'd seen *Smoke Signals* and they'd got married a year later and they've been married ever since.

JH: So people come to you with these stories about their first viewing of this film?

SA: Yeah, which is always great. And then you look on YouTube, people are doing their parodies and their remakes and their mockings of *Smoke Signals*.

JH: You've started writing really deliberately for a young adult audience. . . . Could you talk a bit about writing in this focused way for a young audience — and are you adapting *The Absolutely True Diary of a Part-Time Indian* for film as well?

SA: Yeah, it's optioned and I really like the folks. See once again, I really like them but this book which has sold over three hundred thousand copies, which won ever frickin' award imaginable, incredibly, a huge success . . . and you know, it's not even optioned, because nobody would option it to make it. So I have a handshake deal with these cool producers, and we're going to try to write the screenplay and go out with the screenplay. That's happening again. It just kills me, because you go to these meetings with these producers and these executives and the mucky muck Hollywood folks and they would talk about how much they loved the book and how their kids were reading it in school. A few executives actually called us in because their kids had brought the book home from school telling their dad how much they loved it and how it should be made. Or their mom. And then I'd go into the meeting and nothing would happen.

But in terms of writing the books themselves, my books, particularly *Lone Ranger* and then *Smoke Signals*, have always done really well with young folks, teenage audiences. So young adult publishers have often talked to me, and I get invited to high schools and I've done librarian things for a long time. So it was always brewing, I'd just never really had the idea. I was always thinking outside myself for a YA novel and then realized one day wait, [my first year at Reardon] was pretty goddamned amazing. And it was.

JH: One of the moments you talk about in the opening of the published screenplay for *Smoke Signals*, about the first movie that you remember seeing as a kid, is *The Texas Chainsaw Massacre*, and then you talk about the first day of filming *Smoke Signals*, filming very close to where your father was born. What was that transition like, from being a spectator to being a producer of film?

SA: It's pretty amazing to be in charge of our own images. I'm sure Chris would tell you the same. I think we were immediately aware that we were doing something revolutionary, that it was a revolutionary moment. Yeah, I knew that. I don't remember if Chris and I ever spoke about it directly in those terms. I know how excited we were. We knew it. We knew it. We were doing something amazing. Of course, we hoped it would change the world forever. In bigger ways and more dramatic ways, it didn't. Ten years ago I think it was still possible. I think with the endless resources, the endless opportunities, the endless options now in media, I don't think there's a film that will ever do it again. But in 1998, it was still possible, there weren't as many options.

JH: So when did you know that you first wanted to make movies? Was this just the first one?

SA: Well, that was an earlier thought of mine before I thought about writing books. Making movies seemed to be more of a possibility than writing books. So yeah. I was always in the school plays on the rez. Because I was the best reader and the least shy, I was always narrator or whatever lead. So in the Christmas play I was the narrator and Santa Claus. Because I had a better memory, too, I could play all sorts of people, because I could remember the lines.

JH: When you were scripting the film, how did you imagine the audiences reacting to it? Did you have an imaginary audience when you were writing it?

SA: Uh, you know, Indians. I guess, where was the first time we screened it in its entirety? God, when was that? Oh yeah, it was here, in Seattle, and my mom and my dad and my siblings came. I guess in some sense I was always writing for them, since everything is about us and so biographical and autobiographical. So when they loved it so much, that was probably it.

JH: And then have there been audience reactions that have really surprised you?

SA: Minnesota. Minneapolis. Screened it at the university there and the sound kept going out, going in and out, but there were enough Indians in the crowd who had seen it enough times, they started filling in dialogue. The Rocky Horror Indian Picture Show.

JH: What were your strongest influences when you were writing *Smoke Signals*?

SA: Oh wow, it's so funny, it's twelve years ago. Certainly, you just think about any oddball road movies. But I actually went on this trip. That's the primary influence. My best friend from the rez and I went to Phoenix to get his dad's remains and we drove them back. So at the most basic level the primary influence was what actually happened. And after that it ended up being all the road movies imaginable.

JH: Some reviewers, Roger Ebert for example, sees and writes about *Smoke Signals* as a continuation of *Powwow Highway*—I wonder what you think about that.

SA: Well, it's because it's about Indians and they go on a road trip. So, yeah. And I like the movie *Powwow Highway*, but I think in many ways *Smoke Signals* is actually an antidote to that. *Powwow Highway*: there's some pretty goofy stuff in there, and they take the goofy stuff seriously. Like when they're wading into the stream there in South Dakota in December, which would have killed them. Or when A. Martinez is stopping that police car and all of the sudden he's dressed in warrior gear, there's that fantasy moment. You know when Philbert survives that awful wreck down the side of the road. I think in all sorts of ways Hollywood intrudes on *Powwow Highway* and it doesn't do that in *Smoke Signals*. I think maybe because *Powwow Highway* was made by non-Indians. And also the sense of humor and all that stuff that does make it in that, they borrowed that from us. Not the other way around. That said, when I first saw *Powwow Highway*, that was like "wow." It made me very happy.

JH: What about Lester FallsApart, is that a reference to the Chinua Achebe novel?

SA: You know, I first wrote that guy, Lester FallsApart, in 1987. After I read that fucking book. And you're the first person who's ever asked me that. . . . But that's the thing, I'm an Indian guy, so people wouldn't assume I'd actually read something. . . . The only thing they sometimes do is they'll refer to, that's borrowed from Yeats—

JH: Things fall apart.

SA: Yeah, they'll remember that, they won't go back to the novel. Because I'm a poet, they think I'll be quoting poets and not international novels.

JH: It's your website identity, and it's this incredible character in *Smoke Signals*—people love this character. What's the influence of the novel and why is it so prominent?

SA: Well, really basically that's a Sisyphus novel, and there's no identity in the world more Sisyphean than Native Americans.

JH: Trying to make a movie.

SA: Trying to make a career, trying make a life, and the sand just keeps fucking pouring.

JH: Why the emphasis on cars? Why is the movie so invested in cars and the road trip as a genre, as an icon, as something that's specifically Indian?

SA: Because I live in the West. Most of us live in the West and it takes a long fucking time to get anywhere. It really is that. On a snowy day, it sometimes took me ninety minutes to get to high school. Twice I snowmobiled to high school. At one point in our lives, horses were vitally important to get places. Cars just took their place. That's always the argument. People are trying to change car culture in the United States, the dependence on gas and oil and that stuff, but the point is cars are sacred.

JH: When *Smoke Signals* was first released, what did you think of the press coverage and the reviews? I've read so much really positive stuff.

SA: I'm just the type of guy who always tends to believe the negative ones. I think Michael Atkinson really hammered it in the *Village Voice*, so I really liked that one — just that whole racial inferiority complex. Michael Atkinson's hammer of it just gave me a giant erection. I can't remember the positive ones. Although Peter Travers, he put us as one of his top ten movies of the year. I remember that, that was amazing. I thought, wow, really? Are you sure? Although his also has the saddest note. I read the review again and it said something about "the welcome of a startling new original voice in American film" or something like that and the notion of the hope that there's going to be more. Looking at it now, it's sort of like, it sort of feels like the obituary for a promising athlete who died in a car wreck. That's what it feels like. So those are all my positive memories of the reviews. [laughter]

JH: I want to be more optimistic.

SA: Ninety-nine percent of them were incredible I'm sure. Let me look on Rotten Tomatoes. What is the percentage of positive?

JH: So what will happen? There are a lot more young people interested in movies and making movies and acting than there were.

SA: What I tell them is completely give up the idea of theatrical distribution. Don't even pursue it. You're dreaming you're going to be Angelina Jolie, and it doesn't happen. Our Angelina Jolie is Irene Bedard, and she can't get a fucking role. Nothing. Our Brad Pitt is Adam Beach. He gets nothing. So give it up, don't even try. You have to go utterly independent. And with the technology available now, you can get an HD camera for a couple hundred bucks. You can get Final Cut Express on your computer for a couple hundred dollars. You can get started with about a thousand dollars. Yeah, you have to avoid it, just don't do it. Don't do it. People get mad at me.

JH: Don't do the thousand-dollar independent start up?

SA: Don't even pursue the traditional route. Stay away. Don't be a Hangs around the Fort. Be a Crazy Horse of filmmaking. Be Red Cloud.

JH: What can people do to further pursue and see Native films, in this context of no major distribution — when it's possible to make things on a very low budget but not easy to see them?

SA: Everybody has high speed Internet now. Everybody has a DVD player, and DVD burners are cheap. As I'm saying all this, there's a subtext here of don't be surprised in about six months to a year when my website is featuring something else entirely. We are learning technology. I have bought my cameras.

JH: I really appreciate your insights. Thank you for making the film.

SA: Thank you for this.

Notes

INTRODUCTION

1. Fraser, "An Interview with Sherman Alexie," 67–68. See Alexie's description of learning to read with a Superman comic book as a young child, in the essay "Superman and Me."

2. Clark, "No Reservations," 8.

3. Shohat and Stam, *Unthinking Eurocentrism*, 205.

4. West and West, "Sending Cinematic Smoke Signals."

5. Lehrer, "A Dialogue on Race." In the interview, Alexie also emphasized the extreme poverty of Native communities ("A poor Native American faces more hurdles than a poor anybody") and the importance of education for Native youth.

6. See appendix, interview with Chris Eyre.

7. LaRocque, *When the Other Is Me*, 164, 162.

8. Tatonetti, "Dancing That Way," 3.

9. See Riley, "Sucking the Quileute Dry."

10. Imperialism involves the domination of one people by another as part of a systemic, nation-based territorial and economic expansion. It can also be understood as an ideology and an epistemology, a way of knowing and imagining the world that is transmitted not just by written documents but also, in the twentieth and twenty-first centuries, through audiovisual media. Colonialism is the name for the concrete processes — for example, policies and acts of subjugation, settlement, and resource extraction — that manifest the larger phenomenon of imperialism. Linda Tuhiwai Smith defines colonialism as "imperialism's outpost, the fort and port of imperial outreach" (*Decolonizing Methodologies*, 23).

11. Runningwater, "Smoke Signals."

12. Cox, "This Is What It Means to Say Reservation Cinema," 84–85.

13. For updated figures, see the official websites for the Coeur d'Alene Tribe, http://www.cdatribe-nsn.gov/, and for the Spokane Tribe of Indians, http://www.spokanetribe.com/.

14. West and West, "Sending Cinematic Smoke Signals."

15. For example, the "commerce clause" of the U.S. Constitution acknowledges tribes as separate political entities in articulating congressional authority to "regulate commerce with foreign nations, and among the several states, and with the Indian tribes." See Deloria and Lytle, *Nations Within*.

16. Bruyneel, *Third Space of Sovereignty*, 23–24.

17. Warrior, *Tribal Secrets*, 87, 97.

18. Government boarding schools for Native children were part of a coercive assimilationist program of education from the late nineteenth through the

mid-twentieth century. Book-length studies of the boarding schools include Lomawaima, *They Called It Prairie Light*; Child, *Boarding School Seasons*; Szasz, *Education and the American Indian*; Fear-Segal, *White Man's Club*; and Adams, *Education for Extinction*.

19. Alfred, "Sovereignty," 43.

20. Barker, "For Whom Sovereignty Matters," 26.

21. The quotation was from Clarkson's LaFontaine-Baldwin Lecture of 2007, quoted in J. Miller, *Compact, Contract, Covenant*, 345n. Miller adds that "the phrase was frequently used prior to 2007 by Hon. David Arnot, Treaty Commissioner for Saskatchewan from 1997–2007."

22. See the work of historians such as J. R. Miller and Olive Dickason (Métis) on First Nations treaties and history for discussions of specific commercial pacts, territorial treaties, numbered treaties, the Indian Act, and 1990s treaty laws in Canada, as well as issues of blood quantum, enfranchisement, and assimilation resulting from the "differential legal standing" of First Nations peoples under Canadian constitutional law.

23. Raheja, "Reading Nanook's Smile," 1163.

24. See Singer, *Wiping the War Paint off the Lens*, 2; Cobb, "This Is What It Means to Say *Smoke Signals*," 207.

25. Rickard, "Sovereignty," 51.

26. Lewis, *Alanis Obomsawin*, 175; Raheja, "Reading Nanook's Smile," 1161, 1165.

27. This definition differs, then, from interpretations such as Robert Warrior's articulation of "intellectual sovereignty."

28. Barclay, "Celebrating Fourth Cinema," 9.

29. Columpar, *Unsettling Sights*, 6.

30. See Ginsburg, Abu-Lughod, and Larkin, *Media Worlds*.

31. L. Smith, *Decolonizing Methodologies*, 146–47. Quentin Youngberg also refers to Sherman Alexie's process of "'Indianing' the (white) literary sphere," which he compares to what he describes as Alexie's project of "queering the Native sphere" in the film *The Business of Fancydancing* (2002). See Youngberg, "Interpenetrations," 60.

32. Quoted in L. Smith, *Decolonizing Methodologies*, 146.

33. Specifically, Alexie notes that the word "universalism" is often a coded way of talking in racialized terms about audiences: "When people say universal they mean white people get it. . . . 'Universal' is often a way to negate the particularity of a project, of an art." As an example, he notes that although a broad range of audiences connect to *Smoke Signals*, they respond to its specifics and to its relevance for their own lives: "They didn't say, 'This made me feel like 100 other people.' The creation is specific and the response is specific. Good art is specific. Godzilla is universal" (West and West, "Sending

Cinematic Smoke Signals," 68). In another interview he asserts, "Good art doesn't come out of assimilation — it comes out of tribalism" (M. Williams, "Without Reservations").

1. "INDIANS WATCHING INDIANS"

1. For example, see Buscombe, *Injuns!* 149. See also Egan, "An Indian without Reservations," 18.

2. See Hearne, "'Indians Watching Indians on TV,'" for further discussion of Indigenous spectatorship in *Smoke Signals* and in Chris Eyre's second feature film, *Skins* (2002).

3. This historical aesthetic of ethnographic display is discussed at length in Rony, Raheja, Griffiths, Ginsburg, and Huhndorf.

4. See bell hooks, "The Oppositional Gaze: Black Female Spectators," in *Black Looks*, 115–32.

5. See Cobb, "This Is What It Means to Say *Smoke Signals*," 212.

6. Singer, *Wiping the War Paint off the Lens*, 62.

7. Shohat and Stam, *Unthinking Eurocentrism*, 114.

8. See Prats, *Invisible Natives*, for a discussion of the way Westerns imagine Indian threat to settlers through synecdoche and other visual strategies for rendering Indian absence on screen.

9. Wilkinson, "Colonialism through the Media," 29–30.

10. Such images have a far longer history than can be discussed here, including Scottish Enlightenment theory of the Four Stages of Development developed by Adam Smith.

11. For detailed and eloquent book-length studies of images of Indians, see Dippie, *The Vanishing American*; Berkhofer, *The White Man's Indian*; Churchill, *Fantasies of the Master Race*; Aleiss, *Making the White Man's Indian*; Marubbio, *Killing the Indian Maiden*; and others.

12. See Buscombe's comment in his 2006 book *Injuns!* on Hollywood's lack of obligation to the Native viewers: "Indians . . . make up only 1.5 per cent of the potential audience inside the USA" (143). Buscombe argues that this percentage explains Hollywood's pursuit of profit in Indian movies through the device of inserting white focal characters with whom non-Native audiences will identify (such as John Dunbar, played by Kevin Costner, in *Dances with Wolves*). In this book I am interested in drawing attention to the strategic way that Eyre and Alexie imagine, include, and address their Indigenous audiences, especially Native youth audiences, in *Smoke Signals*. My argument is the opposite of Buscombe's — that Native audiences are important precisely because they are overlooked by the engines of Hollywood profit.

13. An "heirship problem" ensued when these individual tracts were divided

into smaller and ultimately unsustainable plots as they were passed down to multiple heirs.

14. See Hearne, "Telling and Retelling in the 'Ink of Light'"; Raheja, "Reading Nanook's Smile."

15. See P. Deloria, *Playing Indian*; Huhndorf, *Going Native*.

16. See Gaines and Herzog, "The Fantasy of Authenticity in Western Costume."

17. For a discussion of stereotypes, see P. Deloria, "Expectation and Anomaly," in *Indians in Unexpected Places*, 7–10; Shohat and Stam, *Unthinking Eurocentrism*, 178–219; Bhabha, "The Other Question," 66–84. Marubbio, *Killing the Indian Maiden*, examines the specific stock figure in the Western of the doomed "Indian maiden."

18. P. Deloria, *Indians in Unexpected Places*, 8.

19. Konkle, *Writing Indian Nations*, 288–89.

20. Exceptions include Will Sampson's portrayal of Chief Bromden in *One Flew Over the Cuckoo's Nest* (dir. Forman, 1975) and Larry Littlebird's lead performance of Abel in *House Made of Dawn* (dir. Morse, 1972), films that depict Native characters navigating both urban and institutional oppressions.

21. Rosaldo, *Culture and Truth*, 68–69, 70.

22. Hearne, "'The Cross-Heart People.'"

23. Belton, *American Cinema/American Culture*, 248.

24. Standing Bear, *My People the Sioux*, 284.

25. For a detailed account of Native American actors in early Hollywood, see Rosenthal, "Representing Indians."

26. P. Deloria, *Indians in Unexpected Places*, 91. See also Aleiss, *Making the White Man's Indian*; Marubbio, *Killing the Indian Maiden*; A. Smith, *Shooting Cowboys and Indians*; Hearne, "'The Cross-Heart People'"; and Simmon, *The Invention of the Western Film*.

27. Shohat and Stam, *Unthinking Eurocentrism*, 118.

28. Engelhardt, *The End of Victory Culture*, 40. Engelhardt writes, "Like the captivity narrative, the ambush scenario flipped history on its head, making the intruder exchange places with the intruded upon."

29. Tuska, *The American West in Film*, 51.

30. For a discussion of Westerns that allude to Vietnam and the My Lai massacre in particular, see Slotkin, *Gunfighter Nation*, 581–91.

31. See Hearne, "The 'Ache for Home'"; Neale, "Vanishing Americans."

32. See Singer, *Wiping the War Paint off the Lens*.

33. See Kilpatrick, *Celluloid Indians*. New works by Michelle Raheja (*Reservation Reelism*) and Angela Aleiss (*Making the White Man's Indian*) have highlighted the wide range of contributions Native actors, consultants, directors, and crew members made to Hollywood and independent productions.

34. See Singer, *Wiping the War Paint off the Lens*.

35. See Lewis, "*Navajo Talking Picture.*"

36. Several new books take up this subject, including Wilson and Stewart, *Global Indigenous Media*; Wood, *Native Features*; and Columpar, *Unsettling Sights*.

37. See Lewis, *Alanis Obomsawin.*

38. See M. Evans, *Isuma* and *"The Fast Runner."*

39. United Nations Declaration on the Rights of Indigenous Peoples, http://www.un.org/esa/socdev/unpfii/en/drip.html.

40. See Chadwick Allen's essay "The Hero with Two Faces" for an analysis of Lone Ranger productions as a form of "treaty discourse": "Essentially mythic, treaty discourse sanctions White American fantasies of an idealized treaty moment. Central to these fantasies is an available and thus knowable Indianness: an Indianness defined as racially 'pure' but organized in non-Indian terms" (612).

41. John Trudell has also been the primary subject of several films, including Heather Rae's 2005 documentary *Trudell* and Ian Skorodin's 1997 fictionalized drama *Tushka*. He played Jimmy Looks Twice in the 1992 Michael Apted drama *Thunderheart*, a fictionalized account of the American Indian Movement's occupation of Wounded Knee, and has had small roles in dramas like *Dreamkeeper*, a Hallmark production made for television. He was featured in Jonathan S. Tomhave's short film *Half of Anything* (2006), and was the voiceover narrator for Chris Eyre's NMAI/Smithsonian production *A Thousand Roads* (2005).

42. See *Trudell* (dir. Rae, 2005).

43. See appendix, interview with Alexie.

44. Carr, *Running on the Edge of the Rainbow.*

45. King, "Performing Native Humor," 171.

46. V. Deloria, *Custer Died for Your Sins*, 147–48.

47. Several critics have made the specific comparison of Peone with Love Daddy. See, for example, Cummings, "'Accessible Poetry'?" 59.

48. Pratt, *Imperial Eyes*, 4.

49. The Ghost Dance is a ritual circle dance that originated with the Paiute spiritual leader Wovoka (Jack Wilson) and was taken up by many tribes late in the nineteenth century. The ritual was connected to aspirations for spiritual and material renewal and, in the Lakota version, to the retreat of white settlers from tribal lands and the return of lost relatives. The Wounded Knee massacre of 1890 started with the U.S. military's fearful misinterpretation and then deadly suppression of the Lakota gathering to practice the religious dance. In *Smoke Signals*, Thomas's story of a gathering of Native people followed by a destructive fire — a fire likened in a simile to a U.S. military figure — seems to gesture toward this historical and symbolic precedent. For more information

on the Ghost Dance, see Du Bois, *The 1870 Ghost Dance*; Kehoe, *The Ghost Dance*; Osterreich, *The American Indian Ghost Dance, 1870 and 1890*.

50. Kozloff, *Invisible Storytellers*, 63.

51. Kozloff, *Invisible Storytellers*, 1.

52. Strategies of recontextualizing older media forms and revisiting issues of voice, silence, and ventriloquism are not limited to Indigenous media; rather, these are broad trends in minority and feminist cinemas. An example is Spike Lee's film *Bamboozled* (2000), which returns to the trope of blackface minstrelsy both as an exploration of historical representations of African Americans on stage and as a politicized intervention that exposes systemic exploitation of black actors in the contemporary entertainment industry.

2. "THE STORYTELLER IS PART OF THE STORY"

1. See Bauman, "Verbal Art as Performance"; Babcock, "The Story in the Story."

2. Fielding, "Native American Religion and Film." The quote in the heading comes from McDonald, "Interview with Sherman Alexie."

3. Highway, "Spokane Words."

4. Highway, "Spokane Words."

5. Keogh, "Interview with Sherman Alexie."

6. Keogh, "Interview with Sherman Alexie."

7. Keogh, "Interview with Sherman Alexie."

8. Alexie, *Smoke Signals*, ix.

9. Gilroy, "Being Sherman Alexie," 80, 83.

10. Keogh, "Interview with Sherman Alexie."

11. Keogh, "Interview with Sherman Alexie."

12. Highway, "Spokane Words."

13. Highway, "Spokane Words."

14. Hall, "Notes on Deconstructing 'the Popular,'" 239.

15. Cox, *Muting White Noise*, 172; and Cox, "This Is What It Means to Say Reservation Cinema," 76.

16. Alexie, *The Lone Ranger and Tonto Fistfight in Heaven*, 187.

17. Alexie, *The Lone Ranger and Tonto Fistfight in Heaven*, 192

18. Alexie, *The Lone Ranger and Tonto Fistfight in Heaven*, 191–92.

19. Alexie, *The Lone Ranger and Tonto Fistfight in Heaven*, 198.

20. Alexie, *The Lone Ranger and Tonto Fistfight in Heaven*, 160.

21. G. Bird, "The Exaggeration of Despair," 47, 49.

22. Cook-Lynn, "American Indian Intellectualism," 126.

23. Owens, "Through an Amber Glass," 78, 76. Owens argues specifically that Alexie maintains "an aggressive posture regarding an essential 'authentic'

Indianness while simultaneously giving the commercial market and reader exactly what they want and expect in the form of stereotype and cliché."

24. Alexie, introduction to *The Lone Ranger and Tonto Fistfight in Heaven*, xix.

25. Alexie, introduction to *The Lone Ranger and Tonto Fistfight in Heaven*, xxi. Calling his stories "reservation realism" may be a direct response to Elizabeth Cook-Lynn's praise of N. Scott Momaday's "tribal realism" in the same essay ("Native Intellectualism and the New Indian Story") in which she criticizes Alexie's representations as "trash or fraudulent or pop" (132). Neither Cook-Lynn nor Alexie expand upon or define these terms — Alexie writes, "I'll let you read the book and figure that out for yourself" (xxi).

26. See S. Evans, "Open Containers"; Gillan, "Reservation Home Movies"; Coulombe, "The Approximate Size of His Favorite Humor"; and Rader, "Word as Weapon" for further discussion of Alexie's pop imagery and controversial comic representations.

27. Himmelsbach, "The Reluctant Spokesman." In another interview, Alexie noted, "The danger is that I become representational, and my characters and my plots become representational, where if I write about an alcoholic, all of a sudden, it means that I'm saying that Indians are alcoholics" (Gilroy, "Being Sherman Alexie," 83).

28. Dunnewind, "Sherman Alexie Captures the Voice."

29. Fielding, "Native American Religion and Film."

30. James Cox points out in *Muting White Noise* that the band name "Coyote Springs" is probably a play on Tony Hillerman's novel *Coyote Waits*.

31. Rader, "Word as Weapon," 163. References to television as an oppressive force in itself and as a symbol of colonialism are integral to the work of other Native authors as well, particularly Thomas King (in *Green Grass, Running Water*) and Gerald Vizenor (in *Bearheart*) (see Cox, *Muting White Noise*, for a discussion of these books as they illuminate Sherman Alexie's novels *Reservation Blues* and *Indian Killer*). Not coincidentally, these authors, too, have tried to intervene more directly in the media landscape through their involvement in filmmaking (King's screenplay for *Medicine River* [1993], as well as his radio show *Dead Dog Café*, and Vizenor's short film *Harold of Orange*, directed by Richard Weise in 1984).

32. Alexie, *Reservation Blues*, 211.

33. Interview with John Purdy, quoted in Youngberg, "Interpenetrations," 70.

34. Alexie, introduction to *The Lone Ranger and Tonto Fistfight in Heaven*, xxii.

35. Wilton, "Native Son."

36. Part of Thomas Builds-the-Fire's closing monologue, cut from the film, included lines that refer to the way street theater intends to affect viewers' behavior. The passage is from Dick Lourie's poem "Forgiving Our Fathers": "Or he's the one, as in a dream of mine, I must pull from the water, but I never

knew it or wouldn't have done it, until I saw a street-theater play so close up I was moved to actions I'd never before taken" (see Alexie's screenplay, 147). Culture jamming refers to a loosely organized prank- and hoax-inclined movement designed to make "mass media content" into a "carrier of questions." See "Culture Jamming," Center for Communication and Civic Engagement, University of Washington, http://depts.washington.edu/ccce/polcomm campaigns/CultureJamming.htm.

37. Wilton, "Native Son." In fact, Alexie protects Spokane culture by omitting spiritual or ceremonial elements in his fiction and films. We can think of this "aesthetics of omission" as a similar strategy to Hopi videographer Victor Masayesva's attention to Hopi cultural privacy.

38. M. Jones, "Alien Nation."

39. West and West, "Sending Cinematic Smoke Signals."

40. Alexie, *The Lone Ranger and Tonto Fistfight in Heaven*, 73.

41. West and West, "Sending Cinematic Smoke Signals."

42. Vizenor's term "survivance" suggests a more active — and more narrative — continuation of Indigeneity than is indicated by "survival." He calls survivance "the new stories of tribal courage" in face of the legacy of dominance and Manifest Destiny (*Manifest Manners*, 3).

43. Todorov, quoted in Vizenor, "Trickster Discourse," 190–91.

44. Gilroy, "Being Sherman Alexie," 81.

45. West and West, "Sending Cinematic Smoke Signals." For further discussion of Native American humor in general and Sherman Alexie's humor in particular, see Andrews, "In the Belly of a Laughing God"; Basso, *Portraits of the Whiteman*; Coulombe, "The Approximate Size of His Favorite Humor"; and Lincoln, *Ind'n Humor*.

46. Purdy, "Crossroads."

47. Gilroy, "Being Sherman Alexie," 81.

48. Red Shirt, "A Conversation with . . . Chris Eyre."

49. "Chris Eyre."

50. See appendix, interview with Chris Eyre.

51. M. Jones, "Alien Nation."

52. See appendix, interview with Chris Eyre.

53. "Chris Eyre."

54. Fielding, "Native American Religion and Film."

55. Fielding, "Native American Religion and Film."

56. M. Jones, "Alien Nation."

57. Kaufman, "An Eyre of Success." See also M. Jones, "Alien Nation." For a discussion of the emergence of institutional structures for training Native filmmakers, especially the Sundance Institute, see Singer, *Wiping the War Paint off the Lens*.

58. Kaufman, "An Eyre of Success." The Sundance/NHK International Film-makers Award, given at the Sundance Film Festival to emerging filmmakers from the United States, Latin America, Europe, and Japan, carries a prize of $10,000 (along with creative, financial and distribution assistance); the award is a collaboration between the Sundance Institute and NHK, the Japanese Broadcasting Corporation.

59. See appendix, interview with Chris Eyre.

60. See appendix, interview with Chris Eyre.

61. See appendix, interview with Chris Eyre.

62. Alexie, *Smoke Signals*, x.

63. See appendix, interview with Chris Eyre.

64. Kaufman, "An Eyre of Success." Alexie describes his vision for the film this way: "We wanted to show the small domestic lives of these Indians being human. I didn't want to make some New-Age film that people could interpret as these 'Indian magical creatures' — this closeness to the earth, talking to birds and animals. I wanted to make something a lot more subversive than that. Much funnier" (M. Jones, "Alien Nation").

65. See appendix, interview with Chris Eyre.

66. Eyre goes on to say, "I didn't really understand what it meant to be Cheyenne/Arapaho until I got older. I had to keep the faith. I'm an amalgamation of two worlds and I think looking at two sides of things that I can't separate has given me that sensibility called humanity" (Chaw, "Skins Game").

67. See appendix, interview with Chris Eyre.

68. Sterngold, "Able to Laugh at Their People."

69. P. Miller, "Smoke Signals."

70. Alexie, *Smoke Signals*, 163.

71. Egan, "An Indian without Reservations," 18. Alexie may be referring specifically here to Iron Eyes Cody, a.k.a. Espera DeCorti, an Italian American actor from Louisiana who not only played hundreds of Indian roles on film and television but also "passed" as Cree/Cherokee in his public and private life. He is best known as the "Crying Indian" in the Keep America Beautiful public service announcement from the early 1970s.

72. Alexie, *Smoke Signals*, 158.

73. Alexie, *Smoke Signals*, 160.

74. Alexie, *Smoke Signals*, 158.

75. Sterngold, "Able to Laugh at Their People."

76. Interview with Tantoo Cardinal.

77. Becker, "Evan Adams Interview."

78. Kozloff, *Invisible Storytellers*, 45.

79. In an earlier version of the script, Velma and Lucy had additional scenes, and Suzy Song's background was revealed more extensively (Alexie, "This Is What It Means.").

80. See Marubbio, *Killing the Indian Maiden*.

81. Gilroy, "A Conversation with Evan Adams," 47–48. See also Evan Adams's description of his acting in Alexie, *The Business of Fancydancing*, 121.

82. "Chris Eyre."

83. See Lefkowitz, "Dialects in the Movies," for a linguistic analysis of Thomas's intonational speech style.

84. Naremore, *Acting in the Cinema*, 3.

85. James Naremore has theorized the work of acting in reflecting a unified self back to viewers with regard to classical Hollywood cinema in his book *Acting in the Cinema*.

86. Masayesva, "Indigenous Experimentalism," 238. Unlike Alexie, Masayesva excludes popular culture from his conception of an Indigenous aesthetic, asserting that "Indigenous culture — not popular culture — will continue to dominate the North American continent as the clearest manifestation of its soul" (238).

87. Becker, "Evan Adams Interview."

88. Becker, "Evan Adams Interview."

89. Babcock, "The Story in the Story."

90. Cobb, "This Is What It Means to Say *Smoke Signals*," 208. See also Kerstin Knopf's analysis of Thomas's voice-over and on-screen storytelling as metanarrative in *Decolonizing the Lens of Power*, 247.

91. Alexie, *Smoke Signals*, 61–62.

92. Babcock, "First Families," 213.

93. See appendix, interview with Chris Eyre.

94. The on-screen use of a wig to signal the theatricality of performing Indianness is more pronounced (because more deliberate) in the 1934 Warner Brothers film *Massacre*, in which Richard Barthelmess, playing Chief Joe Thunderhorse, removes his wig of long black braids after performing in a Wild West show to reveal his short hair. Because Richard Barthelmess is a white actor playing Indian in redface, the wig, meant to initiate the film's thematic focus on Indian assimilation, is also a prop that signals Hollywood racial masquerade.

95. See Knopf, *Decolonizing the Lens of Power*, 247.

96. See Hearne, "'The Cross-Heart People,'" for a discussion of the ways that costume, hairstyles, and accessories (such as Plains headdresses and Olla-maiden water jars) have substituted in photographs and films for skin color as a visible signifier of Indianness.

3. "DANCES WITH SALMON"

1. See appendix, interview with Sherman Alexie.

2. Independence Day — a national holiday commemorating the adoption of the Declaration of Independence on July 4, 1776, by the Continental Congress

in Philadelphia — has been celebrated with fireworks (along with picnics, parades, patriotic speeches, music, and military displays) since the early 1800s.

3. Armbruster-Sandoval, "Teaching *Smoke Signals*," 129. See also Janice Gould's reading of Louise Erdrich's poem "Dear John Wayne"; Gould argues that John Wayne is "a stand-in for American society, himself a 'great white father'" (quoted in Rader, "Word as Weapon," 154).

4. The documentary film *Boomtown*, directed by Bryan Gunnar Cole in 2002, chronicles the complex contradictions that Independence Day brings for the twenty-six recognized tribes in Washington state that sell fireworks from roadside stands; the treaty rights that exempt tribal lands from certain state laws also transform their communities into a chaotic marketplace for patriotic celebrations. Bennie Armstrong, chairman of the Suquamish Nation and head of a family fireworks business, asks, "After 450 years of oppression, why do we sell fireworks to celebrate the birth of a country that oppresses Indians?"

5. See Houston Wood's description of the film in *Native Features*, 110–14. Wood rightly points out that in the wake of *Smoke Signals*'s blitz of media attention, other early and mid-1990s Native films have been overlooked, including, in addition to *Tushka*, the HBO miniseries *Grand Avenue* (dir. Daniel Sackheim, 1996), based on author Greg Sarris's (Pomo/Miwok) screenplay; and *Naturally Native*, directed by Valerie Red-Horse (Cherokee/Sioux) and funded by the Mashantucket Pequot Tribe of Connecticut. See also Heather Rae's documentary film biography *Trudell* (2005).

6. See Mills, *The Racial Contract*, 3, on the social contract as a "racial contract" in Western political theory.

7. Native Americans were made citizens of the United States by an act of Congress in 1924. However, this apparent gesture of inclusion also constituted a denial and abrogation of Native American tribes' status as nations, a status acknowledged in the many treaties between the United States and individual tribal nations.

8. Haralovich, "Fireworks in Film and TV." Quotation is from Haralovich, "Zombies v. Humans."

9. Allen, *Blood Narrative*, 17.

10. Rogin, *Fathers and Children*, 188. For further considerations of this metaphor, see Rogin's biography of Andrew Jackson, in which he argues that "two dominant cultural symbols formed Jackson's life," consisting of "Indians, embodying a lost childhood world," and "revolutionary fathers" (14). Thus concurrent with the construction of U.S. politicians as "fathers" are infantilizing images of Indians as "children of nature": "Policy-makers had insisted since colonial days on their parental obligations to the Indian tribes. A colonial Massachusetts law, for example, classified Indians with children and the insane. Leaders of the new nation sought from the outset to subject Indians to a

paternal presidential authority. In legal relations, too, Indians were the 'wards' of the state" (188). See Prucha, *The Great Father*, for detailed discussions of U.S. trusteeship and wardship over Native nations, including a discussion of the extension of paternalism in the era of self-determination in the 1970s.

11. I am grateful to David Delgado Shorter for suggesting this reading of the film's trope of fatherhood as a comment on Native relationships to the United States and the Great White Father trope.

12. Clark and Nagel, "White Men, Red Masks," 123. See also P. Deloria, *Playing Indian*; Huhndorf, *Going Native*; Nelson, *National Manhood*.

13. Klopotek, "'I Guess Your Warrior Look Doesn't Work Every Time,'" 265–66.

14. West and West, "Sending Cinematic Smoke Signals." John Clark, in an article for the *Los Angeles Times*, notes Alexie's feeling that Native men suffer disproportionately: "Alexie says . . . their role of provider has been taken away from them. They are lost. They are absentee fathers, wandering sons" ("No Reservations," 82).

15. West and West, "Sending Cinematic Smoke Signals."

16. Alexie, *The Lone Ranger and Tonto Fistfight in Heaven*, 24.

17. Ginsburg, "Indigenous Media."

18. "CAMERA MOVES across bedroom to a CLOSE ANGLE on a blank television set" (Alexie, *Smoke Signals*, 13).

19. Allen, "The Hero with Two Faces," 612. On the structural subordination of sidekicks, see Shohat and Stam, *Unthinking Eurocentrism*, 204.

20. Alexie, *Smoke Signals*, 161.

21. For more broad-based and extensive discussions of music in Westerns, especially in relation to issues of racial delineation and the history of blackface minstrelsy, see Gorbman, "Drums along the L.A. River"; Kalinak, "Typically American" and "How the West Was Sung"; and Stanfield, *Hollywood, Westerns and the 1930s*.

22. The early publication is in James Aird, *Selections*, vol. 3, no. 26, 1788. See also Moore and Lake, *The Poetical Works of Thomas Moore*, 288–89. The history of the song is available in many print and online music history venues, such as http://www.ibiblio.org/fiddlers/GAMB_GAY.htm and http://www.contemplator.com/ireland/gowen.html (where readers can hear the tune).

23. Internet sites disseminating information about the song and story include the following: home pages for the Fourth Squadron of the Seventh Cavalry at Camp Garry Owen, http://www.globalsecurity.org/military/agency/army/4-7cav.htm and http://www.globalsecurity.org/military/facility.camp-owen.htm; sites covering the history of the Indian Wars and the Civil War, such as http://www.indianwars.org/Misc/garyowen.htm and http://www.civilwarmusic

.net/display_tune.php?tune=garryowen; and folk music sites such as http://www.contemplator.com/ireland/gowen.html.

24. Hall, "Notes on Deconstructing 'The Popular,'" 227.

25. Significantly, Chris Eyre's second feature film, *Skins* (2002), screened for free on Native reservations across the United States in advance of its theatrical release, traveling on a specially configured, mobile "cinetransformer" bus. The "Rolling Rez" tour used a film exhibition trailer that could expand laterally to form an indoor one-hundred-seat theater with air-conditioning, restrooms, concession stands, digital projection, and surround sound.

26. See Sherman Alexie's film *49?* (2003), and also the early documentary produced by Larry Evers *Songs of My Hunter Heart* (dir. Carr, 1979), a nonfiction film highlighting the poetry and "49" songs of Harold Littlebird.

27. West and West, "Sending Cinematic Smoke Signals."

28. See hooks, *Black Looks*.

29. Dean Rader's essay "Word as Weapon" contains an excellent discussion of the figure of John Wayne in Native American literature, including Louise Erdrich's widely anthologized poem "Dear John Wayne" and Sherman Alexie's prose poem "My Heroes Have Never Been Cowboys." Rader argues that writers such as Erdrich, Alexie, and Wendy Rose take up resistance against the "movie screen" as the twentieth-century "site of cultural imperialism" (150) and the "inability to unmake the image of Indians that Hollywood has made" (153).

30. Willemen and Pines, *Questions of a Third Cinema*, 8.

31. M. Jones, "Alien Nation."

32. James, *Literary and Cinematic Reservation*, 51–52.

33. The car driving in reverse also suggests (in a literal and ironic way) the history of Western narratives that imagine Indians as uncivilized, literally "backward" or ahistorical. See Fabian, *Time and the Other*.

34. West and West, "Sending Cinematic Smoke Signals," 8.

35. West and West, "Sending Cinematic Smoke Signals," 8.

36. Turim, *Flashbacks in Film*, 10.

37. See, for example, Alexie, *Smoke Signals*, 157.

38. In the published screenplay, Alexie notes that Eyre and director of photography Brian Capener "made the magical flashback transition between Scenes 18 and 19 all the more magical by allowing the adult Thomas and the Young Victor to be on-screen at the same time" (*Smoke Signals*, 157).

39. M. Jones, "Alien Nation."

40. M. Jones, "Alien Nation."

41. Momaday, *The Man Made of Words*.

42. Gilroy, "Another Fine Example of the Oral Tradition?" 38.

43. Jhon Warren Gilroy and others have discussed *Smoke Signals* in terms of Louis Owens's articulation of "frontier space."

44. Highway, "Spokane Words." Responses to the reshaping of the Columbia River have been gathered, with archival photographs, in collections such as William D. Layman's *River of Memory*.

45. I'm grateful to my students in Film Studies 4001/7001, The Western, and particularly to Michael Koscelniak, for their contributions in developing this reading of Arnold Joseph.

46. The varieties of Pacific salmon (sockeye, coho, chinook, chum, and others) are anadromous fish, migrating from freshwater streams out to sea and back again. Juvenile salmon, or smolts, are carried downstream tail-first to the sea by the fast, powerful river currents. Returning loaded with fat after several years of feeding and growing in the ocean, they swim upstream to their birthplaces, fighting the same powerful currents and slowly losing body mass until they die while spawning.

47. "Compilation of Information on Salmon and Steelhead Total Run Size," 15, 19. Alex Sherwood's description of Spokane Falls was given during his courtroom testimony in 1968, when he was seventy-three years old. The Spokane tribe's current website gives a similar description of the falls as central to Spokane tribal geography: "The Spokane Indians fished the Spokane River and used the grand Spokane Falls as a gathering place of family and friends" (http://www.spokanetribe.com/page.php?code=reservation). A single Salmon Chief, from the Spokane tribe, distributed the catch and organized the ceremonies, trading, potlatches, dancing, contests, and other festivities (Fahey and Dellwo, *The Spokane River*, 6).

48. Quoted in Fahey and Dellwo, *The Spokane River*, 50.

49. Vast quantities of fish were dried and cached for winter; at the several fisheries on the Spokane River, during a good season, groups working together could catch eight hundred to a thousand forty- to sixty-pound fish per day using baskets, nets, and spears as well as weirs and other fish traps (Ruby and Brown, *The Spokane Indians*, 16–18). According to John Fahey, the Spokane's "major fisheries were at Little Falls, the juncture of the Spokane and Little Spokane, and the mouth of Latah (Hangman) Creek, as well as at the great falls of the Spokane" (Fahey and Dellwo, *The Spokane River*, 6). The big Spokane Falls and the major fishery at Kettle Falls drew many tribes. For further discussion of Spokane salmon fishing, see Fahey and Dellwo, *The Spokane River*; Ruby and Brown, *The Spokane Indians*.

50. "Compilation of Information on Salmon and Steelhead Total Run Size," 13.

51. Youngs, *The Fair and the Falls*, 17–18. In addition to Youngs, see also Ruby and Brown, *The Spokane Indians*, for discussions of Spokane stories about the origin of the river and falls.

52. One commentator wrote in the *Walla Walla Union* in 1877, "Nature did not intend this mighty water-power for nought." In 1879 a local minister

wrote in a letter that "perhaps there is no better water-power in the world. The impression is that this place will become the Lowell and the metropolis of all this upper country." See Morrissey, *Mental Territories*, 120, 41–42.

53. City planners manifested these beliefs in linked celebrations of patriotism and modernity in various fairs and expositions. In 1876, when the city of Spokane Falls (later shortened to Spokane) hosted a Fourth of July centennial celebration that drew people from the entire region, only one sawmill stood on the banks of the river, followed by a flour mill in 1877. In 1890 the city hosted the Northwestern Industrial Exposition with the theme of "conquest of nature" (an emphasis that was not recalibrated until 1974, when Spokane hosted a world's fair exposition on the site of the falls, the first with an environmental theme).

In preparing for the expo and the urban renewal it fostered, the city worked to restore the falls and established a park on its banks. In Alexie's screenplay for *Smoke Signals*, Thomas Builds-the-Fire says that he visited the bridge over the Spokane Falls "during the World's Fair" (52–53), but the fair was held in Spokane in 1974, two years before Victor and Thomas were born. This temporal slip testifies to Thomas's unreliable narration and is significant, even though it was cut from the film, because it suggests Alexie's interest in building the history of the city and river into the fabric of the film's location during the crucial scene at the bridge. See William T. Youngs's impressive history of the expo, including many interviews with participants and planners, *The Fair and the Falls*.

54. "Compilation of Information on Salmon and Steelhead Total Run Size," 21–22.

55. Ruby and Brown, *The Spokane Indians*, 192. In addition to the Spokane reservation, members of the upper, lower, and middle Spokane bands also settled on the Flathead, Coeur d'Alene, and Coleville reservations.

56. The town commonly referred to as "The Falls" claimed a population of 350 in 1880, which surged to 12,000 by the dry summer of 1889, when much of the city burned down in a catastrophic fire (Morrissey, *Mental Territories*, 43). In a prefiguration of *Smoke Signals*'s discourse of fire, historian Katherine Morrissey writes that settlers' personal accounts of the region's history "use the fire as a community reference point. . . . In memory, the fire of 1889 came to symbolize the emergence of the Inland Empire, 'Rising Phoenix like from the great fire of 1889,' according to many" (46), as residents aggressively rebuilt the town as a modern city.

57. Fahey, *The Spokane River*, 26; see 25–36 for a discussion and chronology of the complicated corporate purchases of land and river current for water power during the intensive dam-building period of the early twentieth century.

58. "Compilation of Information on Salmon and Steelhead Total Run Size,"

24. Also quoted in "Avista Corporation & the Spokane River," http://www
.waterplanet.ws/avista/Avistahome/Avista_&_Spokane_River.html.

59. Bureau of Reclamation, U.S. Department of the Interior, "Grand Coulee
Dam," 2. A year earlier, in 1936, Charles Charapkin (Coeur d'Alene) had peti-
tioned the president of the United States regarding the river, saying, "When I
was ten or twelve . . . the Indians fished with traps in several localities of the
Spokane River, from the Columbia as far as Spokane Falls. There were five
such traps. At each of these traps the Indians caught about 1,000 salmon each
day for a period of 30 days each year. . . . But since the White people came
to these parts, the salmon have rapidly disappeared, until today there are no
salmon at Spokane Falls" (http://www.peopleoftheriver.org).

60. See White, *The Organic Machine*.

61. White, *The Organic Machine*, 90.

62. Sierra Club Upper Columbia River Group, "Death of the Spokane River?"

63. Perhaps the image of Phoenix in the film is a symbolic vision of the Native
spaces created in urban areas during relocation, or perhaps a materialization
of a line of poetry that Alexie credits with inspiring his entry into writing:
"I'm in the reservation of my mind."

64. M. Jones, "Alien Nation."

65. Alexie, *The Lone Ranger and Tonto Fistfight in Heaven*, 69.

66. Alexie, *Smoke Signals*, 108.

67. "Diabetes is like a lover, hurting you from the inside," says the narrator
in "Witnesses, Secret and Not" (Alexie, *The Lone Ranger and Tonto Fistfight in
Heaven*, 217, 221). Articles on the links between commodity foods, convenience
foods, and Native American diabetes include Nabhan, "Diabetes, Diet and
Native American Foraging Traditions," and Miewald, "The Nutritional Impact."

68. Nabhan, "Diabetes, Diet and Native American Foraging Traditions," 236.

69. Clark, "No Reservations," 9.

70. Lawson, "Native Sensibility and the Significance of Women," 100–101.

71. Fielding, "Native American Religion and Film."

72. Weinmann, "Hold Me Closer, Fancy Dancer."

73. Lawson calls the hero-twin story "an archetypal story in the canons of
Native oratory," involving "the violent birth of twin boys who, after many
adventures, eventually return home to find their father gone. They soon learn
their father has become a star, and they climb through the air to join him"
("Native Sensibility and the Significance of Women," 98–99).

74. Alexie, *Smoke Signals*, 85, 163.

75. Alexie, *The Lone Ranger and Tonto Fistfight in Heaven*, 60.

76. Alexie, *The Business of Fancydancing*, 138.

77. Alexie, *Smoke Signals*, 25.

4. "TAKE YOUR DAD'S PICKUP"

1. Wood, *Native Features*, 17.

2. Menier, "Guestbook."

3. Clark, "No Reservations," 8.

4. Clark, "No Reservations," 8–9, 82.

5. Becker, "Evan Adams Interview." Becker's short films include *Conversion* (2006).

6. Gilroy, "Being Sherman Alexie," 83, 84.

7. See appendix, interview with Chris Eyre.

8. See the NMAI Film and Video website, "Native Networks," at http://www .nativenetworks.si.edu/Eng/rose/youth_media.htm.

9. Suggestions from the Weinsteins at Miramax helped shape the film before Sundance, including retitling it *Smoke Signals* and a restructuring of Suzy Song's presence in the film. Trying to increase Suzy Song's magical presence in the film, Alexie and Eyre were moving her scenes earlier; Weinstein suggested the strategy of delaying the audience's first glimpse of Suzy until Victor and Thomas themselves first see her, halfway through the film. Alexie writes that Weinstein's input was "an incredibly simple editing suggestion that radically changed the tone of the film and of Irene Bedard's performance as Suzy Song. She is now much more mysterious and magical because we see her less" (Alexie, *Smoke Signals*, 155).

10. "Chris Eyre." See also Runningwater, "Smoke Signals."

11. McCarthy, review of *Smoke Signals*, 12.

12. Chris Eyre described Miramax's distribution strategy in an interview with @sk Hollywood. See BoxOfficeMojo.com for a domestic summary of the film's first four weekends.

13. See Horn, "DVD Sales Turn Every Film into a Mystery."

14. Knopf, *Decolonizing the Lens*, 239.

15. Box office figures from the Internet Movie Database (imdb.com) and BoxOfficeMojo.com. Kerstin Knopf reports a higher figure of $4 million for the film's budget (*Decolonizing the Lens*, 237).

16. See Angela Aleiss's useful comparative chart in *Making the White Man's Indian*, 161.

17. Ebert, "Smoke Signals"; Peary, "Universal Story"; Maslin, "Film Festival Review"; Stack, "*Smoke* Causes Tears of Sadness, Joy"; Savlov, Review of *Smoke Signals*.

18. See appendix, interview with Chris Eyre; S. Jones, "Smoke Gets in Your Eyes"; O'Sullivan, "Smoke Signals"; Hunter, "Smoke Signals from the Heart."

19. See, for example, Siskel and Ebert, *At the Movies*, June 27, 1998. Among many other instances, John Nesbit compares the opening shots of *Do the Right Thing* and *Smoke Signals* in his review ("Sherman Alexie"), as does De-

nise Cummings in her excellent article on *Smoke Signals*'s relationship with American independent film, "'Accessible Poetry'?" 59.

20. Fleischer, "Gone with the Wind." In another interview, with the London paper *The Guardian*, Alexie notes that although he and Eyre have reconciled, "the momentum has gone" (Jaggi, "All Rage and Heart").

21. Media coverage and subsequent film scholarship on *Smoke Signals* has to some extent also elided the complex collaborations of film authorship, focusing on Alexie as a singular spokesperson for the film.

22. "Chris Eyre"; Clark, "No Reservations"; Keogh, "Interview with Sherman Alexie."

23. Fleischer, "Gone with the Wind."

24. See appendix, interview with Chris Eyre.

25. See appendix, interview with Chris Eyre.

26. Alexie, *The Business of Fancydancing*, 131.

27. Expressing his frustration with standard filmmaking styles — even for the independent production of *Smoke Signals* — Alexie said that "it was so, so nonconducive to creation. . . . Being on film sets felt no different to me than visiting my friends at law firms or at Microsoft. Every decision based on money. Every decision! The whole process itself being so conservative. It was always about fear!" (Brian Miller, "The Road to Utah," *Seattle Weekly*, in Alexie, *The Business of Fancydancing*, 156). Miramax currently holds the rights to *Reservation Blues*.

28. In the stories from cast and crewmembers that follow Alexie's published screenplay for *The Business of Fancydancing*, story after story emphasizes Alexie's unusual directorial style — egalitarian, collaborative, trusting, improvisational, and risk taking, inclusive of friends and social networks. The niche-market distributor for *The Business of Fancydancing*, Outrider Productions, has largely targeted a queer audience, resulting in what film scholar Quentin Youngberg characterizes as the film's interpenetrating codes, "queering the Native sphere" while "'Indianing' the white and queer spheres" ("Interpenetrations," 71, 64).

29. Sheyahshe-Lell, "Native American Film Making," 11.

30. Beach has had well over thirty film roles, including Native-directed films such as *Skinwalkers* and *The Thief of Time*; Shirley Cheechoo's *Johnny Tootall* (2005); as well as mainstream Hollywood and television productions such as *Windtalkers* and *Bury My Heart at Wounded Knee* (2007).

31. Menier, "Guestbook."

32. See Whitt, "Cultural Imperialism and the Marketing of Native America," 139–71, for further discussion of the politics of property value and cultural and commercial imperialism.

33. Alexie, "Death in Hollywood," 9.

34. Alexie, *The Business of Fancydancing*, 7.

35. Moore goes on to link Alexie's resistance to closure with "oral storytelling patterns" that "are often open-ended, even interactive," as well as with "sit-coms and prequel/sequel movies" that are also "open-ended in a more manipulative mode" ("Sherman Alexie," 302).

36. Williams and Zelizer, "To Commodify or Not to Commodify," 373.

37. Quentin Youngberg, considering *Smoke Signals* in light of global counter-cinema and the issue of what he calls "cultural mediation," writes, "In their [Alexie and Eyre's] scheme . . . Native people can be active agents in those complex processes of mediation rather than simply the innocent victims of institutional processes somehow larger than, and outside of, themselves" ("Cultural Mediation," 147).

38. Singer, *Wiping the War Paint off the Lens*, 61.

39. Elsaesser, "Hyper-, Retro-, or Counter Cinema," 124, quoted in Youngberg, "Cultural Mediation."

40. The name may be a play on Kicking Bird, played by Graham Greene, in *Dances with Wolves*.

41. See Barnes, "At Miramax." Miramax was sold to Disney in 1993, and in 2005 the Weinsteins left to form the Weinstein Company.

42. Cieply, "Independent Filmmakers."

43. His developing romance with his sister's Tulsa neighbor, Francie, is also linked to his grief over his father — Francie's name resembles Cufe's father's name, Frankie (Richard Ray Whitman), and she favors the same old-fashioned technology, a stereo system for vinyl records.

44. Jenkins, *Convergence Culture*, 4.

45. aznxflipx91, "frybread."

46. tcheremnykh, "smoke signals rap."

47. stoddyjacob, "smoke signals school rap."

48. jamesGOLDbond, "Interviews on Smoke Signals."

49. Bolter and Grusin, *Remediation*. Wesch ("An Anthropological Introduction to YouTube") argues that YouTube has engendered a new cultural order based on the playful or mocking imitation of existing popular culture forms as a form of veneration. This imitative aesthetic intensifies what he terms the "authenticity crisis" brought on by YouTube's anonymity and physical distance, a "virtual" invitation to role-play.

50. The origin of "How" as imagined Indian speech predated cinematic Indians; Robert Collins, a doctoral candidate in history at Auburn University, argues that it may have originated with settlers' hearing the Muskogee word *hvo*, pronounced "hao," as an "affirmative interjection, something like 'yeah' in English" ("Why Indians Say 'How' and 'Ugh'").

51. See appendix, interview with Sherman Alexie.

52. thebiri, "Hey Victor!"; appendix interviews with Sherman Alexie and Chris Eyre.

53. brinkingright, "Thomas from Smoke Signals."

54. See the sequence beginning with alyssaabbo, "Hey Victor Pt 1."

55. Naficy, "Theorizing 'Third-World' Film Spectatorship," 9.

56. Henry Jenkins (*Convergence Culture*), for example, traces the amplification and impacts of audience participation in media franchises such as *Survivor*, *Harry Potter*, and *The Matrix*.

57. Burgess and Green, *YouTube*, 6; Hall, "Notes on Deconstructing 'the Popular,'" 239.

58. NativeRockers, "Smoke signals our version."

CONCLUSION

1. See appendix, interview with Sherman Alexie.

2. See Leuthold, *Indigenous Aesthetics*; and Kilpatrick, *Celluloid Indians*.

3. See Vivian Sobchack's analysis of the way historical epics have been marketed using claims about excessive production costs and difficulties ("'Surge and Splendor'").

4. Svetkey, "Little Big Movie." *New York Times* reviewer Vincent Canby likened the film to "a vacation in the Rockies" ("A Soldier at One with the Sioux"). For reporting on the production and marketing budget for *Avatar*, see Cieply, "A Movie's Budget Pops from the Screen"; see also Annalee Newitz's analysis of the film's generic story structure, "When Will White People Stop Making Films Like 'Avatar'?"

5. Sheyahshe-Lell, "Native American Film Making," 11.

6. Red Shirt, "A Conversation with . . . Chris Eyre."

7. Sheyahshe-Lell, "Native American Film Making," 11.

8. Wood, *Native Features*, 8.

9. See Buscombe, *Injuns!* 27.

10. Georgina Lighting, personal communication.

11. Hearne and Shlachter, "Pockets Full of Stories."

12. See appendix, interview with Sherman Alexie.

13. See appendix, interview with Sherman Alexie.

14. Native productions can be highly visible without being visible *as* Native productions. For example, Maori filmmaker Taika Waititi's writing and directing for the two-season HBO comedy *Flight of the Conchords* has gone unremarked as Indigenous cinema because its subject matter is not Indigenous.

Bibliography

Adams, David Wallace. *Education for Extinction*. Lawrence: University Press of Kansas, 1995.

Aleiss, Angela. *Making the White Man's Indian: Native Americans and Hollywood Movies*. Westport CT: Praeger, 2005.

———. "Native Americans: The Surprising Silents." *Cineaste* 21 (1995): 34–35.

Alexie, Sherman. *The Absolutely True Diary of a Part-Time Indian*. New York: Little, Brown and Company, 2007.

———. *The Business of Fancydancing: The Screenplay*. Brooklyn NY: Hanging Loose Press, 2003.

———. "Death in Hollywood." *Ploughshares* 26, no. 4 (2000): 7–10.

———. *The Lone Ranger and Tonto Fistfight in Heaven*. New York: Grove Press, 1993.

———. *Reservation Blues*. New York: Grand Central Publishing, 1996.

———. *Smoke Signals: A Screenplay*. New York: Hyperion, 1998.

———. "Superman and Me." *Los Angeles Times*, April 19, 1998. http://www .fallsapart.com.

———. "This Is What It Means to Say Phoenix, Arizona." Reading script, December 10, 1996.

Alfred, Taiaiake. "Sovereignty." In *Sovereignty Matters: Locations of Contestation and Possibility in Indigenous Struggles for Self-Determination*, edited by Joanne Barker, 31–50. Lincoln: University of Nebraska Press, 2005.

Allen, Chadwick. *Blood Narrative: Indigenous Identity in American Indian and Maori Literary and Activist Texts*. Durham: Duke University Press, 2002.

———. "The Hero with Two Faces: The Lone Ranger as Treaty Discourse." *American Literature* 68, no. 3 (1996): 609–38.

Anderson, John. "This Time, the Indians Tell Their Own Story." *New York Times*, August 27, 2006. http://www.nytimes.com/2006/08/27/ movies/27ande.html.

Andrews, Jennifer. "In the Belly of a Laughing God: Reading Humor and Irony in the Poetry of Joy Harjo." *American Indian Quarterly* 24, no. 2 (2000): 200–218.

Armbruster-Sandoval, Ralph. "Teaching *Smoke Signals*: Fatherhood, Forgiveness, and 'Freedom.'" *Wicazo Sa Review* (Spring 2008): 123–46.

Babcock, Barbara. "First Families: Gender, Reproduction and the Mythic Southwest." In *The Great Southwest of the Fred Harvey Company and the Santa Fe Railway*, edited by Barbara Babcock and Marta Weigle, 207–17. Phoenix: Heard Museum, 1996.

———. "The Story in the Story: Metanarration in Folk Narrative." In *Verbal Art as Performance*, edited by Richard Bauman, 61–80. Prospect Heights IL: Waveland Press, 1977.

Barclay, Barry. "Celebrating Fourth Cinema." *Illusions* 35 (2003): 7–11.

Barker, Joanne. "For Whom Sovereignty Matters." In *Sovereignty Matters: Locations of Contestation and Possibility in Indigenous Struggles for Self-Determination*, edited by Joanne Barker, 1–31. Lincoln: University of Nebraska Press, 2005.

Barnes, Brooks. "At Miramax, Deep Cuts in Staff and Filmmaking." *New York Times*, October 2, 2009. http://www.nytimes.com/2009/10/03/business/media/03miramax.html?scp=1&sq=barnes%20%22at%20miramax,%20deep%20cuts%22&st=cse.

Basso, Keith H. *Portraits of "The Whiteman": Linguistic Play and Cultural Symbols among the Western Apache.* Cambridge: Cambridge University Press, 1979.

Bauman, Richard. "Verbal Art as Performance." In *Verbal Art as Performance*, edited by Richard Bauman, 3–60. Prospect Heights IL: Waveland Press, 1977.

———, ed. *Verbal Art as Performance.* Prospect Heights IL: Waveland Press, 1977.

Becker, Nanobah. "Evan Adams Interview." June 2003. http://www.nativenetworks.si.edu/Eng/rose/adams_e_interview.htm#open.

Belton, John. *American Cinema, American Culture.* New York: McGraw Hill, 1993.

Berkhofer, Robert F. *The White Man's Indian: Images of the American Indian from Columbus to the Present.* New York: Random House, 1979.

Bhabha, Homi. "The Other Question: Stereotype, Discrimination and the Discourse of Colonialism." In *The Location of Culture*, 66–84. New York: Routledge, 1994.

Bird, Gloria. "The Exaggeration of Despair in Sherman Alexie's Reservation Blues." *Wicazo Sa Review* 11, no. 2 (1995): 47–52.

Bird, S. Elizabeth. *The Audience in Everyday Life: Living in a Media World.* New York: Routledge, 2003.

Bolter, Jay David, and Richard Grusin. *Remediation: Understanding New Media.* Boston: MIT Press, 2000.

Bruyneel, Kevin. *The Third Space of Sovereignty: The Postcolonial Politics of U.S.-Indigenous Relations.* Minneapolis: University of Minnesota Press, 2007.

Bureau of Reclamation, U.S. Department of the Interior. "Grand Coulee Dam." Washington DC: United States Department of the Interior, 1938.

Burgess, Jean, and Joshua Green. *YouTube: Online Video and Participatory Culture*. Cambridge: Polity Press, 2009.

Buscombe, Edward. *Injuns! Native Americans in the Movies*. Bodmin, UK: Reaktion Books, 2006.

Canby, Vincent. "A Soldier at One with the Sioux." *New York Times*, November 9, 1990. http://movies.nytimes.com/movie/review?res=9 C0CE6DB1338F93AA35752C1A966958260.

Carr, Denny, dir. *Running on the Edge of the Rainbow*. 1978. http:// parentseyes.arizona.edu/wordsandplace/silko.html.

Chaw, Walter. "Skins Game: FFC with Chris Eyre." *Film Freak Central*, October 2, 2002. http://filmfreakcentral.net/notes/ceyreinterview.htm.

Child, Brenda. *Boarding School Seasons*. Lincoln: University of Nebraska Press, 1998.

"Chris Eyre: The @sk Hollywood Interview." Express Video, 1998. http:// www.expressv.myvideostore.com/content/askhollywood/interviews/ chris_eyre/index.phtml?client=expressv.

Churchill, Ward. *Fantasies of the Master Race: Literature, Cinema, and the Colonization of American Indians*. New York: City Lights Press, 2001.

Cieply, Michael. "Independent Filmmakers Distribute on Their Own." *New York Times*, August 13, 2009. http://www.nytimes.com/2009/08/13/ business/media/13independent.html.

———. "A Movie's Budget Pops from the Screen." *New York Times*, November 8, 2009. http://www.nytimes.com/2009/11/09/business/ media/09avatar.html.

Clark, David Anthony Tyeeme, and Joane Nagel. "White Men, Red Masks: Appropriations of 'Indian' Manhood in Imagined Wests." In *Across the Great Divide: Cultures of Manhood in the American West*, edited by Matthew Basso, Laura McCall, and Dee Garceau, 109–30. New York: Routledge, 2001.

Clark, John. "No Reservations." *Los Angeles Times*, June 28, 1998. http:// articles.latimes.com/1998/jun/28/entertainment/ca-64212.

Cobb, Amanda J. "This Is What It Means to Say *Smoke Signals*: Native American Cultural Sovereignty." In *Hollywood's Indian: The Portrayal of the Native American in Film*, edited by Peter C. Rollins and John E. O'Connor, 206–28. Expanded ed. Lexington: University Press of Kentucky, 2003.

Collins, Robert. "Why Indians Say 'How' and 'Ugh.'" A la Rob website, April 14, 2009. http://alarob.wordpress.com/2009/04/14/why-indians -say-how/.

Columpar, Corinn. *Unsettling Sights: The Fourth World on Film*. Carbondale: Southern Illinois University Press, 2010.

"Compilation of Information on Salmon and Steelhead Total Run Size, Catch and Hydropower Related Losses in the Upper Columbia River Basin, Above Grand Coulee Dam." Fisheries Technical Report No. 2. Allan Scholz, Kate O'Laughlin, David Geist, Jim Uehara, Dee Peone, Luanna Fields, Todd Kleist, Ines Zozaya, Kim Teesatuskie. Upper Columbia United Tribes Fisheries Center, Eastern Washington University, Department of Biology, Cheney, Washington, 1985.

Cook-Lynn, Elizabeth. "American Indian Intellectualism and the New Indian Story." In *Natives and Academics: Researching and Writing about American Indians*, edited by Devon A. Mihesuah, 111–38. Lincoln: University of Nebraska, 1998.

Coulombe, Joseph L. "The Approximate Size of His Favorite Humor: Sherman Alexie's Comic Connections and Disconnections in *The Lone Ranger and Tonto Fistfight in Heaven*." *American Indian Quarterly* 26, no. 1 (2002): 94–115.

Cox, James H. *Muting White Noise: Native American and European American Novel Traditions*. Norman: University of Oklahoma Press, 2006.

———. "This Is What It Means to Say Reservation Cinema: Making Cinematic Indians in *Smoke Signals*." In *Sherman Alexie: A Collection of Critical Essays*, edited by Jeff Berglund and Jan Roush, 74–94. Salt Lake City: University of Utah Press, 2010.

Cummings, Denise. "'Accessible Poetry'? Cultural Intersection and Exchange in Contemporary American Indian and American Independent Film." *Studies in American Indian Literatures* 13, no. 1 (2001): 57–80.

Deloria, Philip J. *Indians in Unexpected Places*. Lawrence: University of Kansas Press, 2004.

———. *Playing Indian*. New Haven: Yale University Press, 1998.

Deloria, Vine, Jr. *Custer Died for Your Sins: An Indian Manifesto*. New York: MacMillan, 1969.

Deloria, Vine, and Clifford M. Lytle. *The Nations Within: The Past and Future of American Indian Sovereignty*. New York: Pantheon, 1984.

Dickason, Olive Patricia. *Canada's First Nations: A History of Founding Peoples from Earliest Times*. Norman: University of Oklahoma Press, 1992.

Dippie, Brian W. *The Vanishing American: White Attitudes and U.S. Indian Policy*. Lawrence: University Press of Kansas, 1982.

Dix, Andrew. "Escape Stories: Narratives and Native Americans in Sherman Alexie's *The Lone Ranger and Tonto Fistfight in Heaven*." *The Yearbook of English Studies* 31 (2001): 155–67.

Du Bois, Cora. *The 1870 Ghost Dance*. Lincoln: University of Nebraska Press, 2007.

Dunnewind, Stephanie, "Sherman Alexie Captures the Voice, Chaos and Humor of a Teenager." *The Seattle Times*, September 8, 2007.

Ebert, Roger. "Smoke Signals." *Chicago Sun-Times*, July 3, 1998. http://rogerebert.suntimes.com/apps/pbcs.dll/article?AID=/19980703/REVIEWS/807030303/1023.

Egan, Timothy. "An Indian without Reservations." *New York Times Magazine*, January 18, 1998, 17–19.

Engelhardt, Tom. *The End of Victory Culture: Cold War America and the Disillusioning of a Generation*. Amherst: University of Massachusetts Press, 1998.

Evans, Michael Robert. *"The Fast Runner": Filming the Legend of Atanarjuat*. Lincoln: University of Nebraska Press, 2010.

———. *Isuma: Inuit Video Art*. Montreal: McGill-Queen's University Press, 2008.

Evans, Stephen F. "'Open Containers': Sherman Alexie's Drunken Indians." *American Indian Quarterly* 25, no. 1 (2001): 46–72.

Eyre, Chris. Telephone interview. July 4, 2008.

Fabian, Johannes. *Time and the Other: How Anthropology Makes Its Object*. New York: Columbia University Press, 1983.

Fahey, John, and Bob Dellwo. *The Spokane River: Its Miles and Its History*. Spokane WA: Spokane Centennial Trail Committee, 1988.

Fear-Segal, Jacqueline. *White Man's Club*. Lincoln: University of Nebraska Press, 2007.

Fielding, Julien R. "Native American Religion and Film: Interviews with Chris Eyre and Sherman Alexie." *Journal of Religion and Film* 7, no. 1 (2003): 1–19.

Fleeman, Michael. "Will *Smoke Signals* Open More Doors for Indians in Film?" *Entertainment Today*, July 10, 1998, AMPAS archive.

Fleischer, Matthew. "Gone with the Wind." *LA Weekly*, April 11, 2007. http://www.laweekly.com/2007-04-12/film-tv/gone-with-the-wind/.

Fraser, Joelle. "An Interview with Sherman Alexie." *The Iowa Review* 30, no. 3 (2000–2001): 59–70. http://www.english.illinois.edu/maps/poets/a_f/alexie/fraser.htm.

Gaines, Jane. "White Privilege and Looking Relations: Race and Gender in Feminist Film Theory." *Screen* 29, no. 4 (1988): 12–27.

Gaines, Jane, and Charlotte Herzog. "The Fantasy of Authenticity in Western Costume." In *Back in the Saddle Again: New Essays on the Western*, edited by Edward Buscombe and Roberta Pearson, 172–81. London: British Film Institute, 1998.

Gillan, Jennifer. "Reservation Home Movies: Sherman Alexie's Poetry."
    American Literature 68, no. 1 (1996): 91–110.
Gilroy, Jhon Warren. "'Another Fine Example of the Oral Tradition'?
    Identification and Subversion in Sherman Alexie's *Smoke Signals*."
    Studies in American Indian Literatures 13, no. 1 (2001): 23–42.
———. "Being Sherman Alexie: An Interview." *Bellingham Review* 24, no.
    49 (2001): 79–86.
———. "A Conversation with Evan Adams." *Studies in American Indian
    Literatures* 13, no. 1 (2001): 43–56.
Ginsburg, Faye. "Indigenous Media: Faustian Contract or Global Village?"
    Cultural Anthropology 6, no. 1 (1991): 92–112.
———. "Screen Memories and Entangled Technologies: Resignifying
    Indigenous Lives." In *Critical Visions in Film Theory: Classic and
    Contemporary Readings*, edited by Timothy Corrigan and Patricia
    White, 887–904. New York: Bedford/St. Martin's, 2011.
———. "Screen Memories: Resignifying the Traditional in Indigenous
    Media." In *Media Worlds: Anthropology on New Terrain*, edited by
    Faye Ginsburg, Lila Abu-Lughod, and Brian Larkin, 40–56. Berkeley:
    University of California Press, 2002.
Ginsburg, Faye, Lila Abu-Lughod, and Brian Larkin, eds. *Media Worlds:
    Anthropology on New Terrain*. Berkeley: University of California Press,
    2002.
Gorbman, Claudia. "Drums along the L.A. River: Scoring the Indian." In
    Westerns: Films through History, edited by Janet Walker, 177–95. New
    York: Routledge, 2001.
Hall, Stuart. "Cultural Identity and Cinematic Representation." In *Film and
    Theory: An Anthology*, edited by Robert Stam and Toby Miller, 704–14.
    Oxford: Blackwell Publishers, 2000.
———. "Notes on Deconstructing 'the Popular.'" In *People's History and
    Socialist Theory*, edited by Samuel Raphael, 227–40. London: Routledge
    and Kegan Paul, 1981.
Haralovich, Mary Beth. "Fireworks in Film and TV." Paper presented at the
    MiT4: The Work of Stories conference. Cambridge MA, May 6, 2005.
———. "Zombies v. Humans in 'Land of the Dead': Fireworks and
    Community." *In Media Res: A Media Commons Project*, April 26, 2007.
    http://mediacommons.futureofthebook.org/imr/2007/04/26/zombies
    -v-humans-land-dead-fireworks-and-community.
Hearne, Joanna. "The 'Ache for Home': Assimilation and Separatism in
    Anthony Mann's *Devil's Doorway*." In *Hollywood's West: The American
    Frontier in Film, Television, and History*, edited by Peter C. Rollins and
    John E. O'Connor, 126–59. Lexington: University Press of Kentucky,
    2005.

———. "'The Cross-Heart People': Race and Inheritance in the Silent Western." *Journal of Popular Film and Television* 30, no. 4 (2003): 181–96.

———. "*House Made of Dawn*: Restoring Native Voices in Cinema." Smithsonian Institution, National Museum of the American Indian, Film and Video Center. Native Networks/Redes Indigenas, December 8, 2005. http://www.nativenetworks.si.edu.

———. "'Indians Watching Indians on TV': Native Spectatorship and the Politics of Recognition in *Skins* and *Smoke Signals*." In *Visualities: Perspectives on Contemporary American Indian Film and Art*, edited by Denise K. Cummings, 41–72. East Lansing: Michigan State University Press, 2011.

———. "Indigenous Animation: Educational Programming, Narrative Interventions, and Children's Cultures." In *Global Indigenous Media: Cultures, Poetics, and Politics*, edited by Pamela Wilson and Michelle Stewart, 89–108. Durham: Duke University Press, 2008.

———. "'John Wayne's Teeth': Speech, Sound and Representation in *Smoke Signals* and *Imagining Indians*." *Western Folklore* 64, nos. 3 and 4 (2005): 189–208.

———. *Native Recognition: Indigenous Cinema and the Western*. Albany: SUNY Press, 2012.

———. "Telling and Retelling in the 'Ink of Light': Documentary Cinema, Oral Narratives, and Indigenous Identities." *Screen* 47, no. 3 (2006): 307–26.

Hearne, Joanna, and Zack Shlachter. "'Pockets Full of Stories': An Interview with Sterlin Harjo and Blackhorse Lowe." In *Native Americans on Film: Conversations, Teaching, and Theory*, edited by M. Elise Marubbio and Eric Buffalohead, 319–47. Lexington: University Press of Kentucky, 2012.

Highway, Tomson. "Spokane Words: An Interview with Sherman Alexie." Seventeenth International Festival of Authors, Toronto, Canada, October 28, 1996. *Aboriginal Voices*, January–March 1997. http://www.lang.osaka-u.ac.jp/~krkvls/salexie.html.

Himmelsbach, Erik. "The Reluctant Spokesman." *Los Angeles Times*, December 17, 1996. http://www.fallsapart.com.

hooks, bell. *Black Looks: Race and Representation*. Boston: South End Press, 1992.

Horn, John. "DVD Sales Figures Turn Every Film into a Mystery." *Los Angeles Times*, April 17, 2005. http://articles.latimes.com/2005/apr/17/entertainment/et-dvdmoney17.

Huhndorf, Shari. *Going Native: Indians in the Cultural Imagination.* Ithaca: Cornell University Press, 2001.

Hunter, Stephen. "Smoke Signals from the Heart." *Washington Post,* July 3, 1998. http://www.washingtonpost.com/wp-srv/style/longterm/movies/videos/smokesignalshunter.htm.

Interview with Tantoo Cardinal by RealTVfilms. sxsw/South by Southwest Film Festival coverage of *Older than America.* YouTube. Uploaded March 19, 2008. http://youtube.com/watch?v=x5xLZX2JR1k.

Jaggi, Maya. "All Rage and Heart" (Interview with Sherman Alexie). *The Guardian,* May 3, 2008. http://books.guardian.co.uk/departments/generalfiction/story/0,,2277677,00.html.

James, Meredith K. *Literary and Cinematic Reservation in Selected Works of Native American Author Sherman Alexie.* Lewiston: Edwin Mellen Press, 2005.

Jenkins, Henry. *Convergence Culture: Where Old and New Media Collide.* New York: New York University Press, 2006.

Jones, Michael. "Alien Nation." *Filmmaker: The Magazine of Independent Film* (Winter 1998).

Jones, Scott Kelton. "Smoke Gets in Your Eyes." *Dallas Observer,* July 9, 1998. http://www.dallasobserver.com/1998-07-09/film/smoke-gets-in-your-eyes/.

Kalinak, Kathryn. "How the West Was Sung." In *Westerns: Films through History,* edited by Janet Walker, 151–76. New York: Routledge, 2001.

———. "Typically American: Music for *The Searchers.*" In *The Searchers: Essays and Reflections on John Ford's Classic Western,* edited by Arthur M. Eckstein and Peter Lehman, 109–43. Detroit: Wayne State University Press, 2004.

Kaufman, Anthony. "An Eyre of Success: Director Chris Eyre Sends 'Smoke Signals.'" *Indiewire,* June 26, 1998. http://www.indiewire.com/article/an_eyre_of_success_director_chris_eyre_sends_smoke_signals.

Kehoe, Alice Beck. *The Ghost Dance: Ethnohistory and Revitalization.* Long Grove IL: Waveland Press, 2006.

Keogh, Tom. "Interview with Sherman Alexie." Encarta Encyclopedia, March 1999. http://encarta.msn.com/sidebar_1741587177/interview_with_sherman_alexie.html.

Kilpatrick, Jacqueline. *Celluloid Indians: Native Americans and Film.* Lincoln: University of Nebraska Press, 1999.

King, Thomas. "Performing Native Humor: The Dead Dog Café Comedy Hour." In *Me Funny,* edited by Drew Hayden Taylor, 169–86. Vancouver: Douglas and McIntyre, 2005.

Klopotek, Brian. "'I Guess Your Warrior Look Doesn't Work Every Time': Challenging Indian Masculinity in the Cinema." In *Across the Great Divide: Cultures of Manhood in the American West*, edited by Matthew Basso, Laura McCall, and Dee Garceau, 251–73. New York: Routledge, 2001.

Knopf, Kerstin. *Decolonizing the Lens of Power: Indigenous Films of North America*. Amsterdam: Rodopi B. V., 2008.

Konkle, Maureen. *Writing Indian Nations: Native Intellectuals and the Politics of Historiography, 1827–1863*. Chapel Hill: University of North Carolina Press, 2004.

Kozloff, Sarah. *Invisible Storytellers: Voice-Over Narration in American Fiction Film*. Berkeley: University of California Press, 1988.

LaRocque, Emma. *When the Other Is Me: Native Resistance Discourse 1850–1990*. Winnipeg: University of Manitoba Press, 2010.

Lawson, Angelica. "Native Sensibility and the Significance of Women in *Smoke Signals*." In *Sherman Alexie: A Collection of Critical Essays*, edited by Jeff Berglund and Jan Roush, 95–106. Salt Lake City: University of Utah Press, 2010.

Layman, William D. *River of Memory: The Everlasting Columbia*. Seattle: University of Washington Press, 2006.

Lefkowitz, Daniel. "Dialects in the Movies: Intonation, 'Oral Tradition,' and Identity in Chris Eyre's *Smoke Signals*." SALSA VII, Texas Linguistic Forum 43, Dept. of Linguistics, 2000.

Lehrer, Jim. "A Dialogue on Race." *McNeil/Lehrer News Hour*, July 9, 1998. http://www.pbs.org/newshour/bb/race_relations/OneAmerica/transcript.html.

Leuthold, Steven. *Indigenous Aesthetics: Native Art Media and Identity*. Austin: University of Texas Press, 1998.

Lewis, Randolph. *Alanis Obomsawin: The Vision of a Native Filmmaker*. Lincoln: University of Nebraska Press, 2006.

———. *"Navajo Talking Picture": Cinema on Native Ground*. Lincoln: University of Nebraska Press, 2012.

Lincoln, Kenneth. *Ind'n Humor: Bicultural Play in Native America*. Oxford: Oxford University Press, 1992.

Lomawaima, Tsianina. *They Called It Prairie Light*. Lincoln: University of Nebraska Press, 1994.

Makino, Yuri. "Cinematic Reservations: An Interview with Chris Eyre." In *Filming Difference: Actors, Directors, Producers, and Writers on Gender, Race, and Sexuality in Film*, edited by Daniel Bernardi, 247–60. Austin: University of Texas Press, 2009.

Marsden, Michael, and Jack Nachbar. "The Indians in the Movies." In *Handbook of North American Indians*, 607–16. Washington DC: Smithsonian Institution, 1988.

Martin, Reed. "Native American Films Attempt to Cross Over." *USA Today*, January 27, 2003. http://www.usatoday.com/life/movies/2003-01-27 -native-usat_x.htm.

Marubbio, M. Elise. *Killing the Indian Maiden: Images of Native American Women in Film*. Lexington: University of Kentucky Press, 2006.

Masayesva, Victor. "Indigenous Experimentalism." In *Magnetic North*, edited by Jenny Lion, 228–39. Minneapolis: University of Minnesota Press, 2001.

Maslin, Janet. "Film Festival Review: Miles to Go, and Worlds Apart." *New York Times*, March 27, 1998. http://movies.nytimes.com/movie/ review?_r=1&res=9C07E2D9163BF934A15750C0A96E958260&oref =slogin.

McCarthy, Todd. Review of *Smoke Signals*. *Variety*, January 28, 1998, 12, AMPAS archive.

McDonald, Christine. "An Interview with Sherman Alexie." *Multicultural Review* 11 (2002): 48–58.

Menier, Joe, dir. "Guestbook." Conversation with Sherman Alexie, hosted by Ross Frank, UCSD Department of Ethnic Studies. UCSD-TV, recorded November 29, 2001.

Miller, Heather Anne. "Tonto and Tonto Speak: An Indigenous Based Film Theory." *Journal of Science and Business Research* 1, no. 3 (2006). http:// www.sbrjournal.net/journalsite/archives/FilmTheory/Tonto.htm.

Miller, J. R. *Compact, Contract, Covenant: Aboriginal Treaty-Making in Canada*. Toronto: University of Toronto Press, 2009.

Miller, Prairie. "Smoke Signals: Director Chris Eyre Interview." *Mini Reviews*, January 1, 1998. http://www.minireviews.com/interviews/ eyre.htm.

Mills, Charles W. *The Racial Contract*. Ithaca: Cornell University Press, 1997.

Momaday, N. Scott. *The Man Made of Words, Essays, Stories, Passages*. New York: St. Martin's Press, 1997.

Moore, David L. "Sherman Alexie: Irony, Intimacy, and Agency." In *The Cambridge Companion to Native American Literature*, edited by Joy Porter and Kenneth M. Roemer, 297–310. Cambridge: Cambridge University Press, 2005.

Moore, Thomas, and J. W. Lake. *The Poetical Works of Thomas Moore*. N.p.: Jules Didot Sr., 1829.

Morrissey, Katherine G. *Mental Territories: Mapping the Inland Empire.* Ithaca: Cornell University Press, 1997.

Nabhan, Gary. "Diabetes, Diet and Native American Foraging Traditions." In *Food in the USA*, edited by Carole M. Counihan, 231–38. London: Routledge, 2002.

Naficy, Hamid. "Theorizing 'Third-World' Film Spectatorship." *Wide Angle* 18, no. 3 (1996): 3–26.

Naremore, James. *Acting in the Cinema.* Berkeley: University of California Press, 1988.

Native American Graves and Repatriation Act, 25 USC 3001 et seq., November 16, 1990. http://www.nps.gov/history/nagpra/mandates/index.htm.

Neale, Steve. "Vanishing Americans: Racial and Ethnic Issues in the Interpretation and Context of Post-war 'Pro-Indian' Westerns." In *Back in the Saddle Again: New Essays on the Western*, edited by Edward Buscombe and Roberta Pearson, 8–28. London: British Film Institute, 1998.

Nelson, Dana D. *National Manhood: Capitalist Citizenship and the Imagined Fraternity of White Men.* Durham: Duke University Press, 1998.

Nesbit, John. "Sherman Alexie (2002 Interview)." *Old School Reviews*, October 14, 2002. http://oldschoolreviews.com/articles/alexie.htm.

Newitz, Annalee. "When Will White People Stop Making Films Like 'Avatar'?" io9: We Come from the Future, December 18, 2009. http://io9.com/5422666/when-will-white-people-stop-making-movies-like-avatar.

Nicholson, Heather Norris, ed. *Screening Culture: Constructing Image and Identity.* Lanham MD: Lexington Books, 2003.

Osterreich, Shelley Anne. *The American Indian Ghost Dance, 1870 and 1890.* New York: Greenwood Press, 1991.

O'Sullivan, Michael. "Smoke Signals: A Few Reservations." *Washington Post*, July 3, 1998. http://www.washingtonpost.com/wp-srv/style/longterm/movies/videos/smokesignalsosullivan.htm.

Over, William. "Native American Cinema and Drama: Valuing Identity." In *Social Justice in World Cinema and Theater*, 149–65. Westport CT: Ablex Publishing, 2001.

Owens, Louis. "Through an Amber Glass: Chief Doom and the Native American Novel Today." In *Mixedblood Messages: Literature, Film, Family, Place*, 57–82. Norman: University of Oklahoma Press, 1998.

Painter, Jamie. "Signs of the Times." *BackStage West Drama-Logue*, July 9, 1998, AMPAS archive.

Peary, Gerald. "Universal Story: *Smoke Signals* is a Native American Masterpiece." *Boston Phoenix,* July 6, 1998. http://www.geraldpeary.com/reviews/stuv/smoke-signals.html.

Prats, Armando José. "His Master's Voice(Over): Revisionist Ethos and Narrative Dependence from *Broken Arrow* (1950) to *Geronimo: An American Legend* (1993)." *ANQ: A Quarterly Journal of Short Articles, Notes and Reviews* 9, no. 3 (1996): 15–29.

———. *Invisible Natives: Myth and Identity in the American Western.* Ithaca: Cornell University Press, 2002.

Pratt, Mary Louise. *Imperial Eyes: Travel Writing and Transculturation.* London: Routledge, 1992.

Prucha, Paul. *The Great Father: The United States Government and the American Indians.* Abridged ed. Lincoln: University of Nebraska Press, 1986.

Purdy, James. "Crossroads: A Conversation with Sherman Alexie." Western Washington University, October 4, 1997. http://faculty.wwu.edu/purdy/alexie.html.

Rader, Dean. "Word as Weapon: Visual Culture and Contemporary American Indian Poetry." *MELUS* 27, no. 3 (2002): 148–67.

Raheja, Michelle. "Reading Nanook's Smile: Visual Sovereignty, Indigenous Revisions of Ethnography, and *Atanarjuat (The Fast Runner)*." *American Quarterly* 59, no. 4 (2007): 1159–85.

———. *Reservation Reelism: Redfacing, Visual Sovereignty, and Representations of Native Americans in Film.* Lincoln: University of Nebraska Press, 2011.

Red Shirt, Delphine, "A Conversation with Cheyenne/Arapaho Filmmaker Chris Eyre." *Native People's Magazine,* March–April 2002. http://www.nativepeoples.com/np_mar_apr02/ma02-article1/ma02-article.html.

Rickard, Jolene. "Sovereignty: A Line in the Sand." *Aperture* 139 (November 1996): 51–54.

Riley, Angela R. "Sucking the Quileute Dry." *New York Times,* February 7, 2010. http://www.nytimes.com/2010/02/08/opinion/08riley.html.

Rogin, Michael. *Fathers and Children: Andrew Jackson and the Subjugation of the American Indian.* New York: Knopf, 1975.

Rosaldo, Renato. *Culture and Truth: The Remaking of Social Analysis.* Boston: Beacon Press, 1993.

Rosenthal, Nicolas G. "Representing Indians: Native American Actors on Hollywood's Frontier." *The Western Historical Quarterly* 36, no. 3 (2005). http://www.historycooperative.org/journals/whq/36.3/rosenthal.html.

Ruby, Robert H., and John A. Brown. *The Spokane Indians: Children of the Sun.* Norman: University of Oklahoma Press, 1970.

Runningwater, N. Bird. "Smoke Signals." *Yes! Magazine,* Winter 1999 issue: "Education for Life." http://www.yesmagazine.org/articles.asp?ID=801.

Savlov, Marc. Review of *Smoke Signals. Austin Chronicle,* July 17, 1998. http://www.austinchronicle.com/gyrobase/Calendar/Film?Film =oid%3a138672.

Sheyahshe-Lell, Michael. "Native American Film Making: Chris Eyre and *Smoke Signals." Illusions,* no. 31 (Summer 2000–2001): 9–12.

Shohat, Ella, and Robert Stam. *Unthinking Eurocentrism: Multiculturalism and the Media.* London: Routledge, 1994.

Sierra Club — Upper Columbia River Group. "Death of the Spokane River?" Special report. 2003. Available at http://www.waterplanet.ws/ documents/030917/SpokaneRiver.pdf.

Simmon, Scott. *The Invention of the Western Film: A Cultural History of the Genre's First Half-Century.* Cambridge: Cambridge University Press, 2003.

Singer, Beverly R. *Wiping the War Paint off the Lens: Native American Film and Video.* Minneapolis: University of Minnesota Press, 2001.

Siskel, Gene, and Roger Ebert. *At the Movies.* June 27, 1998. Disney-ABC Domestic Television.

Slotkin, Richard. *Gunfighter Nation: The Myth of the Frontier in Twentieth-Century America.* Norman: University of Oklahoma Press, 1991.

Smith, Andrew Brodie. *Shooting Cowboys and Indians: Silent Western Films, American Culture, and the Birth of Hollywood.* Boulder: University Press of Colorado, 2003.

Smith, Linda Tuhiwai. *Decolonizing Methodologies: Research and Indigenous Peoples.* Dunedin: University of Otago Press, 1999.

Smith, Paul Chaat, and Robert Warrior. *Like a Hurricane: The Indian Movement from Alcatraz to Wounded Knee.* New York: New Press, 1997.

Sobchack, Vivian. "'Surge and Splendor': A Phenomenology of the Hollywood Historical Epic." In *Film Genre Reader II,* edited by Barry Keith Grant, 280–307. Austin: University of Texas Press, 1995.

Stack, Peter. "*Smoke* Causes Tears of Sadness, Joy." *San Francisco Chronicle,* July 3, 1998. http://www.sfgate.com/cgi-bin/article.cgi?f=/c/a/1998/07/ 03/DD61314.DTL.

Standing Bear, Luther. *My People, the Sioux.* New York: Houghton Mifflin, 1928.

Stanfield, Peter. *Hollywood, Westerns and the 1930s: The Lost Trail.* Exeter: University of Exeter Press, 2001.

Sterngold, James. "Able to Laugh at Their People, Not Just Cry for Them." *New York Times*, June 21, 1998.

Strong, Pauline Turner, and Barrik Van Winkle. "'Indian Blood': Reflections on the Reckoning and Refiguring of Native North American Identity." *Cultural Anthropology* 11, no. 4 (1996): 547–76.

Svetkey, Benjamin. "Little Big Movie." *Entertainment Weekly*, March 8, 1991. http://www.ew.com/ew/article/0,,313535,00.html.

Szasz, Margaret. *Education and the American Indian*. Albuquerque: University of New Mexico Press, 1974.

Tatonetti, Lisa. "Dancing That Way, Things Began to Change: The Ghost Dance as Pantribal Metaphor in Sherman Alexie's Writing." In *Sherman Alexie: A Collection of Critical Essays*, edited by Jeff Berglund and Jan Roush, 1–24. Salt Lake City: University of Utah Press, 2010.

Turim, Maureen. *Flashbacks in Film: Memory and History*. New York: Routledge, 1989.

Tuska, Jon. *The American West in Film: Critical Approaches to the Western*. New York: Greenwood Press, 1985.

Vizenor, Gerald. *Fugitive Poses: Native American Indian Scenes of Absence and Presence*. Lincoln: University of Nebraska Press, 1998.

———. *Manifest Manners: Narratives on Postindian Survivance*. Lincoln: University of Nebraska Press, 1994.

———. "Trickster Discourse: Comic Holotropes and Language Games." In *Narrative Chance: Postmodern Discourse on Native American Indian Literatures*, edited by Gerald Vizenor, 187–211. Albuquerque: University of New Mexico Press, 1989.

Warrior, Robert. *Tribal Secrets: Recovering American Indian Intellectual Traditions*. Minneapolis: University of Minnesota Press, 1995.

Weinmann, Aileo. "Hold Me Closer, Fancy Dancer: An Conversation with Sherman Alexie." AMC FilmCritic.com, September 30, 2002. http://www.filmcritic.com/features/2002/09/hold-me-closer-fancy-dancer-a-conversation-with-sherman-alexie/.

Wesch, Michael. "An Anthropological Introduction to YouTube." Presentation at the Library of Congress, June 23, 2008. http://www.youtube.com/watch?v=TPAO-lZ4_hU&feature=fvsr.

West, Dennis, and Joan M. West. "Sending Cinematic Smoke Signals: An Interview with Sherman Alexie." *Cineaste* 23, no. 4 (1998): 28.

White, Richard. *The Organic Machine*. New York: Hill and Wang, 1995.

Whitt, Laurie Anne. "Cultural Imperialism and the Marketing of Native America." In *Natives and Academics: Researching and Writing about American Indians*, edited by Devon A. Mihesuah, 139–71. Lincoln: University of Nebraska, 1998.

Wilkinson, Gerald. "Colonialism through the Media." *The Indian Historian* (Summer 1974): 29–32.

Willemen, Paul, and Jim Pines, eds. *Questions of Third Cinema*. London: British Film Institute, 1989.

Williams, Joan C., and Viviana A. Zelizer. "'To Commodify or Not to Commodify: That Is *Not* the Question." In *Rethinking Commodification: Cases and Readings in Law and Culture*, edited by Martha M. Ertman and Joan C. Williams, 362–82. New York: New York University Press, 2005.

Williams, Mary Elizabeth. "Without Reservations." *Salon*, July 2, 1998. http://www1.salon.com/ent/movies/int/1998/07/02int.html.

Wilson, Pamela, and Michelle Stewart. "Introduction: Indigeneity and Indigenous Media on the Global Stage." In *Global Indigenous Media: Cultures, Poetics, and Politics*, edited by Pamela Wilson and Michelle Stewart, 1–35. Durham: Duke University Press, 2008.

Wilton, Caren. "Native Son, the Sadness and Wit of Sherman Alexie." *NZ Listener* 204, no. 3452 (July 8–14). http://www.listener.co.nz/uncategorized/native-son/.

Wood, Houston. *Native Features: Indigenous Films from around the World*. New York: Continuum, 2008.

Youngberg, Quentin. "Cultural Mediation and the Possibility of a Native Counter-Cinema." *Studies in the Humanities* 33, no. 2 (2006): 140–63.

———. "Interpenetrations: Re-encoding the Queer Indian in Sherman Alexie's *The Business of Fancydancing*." *Studies in American Indian Literatures* 20, no. 1 (2008): 55–75.

Youngs, William T. *The Fair and the Falls: Spokane's Expo '74, Transforming an American Environment*. Cheney: Eastern Washington University Press, 1996.

YouTube Videography

This list of YouTube videos related to *Smoke Signals* should be understood as a snapshot indicating the range of postings at a particular moment in time (2009); given the ephemeral and constantly shifting nature of YouTube's content, some of these posts will be or have already been removed, while new posts will continue to appear.

CLASSROOM/PROJECT VIDEOS

aznxflipx91. "fry bread." Uploaded November 20, 2007. http://www .youtube.com/watch?v=XFEYIiP9NUU.

jamesGOLDbond. "Interviews on Smoke Signals." Uploaded October 20, 2006. http://www.youtube.com/watch?v=msTndZLd_3k&feature =related.

stoddyjacob. "smoke signals school rap." Uploaded June 4, 2009. http:// www.youtube.com/watch?v=rLQT_PABAws&feature=related.

tcheremnykh. "smoke signals rap." Uploaded May 24, 2007. http://www .youtube.com/watch?v=Mla-NI5gnfE&feature=channel_page.

COVERS

Gilnar13. "John Wayne's teeth — Moury Z Roury." http://www.youtube.com/ watch?v=gVotFqbsgzA&feature=related.

pachway1. "John Wayne Teeth." Uploaded July 29, 2008. http://www .youtube.com/watch?v=Ux9Kvj9hBkE&feature=related.

EXCERPTS FROM INTERVIEWS WITH DIRECTOR, DOCUMENTARIES

Framesinmotion2007. "Native American Filmmaking." Uploaded October 20, 2007. http://www.youtube.com/watch?v=pBxxavk9cOU&feature =related.

"HEY, VICTOR" VIDEOS

brinkingright. "Thomas from Smoke Signals . . . wait, that's Mat Salazar!!!" Uploaded February 25, 2007. http://www.youtube.com/ watch?v=l1lnvNmh8fE.

happyveggysan. "Hey Victor (a Japanese question)." Uploaded February 11, 2009. http://www.youtube.com/watch?v=kk3pit21F1Q&feature =related.

Have420Naheed. "Hey Veekdoor." Uploaded January 26, 2008. http://www.youtube.com/watch?v=iV1ty1GZYWY&NR=1.

randomthang. "Hey Victor." Uploaded May 30, 2008. http://www.youtube .com/watch?v=FO9f-2BBIEg&feature=related.

SportsW3. "hey victor spoof." http://www.youtube.com/watch?v
=8fhX7JCG3z4&feature=related.

thebiri. "Hey Victor!" Uploaded September 26, 2009. http://www
.youtube.com/watch?v=m2KNwcPRjqU.

JOHN WAYNE'S TEETH VIDEOS

EmoDirector. "tribute to john wayne's teeth." Uploaded April 20, 2008.
http://www.youtube.com/watch?v=O8OY9zALn6w.

shadowodancer. "John Wayne's Teeth by Eaglebear Singers." http://www
.youtube.com/watch?v=qZYJHeU_2bw&feature=related.

Theatre49. "John Wayne's Teeth." http://www.youtube.com/watch?v
=KaYpDh7ljBs&NR=1.

twinmonsterslayer. "John Waynes teeth." Uploaded December 28, 2007.
http://www.youtube.com/watch?v=9ctLVlkDWRs&feature=related.

REENACTMENTS

alyssaabbo. "Hey Victor Pt 1." Uploaded June 1, 2009. http://www
.youtube.com/watch?v=M-sWks1QS8Y&feature=related.

NativeRockers. "Smoke signals our version." Uploaded March 9, 2007.
http://www.youtube.com/watch?v=s-yH1EM5lYo&feature=related.

Index

Cox, James, 40, 42
Cruze, James, 12
Cummings, Denise, 88
Curse of the Redman, 11–12
Curtis, Edward S., 8
Custer, George, 27, 29, 82, 83, 97
Custer Died for Your Sins, 27

Dances with Wolves, xvi, xxi–xxii,
    xxxiii, 3, 9, 10, 11, 15, 39, 159,
    160; influence of, on genre, 14;
    Native American names and,
    25; as non-Native cinema, 163;
    reference to, in *Smoke Signals*,
    67, 69, 77; Tantoo Cardinal in, 57
Daves, Delmer, 3, 13
Daviau, Allen, 51
Dawes Act, 7
Dead Dog Café Comedy Hour, 26
Dead Man, 57, 88
Deadwood, 14
Death Wish V, 77, 78, 117
de Heer, Ralph, 20
de la Rosa, Shonie, 21
Deloria, Philip, 8
Deloria, Vine, Jr., xxvii, 27
Del Rio, Dolores, 12
DeMille, Cecil B., 10
Denny's (restaurant), 118–19, 153
Devil's Doorway, 13
Dickerson, Ernest, 49
Dippie, Brian, 5
The Doe Boy, 21, 136, 138
Do the Right Thing, 28, 49, 134
Douglass, Frederick, 82
Dreamkeeper, 199n41
Duck Valley NV, 24

Eagle vs. Shark, 20
Eastwood, Clint, 9, 11, 138
Easy Rider, 93, 99

Ebert, Roger, 133, 134, 190–91
Edge of America, 138, 172
Elsaesser, Thomas, 141–42
Englehardt, Tom, 13
Estes, Larry, 52, 170
E.T., 51
The Exiles, 187
Eyre, Chris, xv, xxi, xxiv, xxxi,
    xxxiii, 28, 31, 36, 77, 85, 99,
    128, 130, 132, 152, 166, 199n41,
    207n24; childhood of, 53–54;
    on contemporary Native
    filmmakers, 135; critical reviews
    of work by, 133, 134; on defining
    Native cinema, 161–63; formal
    training of, 49–50; funeral
    rituals depicted by, 124; on
    hairstyles, 71–72, 175–76; home
    dramas of, 49–54, 85; on impact
    of *Smoke Signals*, 177–78; on
    independent filmmaking,
    167–70; location scouting by,
    116–17, 172–74; production
    of *Smoke Signals* and, 50–54;
    on public reception of *Smoke
    Signals*, 130–31; in *Smoke Signals*,
    93, 95; Sundance Institute and,
    35, 50–52; work of, after *Smoke
    Signals*, 124, 137–38

FallsApart, Lester, 24–29, 74
Farmer, Gary, xviii, 19, 57, 58, 88,
    100, 133–34, 174, 184
fast food, 118–20
Federal Bureau of Investigation
    (FBI), 24, 81
Federal Communications
    Commission (FCC), 18
Field, Syd, 140
5th World, 21, 136, 179
Fire with Fire, 180

mainstream media: Fourth World production and, 20–21; images of Native Americans in, xx–xxv, 8–10, 30–31, 33, 67–69, 90–97, 140–41, 154; and imperialist nostalgia, 9; Indigenization of, xvi, xvii, xxxi; journey films in, 99, 100–101; and Sherman Alexie, xvii, 41–42; and silent films, 10–12
Malick, Terrence, xxiii, 136
Manifest Destiny, 13
Mankiewicz, Joseph, 103
Mankiller, Wilma, xxiv–xxv
Mann, Michael, xxi, 13
The Maori Merchant of Venice, 20
Maori Television, 21
Margolin, Stuart, 18
Martinez, A., 84
Marubbio, M. Elise, 6
Masayesva, Victor, Jr., 16, 20, 65
masculinity, 84–86
Maslin, Janet, 133
Mathews, John Joseph, xxvii
Mauri, 20
McCarthyism, 13
McNeil/Lehrer News Hour, xxi
Means, Russell, 18
Medicine River, 16, 18
method acting, 58–63
Metz, Christian, 101
Midnight Cowboy, 99, 111
Mile Post 398, 21
Miles, Elaine, xix, 55
Mineo, Sal, 55
Miramax, 137, 143, 158
The Missing, 12
Mita, Merata, 20
Moffatt, Tracey, 20
Mojica, Monique, xix
Momaday, N. Scott, 18, 104

Moore, David, 125, 140–41
Morse, Richardson, 17, 18
My People the Sioux, 11

Nabhan, Gary, 119
Naficy, Hamid, 154
Nagel, Joane, 85
Naremore, James, 63
narration, 30, 59, 104–5, 147
narrators, film, 3
National Film Board of Canada, 19, 21
nationalism, 97
National Museum of the American Indian (NMAI), 130
Native American actors: advocacy by, 17; American Indian Movement and, 18–19, 81; independent projects and, 17–18; intellectual work by, 65–66; mainstream films and, 138–39, 193; method acting by, 58–63; narration by, 30, 59, 104–5, 147; performativity and, 58–75; in silent era, 17; in *Smoke Signals*, 54–57, 183–84; stylized acting of, 63; and white actors, 11, 54–57
Native American cinema, xxxi–xxxiv; American Indian Movement and, 18–19; analysis of, xvii–xviii; definitions of, 161–65; flashbacks and flashforwards in, 99–105; history of, 16–21; independent projects and, 17–18; intercultural partnerships and, 18–19; mainstream media and, xvi–xvii; marketing of, 158–61; Native directors and, 12, 17, 164–65; performance and, 33–36; storytelling and, 29–30, 59–61;

In the Indigenous Films series

"The Fast Runner": Filming the
Legend of Atanarjuat
Michael Robert Evans

"Smoke Signals": Native Cinema Rising
Joanna Hearne

"Navajo Talking Picture":
Cinema on Native Ground
Randolph Lewis

To order or obtain more information on
these or other University of Nebraska Press
titles, visit www.nebraskapress.unl.edu.

CPSIA information can be obtained at www.ICGtesting.com
Printed in the USA
BVOW040245011012

301696BV00001B/5/P